Compassion Focused Therapy

for dummies®
A Wiley Brand

by Mary Welford

Compassion Focused Therapy For Dummies®

Published by: **John Wiley & Sons, Ltd.**, The Atrium, Southern Gate, Chichester, www.wiley.com

This edition first published 2016

©2016 John Wiley & Sons, Ltd., Chichester, West Sussex.

Registered office

John Wiley & Sons, Ltd., The Atrium, Southern Gate, Chichester, West Sussex, PO19 8SQ, United Kingdom

For details of our global editorial offices, for customer services and for information about how to apply for permission to reuse the copyright material in this book, please see our website at www.wiley.com.

Wiley publishes in a variety of print and electronic formats and by print-on-demand. Some material included with standard print versions of this book may not be included in e-books or in print-on-demand. If this book refers to media such as a CD or DVD that is not included in the version you purchased, you may download this material at http://booksupport.wiley.com. For more information about Wiley products, visit www.wiley.com.

Designations used by companies to distinguish their products are often claimed as trademarks. All brand names and product names used in this book are trade names, service marks, trademarks or registered trademarks of their respective owners. The publisher is not associated with any product or vendor mentioned in this book.

For general information on our other products and services, please contact our Customer Care Department within the U.S. at 877-762-2974, outside the U.S. at (001) 317-572-3993, or fax 317-572-4002. For technical support, please visit www.wiley.com/techsupport.

Library of Congress Control Number: 2016940425

A catalogue record for this book is available from the British Library.

978-1-119-07862-3 (pbk); 978-1-119-07863-0 (ebk); 978-1-119-07869-2 (ebk)

Printed and bound in Great Britain by TJ International Ltd, Padstow, Cornwall, UK

10 9 8 7 6 5 4 3 2 1

Contents at a Glance

Table of Contents

Introduction

You can work through a never-ending list of things you *could* do to improve your wellbeing. Getting more sleep, taking regular exercise, eating a healthier diet, developing a positive mental attitude and drinking less alcohol are just some of the things you may benefit from. Advice comes from the TV, newspapers, self-help books, friends, relatives, colleagues, healthcare professionals and even the chats we have with ourselves!

But it's hard to motivate ourselves to make helpful changes. It's even harder to maintain them. Compassion Focused Therapy (CFT) is here to help. This approach offers life-changing insights into our amazing capacities and also the challenges we face in our everyday lives. By understanding ourselves, we become motivated to act out of true care for our wellbeing. This changes the relationship we have with ourselves and others.

Practicing CFT won't mean you suddenly turn into a 'perfect' version of yourself. It does however mean that you become more aware of the choices you have and you're motivated to make ones that are more helpful to you. And yes, you find plenty of advice in here to guide you on your way too!

About This Book

Compassion Focused Therapy For Dummies contains a wealth of important information that can help you to understand yourself, and others, better. It also introduces you to practices that you can integrate into your everyday life, minute by minute, hour by hour, day by day. . . .

I've used as little jargon and off-putting technical terms as possible, and so you don't need to approach this book with a background knowledge of psychology. Simply put, if you're in possession of a human brain and you'd like to discover more about CFT, this book is written for you.

That said, two factors may motivate you to continue developing your understanding of CFT once you finish this book:

>> CFT is rooted in a scientific understanding of what it is to be human. As such, the approach constantly evolves to reflect the science. In the same way as it's helpful to keep up with advancing technology, it's also good to keep up with advancing our understanding of ourselves.

>> We humans are highly complex. This book simply doesn't have the room to do CFT complete justice – not if you want to be able to lift it up! When you finish reading, you may want to move on to explore the comprehensive work of Paul Gilbert (the originator of the CFT approach), his colleagues and collaborators.

Foolish Assumptions

In writing this book, I've had to make a few assumptions about you. I've assumed that:

>> You're interested in improving your wellbeing.

>> You appreciate that CFT is based on an incredible amount of research – but you don't necessarily want to plough through it all!

>> You realise that I've had to make some tough decisions about what to include and what to leave out. Hopefully most of the choices I've made are right (but thankfully I won't criticise myself if I've made a mistake; I hope you don't either!).

>> You recognise that I'm not trying to pass CFT off as my own creation. Instead, I set out to describe the work of Paul Gilbert and colleagues (of whom I am privileged to be one).

>> You may be selective about which parts of the book you read. As such, I've written this book in a way that allows each chapter to 'stand alone' so that you can pick and choose the content you want to read, and when you want to read it.

>> You're prepared to give new things a go!

If you're a therapist or studying CFT, I also assume that you recognise the importance of learning the approach 'from the inside out', and as such that you'll work through the book with this in mind.

Icons Used in This Book

Icons are handy little graphic images that point out particularly important information about CFT. Throughout this book, you find the following icons, conveniently located along the left margins:

REMEMBER

Remember what follows this icon, as it's important. It helps to return to these points from time to time to help you understand and connect with the approach further.

TIP

The tip icon identifies useful ideas to help you gain more understanding and insight.

WARNING

Take careful note of the advice beside this icon as it's important to your wellbeing.

EXAMPLE

Examples of the ways that people have practised CFT are provided throughout this book. The examples represent real people and real life situations, but details have been altered and at times stories may have been amalgamated.

Beyond the Book

In addition to the material in this book, I also provide a free access-anywhere Cheat Sheet that offers some helpful reminders about the many benefits of CFT. To get this Cheat Sheet, simply go to www.dummies.com and search for 'Compassion Focused Therapy For Dummies Cheat Sheet' in the Search box.

Where to Go from Here

If you're new to CFT, you may find it helpful to start with Chapter 1 before you decide how to tackle the rest of the chapters (you may even decide that you want to read the book from start to finish – but you don't have to take that approach, as you find plenty of helpful cross-references to other useful chapters as you work through each chapter). However you decide to begin, do this at a pace to suit both your understanding and emotional experience.

If you have some experience of CFT, you may choose to skip to a particular topic due to a need or question you may have. If this is the case, use the table of contents and the index to help you find your way to the required information. Regardless of how you find your way around this book, I hope you appreciate the journey.

Finally, CFT aims to assist you to develop a compassionate understanding and relationship with yourself and others. If you find the approach helpful, it's likely to become a way of life. To support your journey, you can access a number of courses to assist you. These course can also connect you with a wider group of people. You can find suitable courses advertised on a range of websites, including www.compassionatemind.co.uk, www.compassioninmind.co.uk and www.compassionatewellbeing.co.uk.

1

Getting Started with Compassion Focused Therapy

Chapter 1

Introducing Compassion Focused Therapy

P eople are more similar than different. We're all born into a set of circumstances that we don't choose, and in possession of a phenomenal yet very tricky brain. We're all trying to get by, doing the best we can. The sooner we wake up to this reality the better.

Compassion Focused Therapy (CFT) is here to help. This approach aims to liberate you from shame and self-criticism, replacing these feelings with more helpful ways of relating to yourself. It helps you to choose the type of person you want to be and to develop ways to make this choice a reality.

In this chapter, I introduce you to CFT, offering you an understanding of how it works and helping you to understand the benefits. I also point out the steps you may take along the way as you work with the information in this book. Finally, I take a moment to help you connect to the wider community around you as you begin this journey.

CFT advocates that you don't rush to 'learn' about the approach but instead allow space to experience and 'feel' it. So take your time with this book as you apply it to your life, and really discover the benefits.

Getting to Grips with Compassion Focused Therapy

CFT was founded by UK clinical psychologist Paul Gilbert, OBE. The name of the approach was chosen to represent three important aspects:

>> **Compassion**, in its simplest yet potentially most powerful definition, involves a sensitivity to our own, and other people's, distress, *plus* a motivation to prevent or alleviate this distress. As such, it has two vital components. One involves engaging with suffering while the other involves doing something about it. Chapter 2 delves into the ins and outs of compassion in more detail.

>> **Focused** means that we actively develop and apply compassion *to* ourselves. It also involves accepting and experiencing compassion *from* and *for* others.

>> **Therapy** is a term to describe the processes and techniques used to address an issue or difficulty.

CFT looks to social, developmental and evolutionary psychology and neuroscience to help us understand how our minds develop and work, and the problems we encounter. This scientific understanding (of ourselves and others) calls into question our experiences of shame and self-criticism and helps us to develop the motivation to make helpful changes in our lives.

CFT utilises a range of Eastern and Western methods to enhance our wellbeing. Attention training, mindfulness and imagery combine with techniques used in Cognitive Behavioural Therapy (CBT), and Person Centred, Gestalt and Narrative therapies (to name but a few), resulting in a powerful mix of strategies that can help you become the version of yourself you wish to be.

CFT is often referred to as part of a 'third-wave' of cognitive behavioural therapy because it incorporates a number of CBT techniques. However, CFT derives from an evolutionary model (which you find out more about in Chapters 3, 4 and 5) and it uses techniques from many other therapies that have been found to be of benefit. As such, CFT builds upon and integrates with other therapies. As therapies become more rooted in science, we may see increasing overlap rather than diversification.

REMEMBER

Compassion can involve kindness and warmth, but it also takes strength and courage to engage with suffering and to do something about it. CFT is by no means the easy or 'fluffy' option. Head to Chapter 6 to address some of the myths associated with compassion.

You may be reading this book because you want to find out more about this form of therapy. Alternatively, you may want to develop your compassionate mind and compassionate self out of care for your own wellbeing. The *why* or your *motivation* for reading this book has a big effect on the experience and, potentially, the outcome. Personally, I hope that whatever your motivation, you consider applying the approach to yourself in order that you can learn it 'from the inside out'.

Defining common terms

You may find that some of the terms used in CFT are new to you. Here are a few common terms that I use throughout this book, along with an explanation of what they mean:

>> **Common humanity:** This refers to the fact that, as human beings, we all face difficulties and struggles. We're more alike than different, and this realisation brings with it a sense of belonging to the human family.

>> **Tricky brain:** Our highly complex brains can cause us problems. For example, our capacity to think about the future and the past makes us prone to worry and rumination, while our inbuilt tendency to work out our place in a hierarchy can have a huge impact on our mood and self-esteem. In CFT, we use the term *tricky brain* to recognise our brain's complexity and the problems this complexity can lead to. We consider our tricky brain in more detail in Chapter 3.

>> **Compassionate mind:** This is simply an aspect of our mind. It comes with a set of attributes and skills that are useful for us to cultivate (I introduce these attributes and skills in Chapter 2). This frame of mind is highly important for our wellbeing, relationships and communities. But just as we have a compassionate mind, we also have a competitive and threat-focused mind – which is highly useful, if not a necessity, at certain times (Chapter 4 takes a look at our threat-focused mind).

>> **Compassionate mind training:** This describes specific activities designed to develop compassionate attributes and skills, particularly those that influence and help us to regulate emotions. Attention training and mindfulness are used as a means to prepare us for this work, and we look at these practices in Part 3.

>> **Compassionate self:** This is the embodiment of your compassionate mind. It's a whole mind and body experience. Your compassionate self incorporates your compassionate mind but also moves and interacts with the world.

>> **Compassionate self cultivation:** Your compassionate self is an identity that you can embody, cultivate and enhance. Compassionate self cultivation describes the range of activities that help you develop your compassionate self. Head to Chapter 10 for more on the cultivation of your compassionate self.

TIP

Engagement in the compassionate mind training and compassionate self cultivation activities provided in this book is often referred to as 'physiotherapy for the brain', as their use has been found to literally change the brain!

REMEMBER

Compassionate mind training and compassionate self cultivation are integral to CFT, but there's so much more to CFT. For many, getting to a point at which you can see the relevance and benefits of compassionate mind training and compassionate self cultivation, and overcome blocks and barriers to compassion, is the most significant aspect of your compassionate journey.

>> **Exercises:** These are activities for you to try. Sometimes they help to illustrate a point or provide a useful insight. Other exercises can give you an idea of what helps you to develop and maintain your compassionate mind.

>> **Practice:** Once you're aware of which exercises are helpful to you, you can then incorporate these into your everyday life. Regular use of these exercises becomes your *practice*.

Observing the origins of CFT

CFT is closely tied to advances in our understanding of the mind and, because scientific advances never stop, the therapy continues to adapt and change based upon it. Much of this book focuses on sharing the science to help develop a compassionate understanding of yourself and a sense of connection with fellow travellers on this mortal coil.

CFT is also born out of a number of clinical observations:

>> **People demonstrating high levels of shame and self-criticism often struggle with standard psychological therapies.** For example, using CBT, many find that they're not reassured by the generation or discovery of alternative beliefs and views and that this doesn't result in changes to the way they feel. Individuals may say 'Logically, I know I'm not bad/not to blame, but I still feel it' and 'I know it's unlikely that things will go wrong, but I still feel terrible'.

>> **What we say to ourselves is important, but *how* we say it is even more important.** Ever called yourself 'idiot' in a light-hearted and jovial manner?

You probably did so without feeling any negative effects. But, have you ever called yourself an idiot in a harsh and judgemental manner? You probably felt much worse on that occasion, perhaps resulting in an urge to withdraw or isolate yourself.

Consider phrases such as, 'look on the bright side' or 'count your blessings'. Sometimes these phrases can be said in a life-affirming way, but using a condescending, frustrated or angry tone represents a whole different ball game. This helps illustrate that your emotional tone is important.

» **Therapy can result in improvement in mood, self-esteem, sense of control and achievement, alongside a reduction in difficulties. However, life events can trigger relapse.** How we relate to ourselves, especially when life doesn't go the way we hope, is pivotal to our ongoing wellbeing.

» **Post therapy, many people report that they never disclosed to their therapist the things that caused them the most distress.** This resulted from their sense of shame and the way they believed others (the therapist) would feel about them. In addition to this, consider how many people simply don't seek help at all because they fear what others think.

» **People struggle to feel loved, valued, safe or content if they've never experienced these feelings.** For some people, these feelings are alien concepts and, most of all, alien experiences, difficult to generate by discussion alone. As such, it's important to develop the emotional resources and skills to deal with difficult emotions without turning to alcohol, food, drugs, work, excessive exercise or particular fixations.

» **Most of us struggle with emotions such as anger, anxiety and vulnerability, but many also find positive emotions extremely difficult, even frightening.** For some people, care, kindness, love and intimacy are terrifying, and to be avoided. People experiencing depression often worry that something bad will happen when their mood lifts. Likewise, feelings of connection and trust often stir up feelings of isolation and rejection, and a fear of loss. These difficulties can interfere with the goals we set ourselves unless we address them.

CFT is an accumulation of years of research, clinical insights and teachings drawn from a broad range of areas. Much of this research and study is summarised and published in scientific papers, textbooks and self-help books by Paul Gilbert and colleagues. A number of websites also provide additional resources. You can find details of these in the Appendix. This book provides you with a starting point for your CFT journey and offers a framework upon which you can hang your future CFT practice – use these resources to develop your practice further.

TAKING A COMPASSIONATELY THERAPEUTIC APPROACH

It has long been established that compassionate, respectful and supportive relationships are key to our wellbeing and integral to effective psychotherapies. A key goal of many therapies is the development of a better relationship with yourself. However, different therapies place emphasis on different methods to account for and produce change, for example:

- *CBT* focuses primarily (but not exclusively) on the link between thoughts, feelings and behaviours and helps you generate new thoughts and behaviours in order to change your feelings.

- *Interpersonal therapy* focuses on your relationships and how they affect you.

- *Psychodynamic therapy* aims to bring the unconscious mind into consciousness, helping you to experience and understand your true feelings in order to resolve them.

In contrast, CFT begins with your experience of compassion from your therapist (in person or through books like this one). This relationship with your therapist is pivotal. It then focuses on the personal development and cultivation of compassion to help you to make beneficial choices for yourself and for others.

With this in mind, this book contains quite a bit of me – as an author, as a psychologist and, most of all, as a human being who struggles too. I hope that the bits of me enhance your experience of reading the words I have chosen to write for you.

Making the Case for Compassion

If we view compassion as 'a sensitivity to our own and other people's distress *plus* a motivation to prevent or alleviate it', we can easily appreciate the many individual, group and societal benefits to developing and maintaining compassion in our lives. It makes intuitive sense and it's the reason why compassion has been a central component of many religious and spiritual traditions across the centuries.

Research studies support the benefits of bringing compassion into your life. Higher levels of compassion are associated with fewer psychological difficulties. Compassion enhances our social relationships and emotional wellbeing: it alters our neurophysiology in a positive way and can even strengthen our immune systems. Research also suggests that CFT can be successfully used to address difficulties associated with eating, trauma, mood and psychosis.

SO I'LL NEVER FEEL BAD AGAIN?

CFT won't rid you of life's difficulties. You won't find yourself day after day serenely swanning around, impervious to life's difficulties.

We practise compassion *because* life is hard. Compassion can assist us to make helpful choices and, when ready, create a space in which we can work through strong emotions, and grieve for things we've lost and wish had been different. With compassion, we relate to our anger, anxiety and sadness with kindness, warmth and non-judgement. This allows us to consider the reasons such emotions are there, work through them and face the issues they are alerting us to.

The development and cultivation of compassion isn't a quick fix. It's a way of living our lives.

However, for me, you can observe the power of the CFT approach in training clinicians. As they discover this approach to help their clients, they often report that the application of CFT in their personal lives can be transformative, leading many clinicians to develop and maintain their own personal practice.

TIP

I believe that personal practice is vital for any clinician. I attribute much of my wellbeing and my ability to engage with other people's suffering to the application of this approach in my life.

Understanding the Effects of Shame and Self-Criticism

Shame and self-criticism are common blocks to wellbeing, and CFT is designed to overcome them. The following sections help you consider how shame and self-criticism can affect you and what you can do to address and overcome these issues.

The isolating nature of shame

Shame is an excruciatingly difficult psychological state. The term comes from the Indo-European word 'sham' meaning 'to hide', and, as such, the experience of shame is isolating. When we feel shame, we feel bad about ourselves. We believe others judge us as inadequate, inferior or incompetent.

The next exercise helps you to explore the nature of shame and how it may affect you. Begin by finding a place you can sit for a short time that is free of distractions. Allow yourself to settle for a few moments. It may help to lower your gaze or close your eyes during the exercise.

1. **Bring to mind a time when you felt ashamed (nothing too distressing, but something you feel okay to revisit briefly).** Allow the experience to occupy your mind for a few moments.

2. **Slowly ask yourself the following questions, allowing time after each question to properly explore your experience:**

   - How (and where) does shame feel as a sensation in your body?
   - What thoughts go through your mind about yourself?
   - What do you think other people thought/would think or make of you if they knew this about you?
   - What emotions do you feel?
   - What does it make you want to do?

3. **Allow the experience to fade from your mind's eye. Recall a time you've felt content or happy, perhaps on your own or with someone else, and let this memory fill your mind and body.**

Depending upon the situation you brought to mind, a sense of anxiety, disgust or anger may have come to the fore. You may feel exposed, flawed, inadequate, disconnected or bad. Maybe you experience the urge to curl up, hide or run away, or perhaps feelings of anger and injustice leave you with the urge to defend yourself or confront someone.

Often, shame results in a feeling of disconnection. We don't like ourselves (or a part of ourselves) and we don't want to experience closeness to others because this may result in rejection. Our head goes down and we want to creep away. In addition, shame can affect our bodily sensations, maybe leading to tension, nausea or hotness. When you combine these negative views of yourself with predicted negative views from others, you create a very difficult concoction of experiences.

REMEMBER

Shame brings with it a range of difficult experiences. Strong physical sensations, thoughts and images are just some of them. Emotions such as anxiety, sadness and anger can race through you as you feel the urge to withdraw, isolate or defend yourself.

Some of the things we feel shame about include:

» Our body (for example, its shape, or our facial features, hair or skin)

- » Our body in action (for example, when sweating, urinating, defecating, burping, shaking, walking or running)

- » Our health (for example, illnesses, infections, diseases or genetic conditions)

- » Our mind (for example, our thoughts, including any intrusive images in our heads, our impulses, forgetfulness and our psychological health)

- » Our emotions (for example, anxiety, anger, disgust, sadness, jealousy or envy)

- » Our behaviour (for example, things we've said and the way we've said them, our use of alcohol and drugs, our compulsions, our eating patterns, or our tendency to avoid other people)

- » Our environment (for example, our house, neighbourhood, car or bedroom)

- » Other people (for example, our friends, family, cultural or religious group, or community)

Exploring why we feel shame

Human beings are social animals and need the protection, kindness and caring of others. Our brains are social organs. We like to feel valued, accepted and wanted by those around us in order to feel safe. There's no shame in this. These needs represent a deep-rooted part of us that's been highly significant in our evolution and survival.

Shame begins in how you feel you live in the mind of another – and it is a social regulator. In other words, we're programmed to try to work out, 'What are they thinking about or feeling toward me?', 'Do they like me?' and 'Who can I trust?' Just to add a further layer of complexity, we also try to work out, 'Do I like myself or this aspect of me?' and 'Can I trust myself?'

REMEMBER

If we perceive rejection from our social group or reject an aspect of ourselves, shame can be the result. Although difficult to experience, shame can trigger us to make helpful changes and others to come to our aid in order to soothe the difficulties we experience.

But what happens if we feel shame about things we are unable to change (such as our appearance, an aspect of our personality or our culture)? What happens if shame is attached to historical events that we blame ourselves for and can do nothing about? What happens when nobody comes to our assistance or we're unable to accept the help offered to us?

Unfortunately, we can find ourselves 'stuck' in shame. We may withdraw and isolate ourselves (physically, emotionally or mentally), predicting rejection from others and often rejecting aspects of ourselves. Alternatively, our experience of shame may lead to over-striving, perfectionism and 'image management', whereby we 'hide' aspects of ourselves. As social beings, this is a very difficult and precarious place to be.

TIP

Perpetual image management is like building a house with no foundations: you may achieve great things, but you attribute them not to yourself but to other factors. It's like living with the perpetual threat of your house falling down!

Similarly, over-striving and perfectionism are all well and good *if* we have the time and energy *and* we can achieve our goals. We feel good and experience a buzz of achievement. However, over a sustained period we can become exhausted and vulnerable to difficulties if we fail to meet our goals or high standards. When this happens we can easily revert back to the experience of shame because underneath our striving and perfectionism is a deep-seated feeling of inadequacy and shame.

Although internal and external shame often come hand in hand, there may be times when you experience them independently (see the nearby sidebar, 'The different types of shame'). For example, you may feel no internal shame about a physical health condition or your body in action, but you may experience external shame if you perceive others feel differently toward you. Alternatively, you may feel internal shame due to an experience of abuse, despite knowing that nobody judges or feels negative things toward you for it.

Beginning to address shame

If the exercise in the earlier section, 'The isolating nature of shame', put you in touch with how shame may affect you, it may be helpful to consider another scenario. The following exercise helps you consider if self-acceptance (which can follow from addressing your experience of shame) may be helpful to you.

THE DIFFERENT TYPES OF SHAME

You can experience different kinds of shame:

- *Internal shame* results from what we feel about ourselves.

- *External shame* relates to what we think others feel about us.

- *Reflected shame* is what we experience as a result of other people's actions. For example, we may feel shame on behalf of a friend or relative. Alternatively, we may feel shame due to the actions of our cultural or religious group or country.

Imagine that you understand and accept yourself, warts and all, with kindness. Imagine you have the confidence to let the key people in your life truly know you. Imagine also that you're able to discard your image management and show vulnerability; give people the opportunity to connect with you, idiosyncrasies and imperfections included; and allow people to get to know you as a whole. Consider what that would be like. Would it be something you'd want to work towards?

If the answer is yes, this is the book for you. Chapter by chapter, exercise by exercise, we'll work towards this aim together.

CFT helps us overcome our experience of shame and then develop self-acceptance. From a place of inner stability, we can begin to relate to ourselves with kindness and encouragement and become better able to look outwards and interact with the world.

REMEMBER

We begin to develop our compassionate mind by seeing ourselves and others in the flow of life and understanding the challenges presented by our tricky brains, our bodies and our social environment (see Chapters 3–5 for more on understanding ourselves). This helps to create the foundation for letting go of shame. We then develop our compassionate self, practice compassion for and from others, and work on our self-compassion to help us further (see Chapters 10–12 for more). This 'flow' of compassion is an important overarching theme that runs throughout this book.

CONFUSING SHAME WITH OTHER CHALLENGING EMOTIONS

Many people use the terms shame, embarrassment, guilt and humiliation interchangeably. Although each is associated with self-conscious feelings, they're very different. To understand these differences, here they are in a nutshell:

- We feel *guilt* when we believe we've done something wrong and feel we need to make amends. Guilt is linked to caring and, as long as it's not misplaced (such as feeling guilty for something that's not our responsibility), it can be a good thing for ourselves, other people and society.

- *Humiliation* brings with it feelings of anger that we've been placed in such a position by someone. We may feel the urge to retaliate to gain back power and control.

- *Embarrassment* happens when we feel judged negatively, but we don't believe the incident sums us up. For example, you may have tripped up in the street, gone out with food in your hair or come back from the toilet with your skirt in your knickers or your flies undone! Any of these sound familiar? We often laugh with others about things that are embarrassing, and this can be a positive, connecting experience.

The burden of self-criticism

Self-criticism is the critical way we talk to ourselves and is associated with emotions such as anger, disappointment and frustration. Relating to ourselves in such a way increases our risk of experiencing a range of psychological problems. Self-criticism has also been found to maintain them. Research suggests that self-critical people may do less well in therapy and experience poorer physical health and relationships.

Self-criticism can take a number of forms. For some, it comes with feelings of inadequacy; for others, self-hatred. Needless to say, whatever form self-criticism takes, addressing the problem is worthwhile.

Becoming familiar with your self-critic

Self-criticism highlights two aspects of ourselves. Our *self-critic* is the part of us that says all those horrible things in our heads (or sometimes out loud!). On the receiving end of the abuse is our *criticised self*.

The following exercise looks to increase your awareness of your self-critic and how it affects you. Begin by finding a place you can sit for a short time that is free from distractions. Allow yourself to settle for a few moments. It may help to lower your gaze or close your eyes during the exercise.

1. **Think back to a recent occasion when you were critical of yourself (nothing too distressing, but something you feel okay to revisit briefly).** It may be something difficult at work, or maybe you lost something or made a mistake.

2. **See the situation in your mind's eye once more. Imagine seeing your self-critic. Ask yourself the following questions:**

- What does your self-critic look like?
- What kind of facial expression does it have?
- What size is it, relative to you?
- What is its tone of voice?
- What is its posture like?
- Is it making any particular movements?
- What emotions is it directing your way?
- Does it remind you of anyone?

3. **Allow the experience to fade from your mind's eye. Now recall a time when you've felt content or happy and let this memory fill your mind and body.**

When we look properly at our self-critic, we often find it's associated with feelings of frustration, contempt, disapproval and anger. It may loom large or take the form of a little gremlin that wags its finger in disapproval. Its tone of voice is hostile, aggressive, patronising or condescending. It can evoke memories from the past, of a person (or people) who was (or continues to be) critical of you and your efforts.

Understanding why we criticise ourselves

What purpose do you think your self-critic serves? Maybe you think it can help you in some way? The following exercise explores this question in more detail.

For a moment, imagine that you take a magic pill and, as a result, you're never going to be self-critical again.

>> What do you think your greatest fear may be?

>> What do you think may happen if you let your self-critic go?

When I conduct this exercise in workshops, it's hard to keep up with the fears shouted out by the audience. Here are the top five answers (but there are many more!):

>> I'll be lazy and I won't get things done

>> I'll become self-absorbed and egotistical

>> I'll make mistakes

>> I won't improve my life or learn anything new

>> People won't like me

As you can see, your self-critic is more than just a finger-wagging gremlin designed to give you a hard time! On the one hand, we know that self-criticism isn't good for our wellbeing and is linked to a number of problems . . . But on the other hand, we think it helps us get things done, makes us a nice person and stops us making mistakes!

We're born without shoes on our feet (thankfully, say all the mothers in chorus!). But most of us consider that shoes are a necessity and therefore wear them. We're also born with a tendency to look out for danger and to signal threats by shouting. Unfortunately, we do this to ourselves in all manner of ways, from calling ourselves an idiot when we've lost our keys (my favourite pastime) to calling ourselves fat when we look in a mirror. Developing your compassionate mind and compassionate self is like putting your shoes on. It supports and helps you navigate the difficulties that life puts in your way.

REMEMBER

Just because we're born like this, it doesn't mean that we need to live our lives like it. With an awareness of what helps us (and what doesn't) we can consciously choose a different way of relating to ourselves. Your self-critic is likely to leave you feeling bullied, down and anxious, while your compassionate self provides you with the strength and courage to face difficult situations and move in a more helpful direction.

Beginning to overcome self-criticism

The exercises in the previous two sections may have illustrated the bullying nature of your self-critic, but they may also have highlighted potential concerns that you may have about letting go of your self-critic.

This next exercise helps you to explore what is motivating your self-critic.

Think back to the situation in which you were self-critical that you identified in the earlier section, 'Becoming familiar with your self-critic':

>> What did your self-critic want?

>> What's underneath its anger, disapproval or disappointment?

>> Is it going about things the right way?

You may discover that your self-critic has your best interests at heart, but it's going about things the wrong way. As such, you may find that it's unhelpful to battle with or respond to your self-critic; instead, it may be helpful to try to develop an alternative way to achieve the things you want to achieve in your life. This is at the heart of CFT. We build a compassionate relationship with ourselves (and with our self-critic too!).

TIP

Certain experiences can lead us to believe we deserve punishment, and this may lie behind self-criticism and self-attacking. For example, children are sometimes told that they have something wrong with them, or they hold themselves responsible for things that aren't their fault. This can make it hard for them to develop self-compassion. Chapters 6 and 7 explore some of the barriers that you may encounter as you develop your compassionate mind and compassionate self. Alternatively, if you think that this is a problem for you, consider speaking to a professional who can assist you in your efforts.

The following exercise helps you to consider whether self-criticism or self-compassion acts as a better guide for you in your life.

Imagine a child for whom you care greatly. It's your first visit to their new school and you go for a meeting with the head teacher. 'There are two classes for each age group,' she says, 'why don't you go and speak to each teacher and observe a bit of their lessons before deciding which class you want your child to join?'

You meet the first teacher. They tell you that they're going to do their best to help your child reach their potential. With a stern voice she says, 'Children improve by the speed at which I correct their mistakes; I use the tone of my voice and tell them off, in no uncertain terms. I often have them sit at the front of the class so that they learn not to repeat their mistakes. I'll find the best strategy to use for your child.'

As the teacher relays this information, a child spills a drink across the table and on the floor. Immediately, the teacher shouts, 'Be careful! Clean up that mess and don't be so clumsy again!' To reinforce this message, the child is told to stand up for the rest of the lesson. The teacher whispers in your ear, 'If they learn that bad things happen after they've made a mistake, they quickly learn not to make them.'

Having said your goodbyes, you enter the other class. The second teacher tells you that they too wish your child to reach their potential. With a warm voice, she says, 'It's very important for children to profit by their mistakes, be open about them, curious about how they came about, and learn to prevent them in the future.'

As you're speaking, a child's knife and fork clatter to the floor. 'Just a moment,' the teacher says to you. As she squats down next to the child, she gently enquires, 'What happened?'

The child replies, 'I was getting my drink and my elbow caught my knife, and that caught my fork, and . . .'. The teacher responds, 'Okay, we need to give this some time and thought, because this keeps happening, doesn't it. How about we have a chat about it?' And so the conversation between child and teacher continues for a little while and in a gentle manner.

Which teacher would you choose for your child?

If the answer is the second teacher, pause for a moment and consider why you're always sending yourself to the first teacher – a critic?

TIP

Learning from your mistakes is very important, but you have a much better chance of doing this, and doing it in a sustainable way, if you encourage yourself with kindness, warmth and non-judgement rather than undermining yourself with self-criticism, frustration and contempt. I'm not sure about you, but if I was a child faced with the first teacher I'd be more likely to deny it was me, blame someone else or wet myself!

In case you're thinking that the antidote to self-criticism is always to be soft and gentle, it may help to consider a different scenario.

Imagine you're a firefighter going into a burning building. What kind of person would you like to give you cover and support as you go? Someone who says with strength and support, 'I've got your back, you can do this' or someone who shouts 'Get in there!' and is quick to criticise if things don't go to plan?

Both people probably lead you to do your job with the same urgency, adrenaline racing through your body, but with the first you're likely to feel supported and part of a team. With the second, you're more likely to feel on your own, with even higher levels of anxiety.

TIP

When things get tough, we need a friend by our side. Someone with our best interests at heart, who is warm, non-judgemental, honest and supportive. We'd look for these qualities in someone else, so why not in ourselves? This is the essence of CFT.

REMEMBER

Someone who truly has your best interests at heart, and is able to act on them, won't just say 'there, there, never mind' if you need to address or confront something. But neither will they beat you up like your self-critic is prone to do. They'll help you reflect, see things from a different perspective and make changes.

DISTINGUISHING BETWEEN SELF-CRITICISM AND COMPASSIONATE REFLECTION

Here are some of the ways self-criticism can differ from compassionate reflection:

Self-criticism	Compassionate reflection
Backward-looking	Forward-looking
Angry and hostile	Warm and non-judgemental
Telling yourself off	Considering personal growth
Punishing and condemning	Encouraging and supportive
Labelling/name calling	Provides perspective
Evokes fear and anxiety, or overwhelms	Evokes excitement and positivity
Increases avoidance and withdrawal	Increases engagement with life's challenges

Although it can seem as if our self-critic has our best interests at heart, it actually stimulates difficult emotions over and over again. In Chapter 4, you find out about how self-criticism can trigger your threat system.

A NOTE TO OTHER CFT THERAPISTS

Imagine a surgeon getting ready to operate. They'll make sure that the instruments they use are the best they can be. This involves preparation and sterilisation.

Many of us use our minds and bodies to help those in need, and so it's important to make sure that the instruments we use are the best they can be too. As therapists, we need to look after ourselves, developing and maintaining our compassionate minds and compassionate selves to do this work. It's helpful to use practices throughout the day to refresh and replenish ourselves so that we can be the best we can be.

In the following exercise, you contemplate living in a mind that's not condemning and critical but that's instead supportive of you and your efforts.

Imagine what would happen if you committed yourself to generating a friendly voice in your head that is always supportive and forward-looking. A voice that can quieten your self-critic, is strong and instils courage in you for facing life's difficulties. Would this be a worthwhile endeavour?

Saying goodbye to self-criticism doesn't mean that you never reflect on your thoughts, emotions and actions. Instead, you discover how to reflect compassionately on your life and your experiences. Check out the nearby sidebar 'Distinguishing between self-criticism and compassionate reflection' for more on the differences between the two.

Using CFT to address shame and self-criticism

Shame and self-criticism are associated with difficult psychological experiences. They can leave us feeling low, anxious, disconnected and sapped of energy. Shame and self-criticism can result when we act in response to a threat (see Chapter 4 for more), which can cause us considerable problems.

REMEMBER

CFT therefore helps us understand ourselves in order to address shame and self-criticism. CFT develops our compassionate mind, recruiting our full brain potential (instead of just our threat system) and our compassionate self in order to relate to ourselves and the world around us in a more helpful and meaningful way. This is beneficial for our own wellbeing and that of others.

Identifying the Steps Involved

CFT begins with discovering more about ourselves, our amazing capacities and the challenges we face. This understanding starts at an intellectual level but, by allowing space for it to 'sink in', we also experience it at a profound emotional level. These experiences help us to address our tendency for shame and self-criticism. They also help us to make sense of difficulties we may experience with emotions, behaviours, thoughts and relationships. Parts 1 and 2 of this book focus on understanding the challenges we face in our lives, and understanding ourselves and how we can work to manage these challenges.

As we begin to understand ourselves better, we start to realise the choices we have. Who do we want to be? Which parts of us do we want to nurture? We become aware of the commitment that making changes requires and develop the motivation to make these changes.

If we're motivated to develop and cultivate our compassionate self, we can use a whole range of practices to help us improve our wellbeing. Parts 3 and 4 delve deeper into CFT, introducing further compassionate practices and offering guidance on widening our experience of compassion.

Connecting with Compassion

Although we're each unique, we're actually more similar than we realise, and we share a common humanity: we're all trying to get by in life, as best we can. With this in mind, we look at a simple exercise that can help to connect you with the wider CFT community.

Close your eyes or lower your gaze, and for a few minutes simply bring your awareness to all the other people who have read or are reading this book. Consider that they, like you, are trying to discover information and practices that may be of benefit to themselves and others. Experience a sense of connection with them.

Bring your attention to me, as I write these words, and my own journey through life's struggles and amazing experiences. Move on to consider those individuals who haven't come across CFT as yet, but who you hope will gain benefit from experiencing compassion in their lives.

Simply sit with this sense of common humanity and, over the coming weeks, months and years, continue to connect with it.

Chapter 2

Understanding Compassion

O ver the centuries compassion has been defined in slightly different ways. Compassion Focused Therapy (CFT) understands compassion to be a sensitivity to distress (be it our own or that of other people) paired with a motivation to prevent or alleviate distress. As a result, we see two distinct yet related psychologies associated with compassion: tuning in to distress and doing something about it.

We can get an insight into how the brain operates when individuals are in a compassionate frame of mind by using modern-day brain-scanning techniques. We can literally observe how compassion affects our brain! We can also study how compassion affects us physically.

In this chapter, we focus on the development of six attributes that make up your compassionate mind and look carefully at six skills. We explore how compassion feels physically and emotionally. (Later in this book, we look at the embodiment of your compassionate mind in more detail. In CFT, this is referred to as your compassionate self.)

REMEMBER

You may find that you have attributes and skills aplenty in certain areas of your life, but not in others. This is unique to you: it differs from person-to-person, situation-to-situation, day-to-day and even minute-to-minute. Noticing such things provides you with an opportunity to consider why this is the case for you, and to discover more about yourself and other people.

You may struggle at first to apply the attributes and skills of compassion to yourself and your own situation. Developing self-compassion is key to the development of your compassionate mind, and this is the focus for much of this book.

Learning from Experience

Compassion affects us in a range of different ways. In this section, we explore these effects using three brief exercises. (In Chapters 10–12, we expand on these exercises further in order to enhance your compassionate mind and compassionate self.)

The first exercise helps you to notice how compassion for someone or something else affects you:

1. **Close your eyes and imagine that you're in the presence of a child or an animal in distress.** Try not to think of anything too upsetting. Maybe the child has fallen and grazed their knee or the animal has been startled by the bang of fireworks and is showing signs of anxiety.

2. **Consider your physical and emotional response to the distressing image.** What do you notice in your body? Are your feelings concentrated in any particular area? What do you feel motivated to do?

3. **Allow the image to fade, and then bring to mind something that makes you smile slightly.** Maybe think about the memory of a beautiful view, a happy time with someone you care about or a good film. Allow this experience to sink in, and, as you relax, you may notice that your breathing becomes slower and deeper than usual.

During this exercise, you're likely to have focused on the feelings of the child or animal. You probably didn't focus your attention on yourself. You may have experienced a pull towards the child or animal, perhaps feeling this in your chest or your stomach. In addition, you may have felt motivated to step in, intervene or comfort them. This sense of courage and this motivation to take action is key to our experience of compassion.

The exercise helps us realise that compassion isn't a warm and fuzzy feeling (although there are situations when compassion can make us feel like that). Engaging with our compassionate mind often brings difficult emotions and bodily sensations. Head to Chapters 6 and 7 to explore some of the myths about compassion.

The experience of compassion for a child or animal is likely to differ from that for a friend or relative. You can explore this in the following exercise.

1. **Close your eyes and imagine that someone you care about is in the throes of loss.** Imagine sitting with them as tears roll down their face.

2. **Consider your physical and emotional response to this unsettling situation.** What do you notice in your body? What do you feel motivated to do?

3. **Allow the image to fade and consider this person in a more content situation and a happier frame of mind.** Allow the experience of them being content and happy to sink in. You may experience a sense of warm connection and maybe joy in your relationship with this person.

Once again, your mind may focus on the other person rather than yourself. You're likely to feel emotionally moved by their distress. An emotional pull towards this person may also be present; however, what you feel motivated to do may have changed. In a situation like this, you may feel motivated to 'be with' the person in their distress rather than to 'do' something or to intervene in any way.

REMEMBER

The specifics of a situation guide us in a certain way. Sometimes we may be motivated to take clear action, and sometimes our actions may be more subtle. However you react, the common aim is to alleviate distress.

Consider one more exercise to help you explore the impact that a compassionate response has on you:

1. **Close your eyes and bring to mind a dilemma, a disagreement or something that caused you to be upset, angry or anxious.** You don't need to think about anything too distressing, just something that brings with it a degree of discomfort.

2. **Imagine that someone is with you to support you through this situation.** How does that feel? Where do you feel it? When you're in their presence, do you feel motivated in a different way?

3. **Allow this experience to fade from your mind's eye and then recall a time when you have felt a sense of contentment.** You may find that you experience a sense of warmth or feel a slight smile appear on your face, and you may also notice that your breathing is slower and deeper than usual.

When we imagine a compassionate response from someone else, some of the difficulties we're struggling with seem to fade slightly. We may experience differences in our emotions, in our bodies and in our motivations as a direct result of this compassionate response.

Our attention moves from the situation we're experiencing and towards the other person and our sense of connection with them. You may have experienced a feeling of warmth. Perhaps for a fleeting moment you felt that you're not alone with your problems, and that, instead, your problems are shared. This can provide clarity, greater perspective and a clearer mind to help you think things through.

REMEMBER

Compassion affects us in many ways. It guides our attention and changes how we feel both physically and emotionally. It motivates us to tune in to and do something about the difficulties that others experience. It can also motivate us to be aware of the difficulties in our own lives, and to act in a way that is helpful to us.

Taking a Look at Compassionate Attributes

The exercises in the preceding section remind you what compassion feels like. In order to begin to build our compassionate mind, it's helpful to further define what compassion is composed of. It's a bit like knowing the ingredients that make up a chocolate cake – it's all well and good saying we like the cake as a whole, but it helps to consider what goes into it, especially if we wish to recreate it.

Based on decades of research, Paul Gilbert outlined, in his bestselling book *The Compassionate Mind* (Constable & Robinson Ltd), six *attributes* (or qualities) of compassion that are experienced in the context of emotional warmth. Warmth is key, as it can help us change a cold and intellectual concept into something that is more meaningful – something that we feel rather than just think.

Each of the six attributes are distinct from each other, but they're also closely related and complementary. In this section, I introduce you to each attribute in turn.

TIP

As you read about these six attributes of compassion, you may be aware of personal sticking points with respect to one or more of them. If this is the case, spend a little time exploring your concerns and fears.

The chapters in Part 2 of this book may help you understand the reasons why you experience difficulties with certain attributes, and explore and address some of these difficulties.

Care for wellbeing

Caring for the wellbeing of others requires motivation and a commitment to act in a way that has others' best interests at heart. However, compassion also involves caring for your own wellbeing.

Imagine that you've been avoiding making a phone call for a week or more due to the feelings associated with a potentially awkward conversation. Maybe this is something you're familiar with – or maybe you tend to avoid some other situations that you can bring to mind.

Motivated by care for your own wellbeing, consider if it's helpful to continue to avoid the situation or conversation. Could it be that the most helpful thing to do involves picking up the phone or facing the situation?

REMEMBER

Many people mistakenly believe that they need to make a choice between prioritising themselves or other people. In fact, compassion can involve holding both ourselves and other people in mind. The next exercise helps us to consider this in a different way.

Imagine that you've been invited to a close friend's party. You've been looking forward to it for weeks, but as the date draws closer you realise that you're run down, you feel exhausted and you crave a night at home to relax and re-energise. What do you do?

Your anxious mind (head to Chapter 17 for more on your anxious mind) may lead you to avoid making a decision until the last minute, fearful of an awkward conversation. You may then push yourself to attend and arrive in a stressed frame of mind. Alternatively, you may create an excuse for not attending or simply not show up. It's unlikely that you'll have a relaxing night in!

Your compassionate mind helps you to calmly and warmly consider all of the different pieces of information and guides you towards the most helpful action to take.

This may result in you sending your apologies. However, it may also mean that, on balance, you decide that it's better to go to the party and give yourself permission to leave earlier than you initially planned, and to make sure that you have a good night's sleep the night before.

REMEMBER

In a compassionate frame of mind, you see things from multiple angles. This is in stark contrast to an anxious state of mind, whereby you may spend a lot of time worrying and may not make the best choice for both yourself and your friend.

In Chapter 4 you become familiar with your different states of mind and how they can affect everyday situations.

Caring for your wellbeing as well as the wellbeing of others can help you to develop the motivation and courage to face things. It can also allow you to see things from different perspectives and, with this wider view of the situation, decide the most helpful action to take.

Sensitivity

Our lives can be so fast-paced that we don't open ourselves to moment-by-moment experiences. We may not pay attention to our feelings and needs, or those of others. At other times, we may be aware that it can be helpful to work on certain things, but we don't 'go there' – we may instead focus on the never-ending treadmill of other routine demands, for example, to distract ourselves. As a result, we can ignore a lot of distress.

Of course, at times it's helpful and even necessary for us to keep a lid on strong emotions, until a time when we can notice, explore and work through them.

When we're ready to address these strong emotions, sensitivity is essential. It allows us to calmly and courageously open our minds and notice what is within and around us. We do this gently, with a sense of curiosity and emotional warmth. You discover how to do this as you work through this book and develop both your compassionate mind and compassionate self.

Being sensitive to your needs and feelings, and those of others, takes courage and strength. This is because it can put you in touch with emotions you may initially want to avoid, such as sadness, anger and anxiety. Your compassionate mind can help you to engage with and work through such experiences.

Sympathy

Sympathy involves being emotionally moved by the distress we tune into, whether it's our own or someone else's.

Sympathy is the attribute of compassion that people often struggle with. This is because they confuse it with 'pity' or a sense of 'looking down on someone'.

Contrary to this misconception, allowing ourselves to be emotionally moved by our own distress or that of others can take incredible courage. In such experiences we feel pain and a sense of common humanity and connection: we experience a sense of 'togetherness'.

In Chapter 6 we spend some time exploring this confusion between sympathy and pity.

COPING MECHANISMS FOR PHYSICAL AND EMOTIONAL DISTRESS

Human beings are amazing and can cope with an inordinate amount of pain and suffering. Sometimes the way that we cope and deal with things is automatic, and at other times we may consciously choose a certain strategy.

A few examples can help to illustrate our strengths:

- At the 2012 London Olympics, Manteo Mitchell broke his leg during the 4 x 400m relay. In a later interview, he said, 'I didn't want to let the three guys or the team down, so I just ran on it. It hurt so bad.' (More common and much less extreme stories, illustrating temporary insensitivity to physical distress, may involve blisters and pulled muscles.)

- Children growing up in difficult environments may show amazing resilience and adaptations. Of course, this can result in them being withdrawn, behaving aggressively, eliciting care from other sources, engaging in self-harm or being very driven, but all of these adaptations can be seen as functional given the environment in which they develop.

- Health professionals working in areas of conflict may see horrific suffering on a day-to-day, hour-to-hour basis. Despite (or maybe because of) this, they're able to dissociate from their own and other people's pain and suffering in order to carry out their job.

- You may have had the experience of 'putting a face on' when you're actually going through some difficult times or pushing through stress, tiredness and even illness. For example, have you ever found yourself preparing for a much-anticipated holiday, only to find that you wake up to exhaustion and even ill-health a day or two into your trip?

Timing and frame of mind are key to whether we're able to be sensitive to our needs and feelings and to deal with these as they arise, or whether it's more helpful to 'push though' or 'keep a lid on it'. It can be helpful to allow time to check in with yourself and others and to consider what's helpful. Difficulties often occur when we continually fail to tune into ourselves or other people and we overlook problems that require our attention.

If we see our own and other people's strengths in the context of our own and other people's struggles, we're likely to relate slightly differently to the distress we feel or see. Compassion, rather than pity, comes to the fore.

Empathy

Empathy allows us to think about and understand ourselves and other people. It helps us consider how others may feel, and to understand what motivates them. It enables us to see things from different perspectives and, in the context of our difficulties, think about what we, or someone else, may need.

REMEMBER

Empathy differs from sympathy. Sympathy involves being moved by our own or another person's distress. Empathy allows us to consider what to do in order to alleviate this distress.

Although many programmes in schools and prisons have focused on the cultivation of empathy, on its own it doesn't necessarily bring about positive changes in behaviour or increased social-connectedness. In fact, taken to its extremes, empathy can be used for great cruelty. For example, 'victim empathy' programmes can help individuals bring to mind what others may feel and how they might behave, but if this isn't paired with a sense of warmth, care and compassion for the other person, it's not likely to change the offenders' behaviour because they're not moved by the person's distress. In stark terms, a non-empathic torturer may put a gun to your head, but an empathic one may instead point it at someone you love.

Non-judgement

The wiring or set-up of our brain means we often make judgements – some are helpful, others not so helpful. Much of this is fuelled by our need to feel safe, secure and part of a group. Our judgements can create a sense of certain groups being 'bad', 'wrong' or different to us. We may view teenagers in hoodies as sinister or people with a certain diagnosis as dangerous, for example. We may perceive these judgements or views as helpful, but they can often be negative and extremely unhelpful.

Judgements can increase our anxiety or anger. They may make us defensive or avoidant, leaving us less open to others.

When we're in a compassionate frame of mind, we're aware of the challenges our brain places in our path; these challenges are outlined in Chapter 3. We're able to reflect on the judgements that we tend to make. We also become aware of the judgements that others are making and what fuels them. A non-judgemental stance means that we're not condemning and critical of others or ourselves – even when we notice that we have been critical and judgemental!

REMEMBER

Taking a non-judgemental stance creates space for reflection and provides an opportunity to consider a different perspective.

Imagine that you have three colleagues:

>> One holds strong negative views about certain things. She talks with distain about those she labels as needy and attention-seeking. She says people should get a grip and get on with things instead of moaning.

>> The second is curious and non-judgemental about people and their experiences. She's also open about some of her own difficulties and, from time to time, shows her emotions.

>> The third is extremely attentive when anyone shows that they're having any difficulty. She constantly asks how they are – in person, by text and by email. Even when things are going well she continues to probe for information.

Who are you more likely to open up to if you're having difficulties? Why is this?

Of course, we're all different – and different situations sometimes require different approaches. But it's unlikely that you'll risk opening up to the first colleague for fear of negative judgement.

You may decide to open up to the third – but this may prove tricky, as her judgment about your ability to cope may feel overwhelming. Her behaviour and emotional state may mean that you feel worse about yourself, because you're reminded of your difficulties, and you may then question your ability to cope.

In contrast, many people are more likely to open up to the second due to their non-judgemental, curious and open stance.

Of course, these examples are extremes, designed to make a point, because most people can behave differently in different circumstances. However, it hopefully illustrates that when we're with someone who isn't judgemental, we're more likely to explore our issues, consider our own role in situations and develop the motivation and courage to do something helpful. When we judge ourselves or others, we provide fewer opportunities for new discoveries.

Openness, curiosity and a non-judgmental stance are the attributes we may choose to have in our friends, family, and almost certainly in a therapist.

REMEMBER

Distress tolerance

Distress tolerance requires you to experience difficult emotions, despite the urge to suppress them or push them away. Such emotions may include anxiety, sadness, anger, jealousy or guilt. As we discover in Chapter 7, distress can also be paired with experiences such as compassion, happiness and joy.

SOFIA'S STORY: CONNECTING WITH DIFFICULT EMOTIONS

Sofia had a difficult relationship with her mother. Growing up, she benefitted greatly from the support of her friends and some of their parents. She coped in one way or another throughout her life.

Sofia met her partner, Jude, at the age of 21 and, keen for their relationship not to be tarnished by her complex family dynamics, she kept her relationship with Jude quite separate from the rest of her family. When Jude suggested that they move 200 miles away, she jumped at the chance. At 25, Sofia gave birth to a beautiful baby boy. Consumed with an urge to protect and care for him, she began to think more and more about her own childhood. She began to feel angry about the things that had or hadn't worked out well for her.

Sofia started to tell herself off, with thoughts such as, 'Stop it . . . you're just going to be like *her*.' When she was feeling sad, she worried that she would become overwhelmed, and when she was feeling anxious, she told herself to 'snap out of it.'

During the first two years of her son's life, Sofia worked hard to keep all of her emotions at bay, but doing so began to take its toll on her wellbeing. She felt tense, low and angry, and she began to wonder what kind of mother she was to her son. Sofia was tearful much of the time and felt a sense of hopelessness and helplessness.

After an emotional GP appointment, Sofia agreed to be referred to the local psychology service. At her first appointment with her therapist, Sofia said she just wanted to feel better and wanted some coping strategies. She was especially fed up with feeling angry and sad, and said that she felt stuck. During subsequent appointments, Sofia began to realise that she hadn't given herself time to properly work through the strong emotions she felt because she was constantly pushing them away.

By developing care for her own wellbeing, Sofia made an active choice to connect with her anger and sadness. She began to voice her frustration and cry. As time went on, Sofia's hopelessness, helplessness, frustration and anxiety began to subside. She began to connect once more with her son, and her relationship with Jude also improved as she began to open up to him and to explain the difficulties she'd experienced in her life.

Although at times it may be important to keep difficult emotions in check, it's imperative that we don't do this all the time, as long-term avoidance of our emotions is widely considered to lie at the root of many psychological difficulties.

TIP

Emotions are there for a reason, and it can be helpful to view them as our friends. They guide us towards our goals and can alert us to realise when our goals are blocked. They can also help us process loss: when we allow ourselves to grieve, we allow ourselves to begin the process of healing.

REMEMBER

As we develop our compassionate mind, we discover how to approach and work through the distress we feel step by step.

Exploring the Skills of the Compassionate Mind

Compassion isn't all hearts and flowers. It involves being both sensitive to distress and doing something about it. It requires us to turn towards difficult emotions and physical sensations and address them – which can be difficult.

Our compassionate mind and compassionate self require certain skills that we need to develop and maintain. Just as you learn to swim in shallow water, I recommend that you learn the skills when you're in a relatively calm frame of mind (and not battling torrential rain!). As John F Kennedy famously said, 'the time to repair the roof is when the sun is shining.' As time goes by you'll find you can increasingly apply a compassionate approach to difficult times in your life – when the storm clouds appear.

Using compassionate attributes as a base (refer to the earlier section, 'Taking a Look at Compassionate Attributes'), Paul Gilbert, in his book *The Compassionate Mind* (Constable & Robinson Ltd), defined six *skills* (or things to do) to help harness and maintain your compassionate mind.

TIP

Thinking of compassionate attributes and skills in the following way can be helpful.

Imagine a six-legged stool, with each leg representing one of the six attributes of compassion. This structure provides a solid and strong base. Remove any of the legs and the structure is still stable (but perhaps a little less so). Now imagine that the seat itself is made up of a tight six-way cane weave, each strand representing one of the compassionate skills.

The compassionate attributes and the skills are integral to each other – the structure wouldn't be a stool without either the base or the seat. Figure 2-1 shows how you can think of the compassionate attributes and skills as this stool.

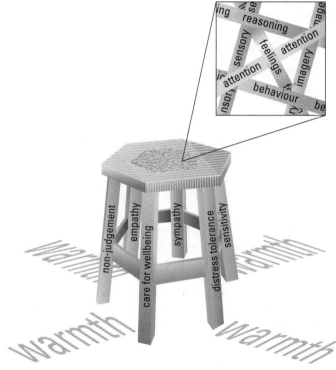

From Welford, The Compassionate Mind Approach to Building Your Self Confidence (2012),
reprinted with permission from Little, Brown Book Group

FIGURE 2-1:
A six-legged stool illustrates the relationship between compassionate attributes and compassionate skills.

It may help to think of another analogy to illustrate the importance of these attributes and skills. Imagine that you have a broken arm and go to the hospital. The nurse who sees you shows warmth and sensitivity, yet does nothing to practically alleviate your pain. A second shows no warmth at all and rather insensitively pulls your arm around in order to set the break. It's clear that both nurses approach you in a way that may be beneficial, but it's the combination that's the most potent mix: sensitivity to distress, plus the application of the skills to address it.

The attributes and skills combine effectively to allow you to build and maintain your compassionate mind and compassionate self. The more you develop and use them, the more robust your compassionate mind and its embodiment as the compassionate self becomes. You may choose to focus initially on what you find relatively easy, and then, gently and courageously, begin to consider the areas that you find difficult.

Each skill is distinct, but they're also closely related and complementary. In the following sections, I introduce you to each skill in turn. I also direct you to other chapters in this book that explore these skills in far more detail.

Compassionate reasoning

Practising compassionate reasoning involves understanding ourselves and the situations we subsequently find ourselves in. This is also something we can develop in relation to other people's feeling and behaviours.

The foundation of compassionate reasoning can be found in attributes such as empathy and sensitivity to distress (for more on these attributes, check out the earlier section, 'Taking a Look at Compassionate Attributes'). Being non-judgemental is also crucial. As you develop your compassionate reasoning skills, you begin to see how the relationship between attributes and skills works to strengthen your compassionate mind.

In Chapter 5, we focus on your life story, and the things that you currently find difficult, in order to help you develop this skill. You can then apply this skill to other situations and, if appropriate, other people.

In Chapter 13, we focus on identifying the thoughts you have, considering whether they're helpful and cultivating new ways of thinking. This type of compassionate reasoning can be extremely helpful in the development of your compassionate mind.

Compassionate imagery

When we're anxious, it's easy to generate frightening images in our minds – whether these are images from the past or from the predicted future. Self-criticism, shame and low mood can also evoke difficult images.

In contrast, compassionate images (such as the one generated in the third exercise in the earlier 'Learning from Experience' section) are supportive, understanding, kind and encouraging. Compassionate imagery is a key focus in Chapters 10–12.

Compassionate attention

What we attend to can have a great bearing on the thoughts and images that occupy our mind, how we feel physically, what we're motivated to do and the emotions we feel. Although much of our attention is automatic, we can discover how to consciously bring our attention to the things that are helpful to ourselves and others. Chapter 8 explores compassionate attention in more detail.

Compassionate sensory experience

The sensory qualities of compassion are not confined to our feelings. They include the tone of voice that we use and hear, and how we feel in our body and in relation to the things around us.

I refer to the importance of our tone of voice throughout this book, and Chapter 9 focuses on posture and breathing, as well as mindful awareness – all of which can alter and enhance our sensory experience, and therefore increase the capacity of our compassionate mind and its embodiment as our compassionate self.

Compassionate behaviour

Compassionate behaviour emerges from the compassionate motivation to alleviate and prevent suffering. It involves embodying our compassionate mind and behaving in a way that's beneficial for our own wellbeing and for the wellbeing of others. We refer to your compassionate mind in action as your *compassionate self*. You discover more about your compassionate self in Chapter 10 and compassionate behaviour in Chapter 15.

Compassionate feelings

You aim to cultivate and enhance feelings of warmth, kindness and connectedness. At times, as you focus your compassionate mind on suffering, be it your own or other people's, you're likely to feel emotionally moved. At other times, compassionate feelings may involve a sense of excitement or enthusiasm in relation to what you're motivated to do and the efforts you're making.

TIP

Maybe you haven't realised it before, but your feelings can be nurtured and developed. They're not something you simply have or haven't got. Feelings are a pivotal component of our compassionate mind, and so you can consider them as a skill that you can develop and utilise.

Although many of the chapters in this book aim to foster compassionate feelings, Chapters 9–11 pay particular attention to their development.

Chapter 3

Making Sense of Life's Challenges

Our experiences, influences and biology can mean our *lives can live us* rather than *us living our lives*. We're prone to shame, self-criticism, acting on impulses, negative judgements of others and an array of psychological difficulties. Sometimes we embark on destructive and addictive behaviours in an attempt to adapt and cope with the challenges around us.

CFT reminds us that we're the product of evolution, of repeated patterns that have been created and developed in our brains over millions of years. The functions and capacities of our evolved brain have been hugely important for the creation and survival of our species – but they come with drawbacks.

Each one of us is not the first and we won't be the last to have certain experiences, feel particular emotions, have certain thoughts or behave in particular ways. Waking up to this, we begin to feel connected to others rather than different.

Understanding the influences of our environment, experiences and biology allows us to press the pause button on our hectic lives and make choices. Do we want to live on automatic pilot, or instead put our efforts into cultivating our compassionate mind and compassionate self?

By looking to your compassionate mind for guidance, you can begin to consciously *grow through your life* in a way that's helpful to you, choosing the version of yourself that you want to be.

In this chapter, we consider how and why our brains have evolved such complicated and tricky response mechanisms, and what the implications are for our lives. We also reflect on our individual nature, and consider the impact that our close environment and the wider world around us has on our state of mind.

REMEMBER

With this understanding of how our brains work and why we deal with life's challenges in the way that we do, we can more effectively open ourselves to compassion. Without this understanding we can too easily fall into the trap of negative judgements, self-criticism and shame.

Recognising That You Have a Tricky Brain

In this section, I look at some of the problems that we encounter due to the design and functioning of our brains. We use the term *tricky* to reflect our brains' complexity but also the problems our brains can cause us. We also consider how you can have mixed emotions, fall into specific roles and relate to yourself in unhelpful ways. I provide lots of exercises and examples to help you appreciate just how complicated we are and how many challenges we face. Some of them may bring a knowing smile to your face as you see the common traps that you yourself may fall into.

Considering evolution, from reptile, to human

Evolution builds on previous designs and doesn't allow a return to the drawing board. As such, the human brain is built upon the mammalian brain, which, in turn, is built on the reptilian brain.

To help you visualise this development process, check out this exercise. It's based on a simplified evolutionary understanding and helps to illustrate the complex biological basis for our more instinctive behaviours, thoughts and emotions.

Draw an oval in the centre of a piece of paper. This oval represents the brain of a reptile (it may help to bring to mind a lizard or turtle). Making sure that your oval is big enough, make a note within it of all the things that reptiles are interested in and the skills they have. The following list gives you some ideas to choose from. (*Note:* You will return to this list throughout this exercise!)

Possible skills and interests for reptiles, mammals and humans

Acquiring food	Alliance building
Displays of aggression	Forming hierarchies
Forward planning	Gaining and defending territory
Impulsiveness	Keeping away from others
Living in groups	Mating
Nurturing young	Play
Rapidly detecting threats	Reasoning and reflection
Self-awareness	Symbolism and creativity
Thinking about the past and future	Thinking about thoughts
Thinking about what others are thinking	Water and shelter

Now draw a larger oval around the first oval. This larger oval represents the mammalian brain (it may help to bring to mind a monkey). Using the preceding list of possibilities, make a note of what you think a mammal's skills and interests may be in the doughnut–shaped space around the reptilian brain (no need to include the things that you've already noted in the inner reptilian brain oval).

TIP

It may help to put a line though each of the skills and interests from the earlier list as you use them.

Finally, draw a third, larger oval around the first two ovals. This final encompassing oval represents the human brain. Use the preceding list to fill the newly created doughnut–shaped space around the mammalian brain with all the additional things that humans are interested in and the unique skills that we have (once again, there is no need to include the things that you've already noted for reptiles and mammals and that humans also share).

Stand back from the image that you've drawn and the accompanying words within it. Consider what you and every other person is up against. In one form or another *all* these skills and interests are part of us: we can be territorial and detect threats very rapidly; we spend time working out our place in the pecking order; we require the nurturing of others; we think about the past and future; we think about thought itself; and we even worry about what everyone else is thinking!

EVOLUTION: FACT OR THEORY?

Compassion Focused Therapy (CFT) draws heavily on the concept of evolution and the impact it's had on our bodies – especially our brains. Central to evolution is the belief that humans evolved from single-celled organisms, and from reptiles and apes. The process of natural selection makes certain traits, characteristics, physical attributes and skills more common and others less so.

However, you can find other theories on how we came to be. For example, many people believe in the idea of 'intelligent design' (that is, the belief that there's an intelligent cause or force behind the features of the universe and living things, rather than natural selection). Others believe that human beings were created and that we didn't descend from any other animal life.

Instead of seeing the differences between each theory and discarding any idea that doesn't seem possible, it's helpful to look towards the similarities between theories and to respect differing views. Hopefully, we can all agree that we have a very tricky brain that has evolved at least since human beings existed (and that in itself is a very long time). In addition, perhaps we can also agree that our brain development is influenced by our experiences, and in this book we look at this aspect in a lot more detail.

Looking at old motives and new capacities

Our evolved brain creates a tendency for mental loops and conflicts (as one reaction leads to another, much like a pinball). Here are a number of scenarios that demonstrate the challenges that your evolved brain can present you with – see if any of them are familiar to you!

TIP

It may help you to recall the oval diagram that you drew in the exercise in the preceding section as you work your way through each of the following scenarios.

Consider the following:

>> Imagine that you're the first to board a train. The second passenger sits directly in front, behind or next to you. What happens then? It's likely that your territorial brain has a lot to say about it. You may feel anxious or angry and have related thoughts about that person and yourself.

Intellectually, you know that there's nothing wrong with someone sitting so close to you. They may be trying to be more sociable because they're lonely or they may always sit there as a matter of routine. However, your territorial brain generally gets the better of you and, until getting off, you're likely to continue to feel wound up in one form or other.

When a lizard's territory is breached, it takes a defensive stance and may become aggressive. In the same way, the reptilian aspect of our brain reacts to a range of situations, including the one in the preceding example – but then it triggers our amazing human brain's capacities, such as imagining what may happen next, predicting what someone else is thinking, and maybe also judging ourselves.

This toxic mix of reptilian territorialism and our human capacities can result in arguments, road rage, boundary disagreements and acts of revenge – even wars. We may then employ lethal weaponry that we've spent money and time developing. Meanwhile, the lizard doesn't have such capacities at its claw-tips!

>> Imagine that you've got your favourite food in the house. Maybe it's chocolate, nuts, crisps, sweets or cream cakes. How long are you able to resist its call from the cupboard? Maybe you have just one or two at first, but this then turns into one more, and then another one?

With a full belly you may tell yourself off, even beat yourself up. This is your human brain stepping in and reflecting on what you've eaten and predicting weight gain and maybe ill health in the future. Left to its own devices, the human aspect of your brain sees this over-indulgence as a threat and takes a negative and critical tone.

>> Imagine a dog, having sneaked a string of sausages and wolfed them down, thinking 'I'm so greedy' or gazing at its reflection in a window and thinking 'Gosh, I look so fat!' Not very likely, is it! A dog's brain is simply not designed like ours. Lucky dogs!

For much of human evolution, food was scarce. It was beneficial for humans to eat whenever they had the opportunity, and for this reason we developed a tendency to 'see food and eat it'.

But now, in many parts of the world at least, you have never-ending opportunities to eat, meaning that food is often difficult to resist. (While driving, I have been known to throw half-eaten bars of chocolate onto the back seat of my car as an attempt to stop me finishing the bar – and even then I sometimes stop and retrieve it 'because I have to'!)

>> Imagine that you find someone attractive but you're already in a relationship. Maybe the person isn't the gender you're usually attracted to or not generally your type. How likely are you to tell yourself off about it, worry about what this means or monitor others to see if they're aware of your attraction?

Of course, it's perfectly normal for us to be attracted to others. It's also helpful to stop ourselves acting on our urges if doing so would be damaging to us or other people – but we can also create rules that are unhelpful and can damage our sense of self. If we don't understand ourselves, we're more likely to relate to ourselves in a hostile way. It's better if we compassionately understand our urges and then make helpful choices.

>> Imagine that you've got an interview or date. Just thinking about it may make your heart race. But your awareness of the importance of your performance in this scenario can actually get the better of you and may be your undoing.

You know that it's helpful to keep a calm head, but you can't stop your mind flitting from one thing to another, making negative predictions and monitoring other people's reactions. You may then become aware of your own anxiety and start to monitor it and to worry that it's beginning to show – and so the negative loop of automatic reaction and monitoring is reinforced, becoming even stronger.

After the event, you may go over and over it in your mind. Negative images – some real, some imagined – may pop into your head and you may berate yourself for the stupid answers you gave while performing under pressure.

>> Imagine pulling out of a junction and suddenly hearing a horn blare, alerting you that another car is approaching. The car swerves and narrowly misses you. Your heart races, but you're also relieved that you somehow avoided a serious accident.

Hours, days and even months later, your mind returns to the near miss. You think about what could've happened and experience a surge of panic all over again. You may tell yourself off repeatedly and begin to avoid driving, judging yourself not safe to be on the road.

Unfortunately, although experiences come and go, we're prone to rumination, and we worry and judge ourselves. Experiences can stay with us for life, undermining our wellbeing.

REMEMBER

A cat won't sit and ruminate about a near miss or worry about what it means for its future. Your average moggy simply finds some other mayhem and mischief to get involved with!

>> Imagine that you've overslept and you find yourself running for a rush-hour train. You board just in time. Out of breath and sweating, you squeeze down the carriage to get some air. Aware of your dry mouth, heavy breathing and light-headedness, you worry that you won't be able to swallow, you'll struggle to catch your breath or you may even faint. You wonder what others are thinking of you. What happens to your anxiety then? Panic is likely to set in, and it becomes a battle to keep it under control.

REMEMBER

Lizards don't plan their day, consciously working out how to get from A to B, or worry about getting somewhere on time. Nor are they aware of their breathing, busy checking their pulse or worrying about what other lizards are thinking of them!

Our amazingly complex and tricky human brain consciously monitors others and ourselves, and worries or gets angry about the things we become aware of. We even worry about worrying, and get angry about being angry! This is all perfectly normal, but it can become problematic.

TIP

Being aware of these human responses gives us the choice and opportunity to address feelings of shame and being self-critical. An in-depth understanding of ourselves, that includes understanding why we behave, feel and think the way we do, provides the foundation of compassion for ourselves and others.

REMEMBER

Our tendency for conflict and self-monitoring can result in all sorts of difficulties. We may struggle in anxiety-provoking situations and not achieve our goals. We may ruminate or criticise ourselves and become depressed. We may worry and experience panic attacks.

Obsessive compulsive disorder (OCD), post-traumatic stress disorder (PTSD), social anxiety, health anxiety and low self-esteem are just some of the difficulties we may struggle with as a consequence of our brain design.

Regulating our emotions: The three circles

Three brain systems have evolved within us to help organise our mind, and each gives rise to different emotions, feelings, urges and desires that influence both our minds and bodies. CFT refers to these systems as the *three circles*.

The relative development and strength of each system, or circle, has a strong impact on our everyday lives because one or two of these may begin to dominate or 'rule the show'. If your three circles become imbalanced, this can have a negative impact on your wellbeing.

The three circles deserve a chapter in their own right: we look at them in more detail in Chapter 4.

Appreciating your mixed emotions

Ever find that you're excited about something you're scared to death about, angry with someone you love or relieved about something that's incredibly upsetting? It's all perfectly normal, but if you're not aware of it, you may tell yourself off and feel confused.

Consider the following scenarios to explore this concept further:

>> Imagine that your boss criticises your work in a hostile manner. You may feel anxious that you'll lose your job, angry that your boss doesn't appreciate your effort and sad because you feel that you're not good enough.

> » Imagine that you're caring for your frail partner. Having asked them to move so that you can change the bed for them, they snap at you. You feel angry with them, yet, aware that they're easily frustrated, you also feel a pang of guilt and sadness. This is quickly followed by anxiety about how long you can continue to care for them.

> » Imagine the day before your wedding. You're excited, but you're also anxious about whether things will go okay. Fleeting doubts pop into your mind and you become frustrated with yourself for even entertaining them. Excitement, anxiety and frustration seem to roll into one and you end up feeling detached and exhausted.

Tricky, isn't it? We can feel multiple emotions about a single event, and when they come fast and furious it can pave the way to self-criticism, shame and feelings of being overwhelmed. It's like a game of pinball – but now it's 'multipinball', with large ball-bearings clashing against each other in all manner of ways. It's not your fault, however; it's a consequence of the tricky brains that we all have.

Chapter 17 helps you to further consider the impact of multiple and often competing emotions.

Understanding our social roles and relationships

Different relationships draw out different aspects of us. For example, at times we're in a dominant role, in others we're subordinate; we may be care-giving during one period or in one relationship, and care-receiving in another. Paul Gilbert, the founder of CFT, refers to these various aspects of ourselves as our *social mentalities*, and each organises the brain in a different way to help us achieve certain goals. We're born with the capacity for many of these roles, and they develop dependent upon our experiences and environment (see the nearby sidebar 'Paul Gilbert's social mentality theory' for more information). We may use them consciously or unconsciously, depending upon our situation.

Our wellbeing is related to how well we can move between, adapt and develop these different brain states. If we get stuck in one role, type of relationship or strategy, we may not be able to adapt to changes in our life or our circumstances.

PAUL GILBERT'S SOCIAL MENTALITY THEORY

Paul Gilbert first proposed *social mentality theory* in 1989. The theory explains how our mind organises itself to form different relationships. Different mentalities motivate and prepare us for different interactions with others. They organise our attention, emotion, cognition and behaviour in pursuit of our goals. In simple terms, our social mentalities are associated with the goals of gaining or giving care, co-operation, competition, or sexual goals.

Imagine your goal is to have sexual contact with someone. This will affect where you look, what thoughts occupy your mind, the emotions you feel, how you act and the way your body feels. Now contrast that with a situation in which you're motivated to care for someone. Consider what you attend to then – the thoughts you have, your emotions, your behaviour and your physical sensations. Finally, if you're in a competitive mentality (where your goal is to outsmart or outrun someone else), consider how that may affect your attention, thoughts, feelings, behaviour and body.

Understanding our own and other people's mentalities can help us account for seemingly unusual behaviour. For example, seeing someone cry is likely to trigger a caring mentality; however, if we're in a competitive state of mind, someone else's tears may be experienced as a triumph. Our mentalities, or other people's motivations, can also be misread and cause problems. For example, men report that they may think twice about approaching a child who is lost and distressed for fear that others will see their contact with the child in a negative way.

Our social mentalities impact not only on ourselves but also on other people. Consider two contrasting examples:

- If you're highly competitive (be it with yourself or others), you're less likely to help others, and this will affect your day-to-day life and the lives of those with whom you're competing.

- If you're mostly in a care-giving mentality, this may impact on your own wellbeing and, if taken to an extreme, you may become exhausted. It may also prevent others from developing their confidence (because they fail to learn things they could do for themselves).

The key to social mentality theory is that we're all constructed in particular ways dependent upon the goals we and other people are motivated towards. Social mentalities are extremely helpful to us but can cause us problems if we misread other people's intentions, become fixed in one way of relating to ourselves or are on the receiving end of particular mentalities from others.

Here are a few examples of the problems that can arise if we struggle to move between different social mentalities:

>> If you're a professional footballer and you've trained your brain to be competitive with yourself and with others, it's unhelpful for you to then be competitive when you're playing football with your seven-year-old child. It's more helpful to put your competitive mentality to one side and to think about what your son or daughter needs to develop their own confidence and skills.

>> If you've spent much of your life caring for others, and resisted any opportunities to be cared for yourself, you may find it a struggle when you become unwell and require treatment.

>> If you've been cared for during much of your life, it may be difficult to switch into a care-giving or dominant role if the need requires it.

>> If you've spent years looking out for and pursuing sexual partners, it can be difficult to commit to a monogamous relationship and interact with others without flirting.

Understanding the roles that we fall into and develop is helpful to us because, by better understanding ourselves, we're less prone to shame and self-criticism and more open to viewing ourselves with compassion. This insight, and the knowledge that we can train our brain in a way we can choose, can result in helpful changes.

Understanding your sense of self

Our sense of self is linked to our experiences and memories and to a feeling of consistency in our views, values, behaviours, relationships and emotions. The brain gets used to itself – what we're likely to do, say and feel in a range of situations. It's similar to us getting used to other people: we have a sense of others that's based on a catalogue of information we have about them.

Being aware of ourselves as 'I' or 'me' comes with an awareness of other people as being separate to us, with different views and motivations. This self-awareness, together with our tendency to place ourselves in hierarchies (for example, to judge ourselves as less attractive, able or intelligent than others), means that we compare ourselves to others in a more complex way than other species do.

But, as we discover in Chapter 1, we're more likely to judge ourselves negatively, and predict this to be the view that others hold of us. We judge ourselves as 'inferior' and may label ourselves as a 'failure'. Shame, anger, frustration, anxiety, disappointment and depression may follow. We may then engage in self-criticism, strive 'to prove' ourselves, avoid situations, and withdraw from other people. These behaviours can not only affect our relationships with others but can also have a big impact on the relationship we have with ourselves. Once again, an amazing human capacity (our sense of self) leaves us open to incredible difficulties.

REMEMBER

Your sense of self creates an inbuilt tendency to protect and defend itself (even if we don't like the self we believe we are!). It also creates the tendency to judge, criticise and attack others. From an evolutionary perspective, it provided a way for our ancestors to ensure that genes would be passed on, and it's how we also ensure that our genes are passed on today. By understanding our tendency to defend ourselves and judge others (due to our tricky brain), we open our mind to a more compassionate understanding of ourselves and others.

Your sense of self can give you an incredible experience of aloneness. This is because you may feel judged and have a sense of being 'other' or an 'outsider'. But it's also the birthplace of your motivation for connecting with others.

REMEMBER

CFT is not about thinking 'I'm brilliant' or that you're better than others. It's about seeing yourself, in the context of your life and evolution, as connected to others and every other living thing. Your compassionate mind can then help you to consider what would be helpful and to commit to making meaningful changes in your life.

Your sense of self can make you incredibly vulnerable to a sense of aloneness, but it's also the birthplace of your desire for connectedness.

REMEMBER

CFT asks you to first consider the version of your 'self' that you want to be. Through a range of practices, you can then work to develop and strengthen this version of yourself. You discover how to move your attention, and to develop your thoughts, feelings and behaviours. Each chapter of this book takes you through an aspect of this process. It takes time and effort, but it can have an immeasurable impact on your wellbeing.

THE DIFFERENT VERSIONS OF ME

Imagine if I'd been born to a different family and parented differently. Imagine if I'd grown up in a different country, with different values and views. Would I be the same version of Mary Welford that I am today? Imagine if I'd been accepted to study genetics rather than psychology. Would I be the same or different?

From the moment of our conception, so many things influence us – this version of me is the product of so many different factors. But by the same token we can choose to be different. Committing time and effort to this means that we can change our brain and change our lives.

Acknowledging Human Needs

Your experiences in life can affect your wellbeing and influence whether your needs are met. Following birth, we remain dependent upon others (usually our parents) for longer than any other species. The care we receive allows our basic needs to be met while our brains and bodies grow and mature. The nature of the relationship we have with our primary care-givers, often referred to as our *attachment*, influences the way our brain develops.

The nearby sidebar 'Genotypes, phenotypes and neuroplasticity' explores the impact experiences have on our minds and bodies.

GENOTYPES, PHENOTYPES AND NEUROPLASTICITY

The human brain is a social organ and needs input from and connectedness with other brains to develop. What you experience influences how your brain develops and the kind of person that you'll become.

Our *genotype* (or DNA sequence) gives us our potential for factors such as intelligence, speed over 100 metres and body shape, but our experiences influence which of our potentials are realised. This combination of biology and environment is termed our *phenotype*. For example, we all possess certain genes for height, but if we don't receive adequate nutrition we won't reach our potential. Similarly, we have the potential for feeling soothed and safe in our social group, but if our experiences in such groups haven't been positive we may develop a very watchful and untrusting way of being with others.

Our biology and experiences create a blueprint for how we form and manage future relationships. Our brains become 'wired' in a particular way. We react to things in a way that may make sense based on our past but that may become problematic in the present.

For example, a baby who's soothed when distressed develops feelings of safeness and security, an awareness of what helps calm them down and skills needed to seek out others or help themselves. Kindness, warmth and compassion from our primary care-givers results in the development of confidence and an ability to feel content or 'happy in our own skin'. It even improves our immune system and results in our brain developing in a way that allows the states of wellbeing and trust in others.

In contrast, a lack of kindness, warmth and compassion, especially in our formative years, and living in threatening environments are associated with increases in stress hormones and a poorer immune response. Anxiety and anger become familiar, preparing us to deal with threats. We become wary and mistrustful of others, have difficulty feeling secure, and find others 'hard to read'. The developing brain, and the brain of the subsequent adult, reflects this.

Of course, all of this can be further complicated when kindness, warmth and compassion are so alien or associated with difficult memories that they trigger fear or anger. Chapter 7 focuses on such difficulties and provides ideas relating to how they may be overcome.

Thankfully we can change things for the better if we're motivated and have the know-how. CFT relies on our brains' *neuroplasticity*. In other words, our brain can make adaptive changes whatever our age – we can stimulate new pathways and make new neurological connections. Many of the practices in this book help you do this.

OUR NEED TO CARE

Experiencing warmth, affection and a connection with others creates an environment for optimal brain development and emotional wellbeing. But what about our human need to *give* care?

The circumstances of our lives and our health (both physical and psychological) can mean that we're unable to help and care for others. As a result, we may then feel that we're not needed or of any use to anyone. If left unchecked, hopelessness, isolation, loneliness and depression can set in. Such experiences are common in those who are physically less able due to age or ill health.

Therefore, it's helpful to first recognise that the giving of care is a basic human need, instead of feeling shame about it. You may wish to then think about ways in which you can still provide care and therefore feel a sense of purpose. Chapter 12 can help you develop self-compassion in relation to difficulties you may have, while Chapter 15 may help you consider some helpful changes that you can make to ensure that your care and kindness has an outlet.

Recognising the Frailty of Life

With health and circumstances on our side, we live for approximately 30,000 days. But our bodies, like our brains, have also developed from an earlier evolutionary model. Our skeleton was originally designed for life in the water. Standing upright, on land, means that we're prone to problems with our backs, hips and knees. It also means that more human mothers and babies die in childbirth, if medical interventions are unavailable, than any other species.

As we age we get more aches, pains and illnesses. Many of us die young as a result of genetic factors or suffer from life-limiting conditions. Viruses, bacteria and parasites reproduce in order to survive and use us as hosts. This can result in disease, deformity and even death. We lose people close to us and see them suffering.

The way that people are with each other can offer wider challenges too. Human beings can inflict horrible pain and suffering on each other and on ourselves due to our capacity for cruelty and violence. The genocide in Rwanda is just one example of how we can turn on each other and commit horrendous acts.

Not wanting to face these realities, we often dissociate ourselves from them. We fall prey to addictions, such as to alcohol and drugs, gambling and an excessive focus on the attainment of material possessions and wealth. Addictions come at a personal cost, while on a wider scale, factory farming, sweatshops and industrialisation lead our world to further pain, suffering and the depletion of the natural environment. And if we don't turn away from these issues, we may instead ruminate and worry about the future challenges that these global problems bring with them.

Until relatively recently (on the scale of human evolution), we had little insight into the impact of such global challenges, but our awareness of tragedies, our impermanence and the role we play makes living with them all the more difficult.

REMEMBER

An awareness of our suffering, and that of others, as well as the associated anger and sadness, can overwhelm us. It can also motivate us to act. This is the birthplace of compassion.

2

Understanding Ourselves

IN THIS PART . . .

Explore the three key emotional systems and consider their influence on our lives.

Get to know yourself compassionately by developing your 'life story'.

Consider the views that may prevent us from cultivating our compassionate mind and compassionate self.

Understand how emotions and other people may block our progress.

Chapter 4

Introducing the Three Circles

Human beings put a lot of effort into managing their lives so that they survive and prosper. We strive to achieve certain goals and keep out of harm's way. We rely on our motivations and emotions to guide us safely through the maze of life.

Compassion Focused Therapy (CFT) aims to help us understand ourselves better, and this includes knowledge about our emotions, behaviour, thoughts and attention. By better understanding ourselves, we become less prone to shame and self-criticism. In this chapter, we discover the 'three circles' (our three core emotional systems) and consider how an understanding of these systems can help us manage our emotions.

TIP

You may find this chapter a bit tricky as many of the words and phrases may be new to you. However, many people who've applied CFT to their lives report that knowledge of the three circles had the greatest impact on them. They began to notice how their mind and body works, and to understand the impact their environment has on them, and why they react and feel the way they do. Ultimately, this self-awareness decreases shame, self-criticism and confusion and replaces it with knowledge and choice.

Getting to Know the Three Circles

Recent research in neuroscience shows that at least three related parts of the brain work together to control and maintain our emotions. We call these our *emotional regulation systems*. In CFT, we refer to these three systems as the *three circles*. Of course, we don't actually have three circles in our head, nor are things so simple, but thinking about our emotions systematically helps us to navigate and understand our emotional world.

The three circles (or systems) are:

>> The *threat system*, designed to help us detect and respond to threats in our lives.

>> The *drive and resource acquisition system*, designed to help us detect, be interested in and take pleasure from securing important resources.

>> The *contentment and soothing system*, designed to help calm and balance the other two systems, giving us positive feelings of peaceful wellbeing and contentment.

TIP

Our threat system is our 'default factory setting' and it can become very sensitive, creating difficult emotions, physical sensations, thoughts and images. We can also get caught up in feeding our drive and resource acquisition system, and at times this can be to our own detriment. Our contentment and soothing system can help us create a sense of wellbeing and keep the other two in check.

Figure 4-1 shows the three circles: the threat system is represented by the bottom circle; the left circle is the drive and resource acquisition system; and the contentment and soothing system is on the right.

You can't see it in Figure 4-1, but the three circles are actually colour-coded. The threat system is red, the drive and resource acquisition system is blue and the contentment and soothing system is green. (The colours lend themselves to statements such as 'I'm in the red!' and 'I need a bit of green!'.)

REMEMBER

Although the diagram shows three distinct circles, the three systems are continuously interacting. The arrows represent this relationship. Sometimes we move slowly from one system to another (for example, a soothing friend may allow us to open up and talk about the things we feel anxious or angry about) and at other times two of the systems may appear to be simultaneously active (such as at times with our primary care-givers, when we experience both soothing feelings and joyful exhilaration). At times, it can even feel as though we're rapidly moving from one system to another. This may be experienced during competitive sports, when we feel a sense of threat from opponents followed very quickly by an intense drive to win – and back again!

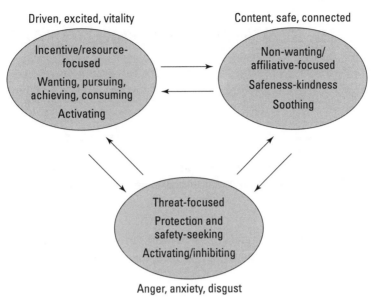

FIGURE 4-1:
The three circles.

From Gilbert, The Compassionate Mind (2009), reprinted with permission from Little, Brown Book Group

No one system is good or bad – what's important is to strive for balance across our life, so no one system rules the show.

To keep things simple, I refer to each of the three circles as the threat system, drive system and soothing system. The following sections explore each system in turn.

The threat system

We need to be aware of danger to ourselves and, if we live in groups, to detect things that are potentially harmful to others too. Our ability to detect danger and respond quickly has significantly contributed to the survival of our species. Possible responses may be to defend (fight), run away (flight) or avoid detection (freeze).

The hormones adrenaline and norepinephrine are released once the brain identifies a threat. Cortisol also plays a powerful role – but its production lags slightly behind the rapid production of the first two hormones.

Over much of our evolution, the major threats were predators. Nowadays, human beings face few predators, but our threat system is triggered by a range of different things that may be harmful to us. In particular, we can become preoccupied by detecting and responding to *social threats* – signs and signals that someone is judging us negatively or may cause us harm. We're also vulnerable to *internal threats* – these may be thoughts and images, physical sensations and emotions that we'd rather not have.

THE BENEFITS OF AN EMOTIONAL MAP

Designed by Harry Beck, and published in 1933, the London Underground Map is a design classic. It depicts the way the tube lines work and how they're interconnected. That said, the map doesn't provide a true geographical representation of the capital city.

It's scary to think just how many people have used it and how many people recognise it instantaneously across the globe. So, if it's useful to have a map of the London underground (that we may only use from time to time), it makes sense that we may benefit from a map for our emotional systems – one that we can use all the time!

Our *threat system* refers to the networks in our brain that quickly detect threats and co-ordinate a response.

When our threat system is triggered, we're likely to experience a change in our emotional state. The most common emotions are anxiety, anger and disgust. To better understand the way the threat system works, try the following exercise.

Imagine that you lose your footing as you're rushing to board a train. The doors beep to signal that they're about to close just as your foot hurtles towards the gap between the train and the platform. You don't have much time for thought. You do, however, experience a surge of panic.

Now, imagine it's lunchtime and you're looking forward to your packed lunch. Opening the box, you're hit by the stench of rotting meat. You may well feel an overwhelming sense of disgust.

Finally, imagine that you're running late – and then realise that, for the second time that week, you've misplaced your keys. What do you feel then? You may feel a sense of anger and frustration towards yourself.

REMEMBER

In addition to surges of emotion, the threat system also affects us physically. For example, in the preceding exercise you may have had a 'heart in mouth' experience as you imagined your foot plunging towards the gap between the train and the platform; you may have begun to retch as you imagined observing your rotting lunch; and you may have felt tension in your muscles as you imagined contemplating the whereabouts of your missing keys. Simply *imagining* these scenarios may have brought about these physical sensations.

Of course, people react differently, and are likely to respond to different threats in a range of ways. This physical response is completely automatic, and part of the brain's basic design.

It's ironic that the threat system that's wired to help us survive is exactly the same system that can make life so difficult for us. Our task is to become more consciously familiar with our threat system, to know what its triggers are, to identify when it's been triggered and to discover what, if anything, we can do about it. In 'taming' it, we can use it to assist rather than impede us.

The following sections look at the threat system in more detail, exploring some of the different ways in which our threat system may create problems for us.

Our tendency to overestimate threat

Ever been told that you're over-reacting or being irrational? You may have even criticised yourself for behaving in these ways. If so, it may reassure you to know that your brain instinctively overestimates danger in a range of different situations. It works on the principle of 'better safe than sorry', and so it's wired to be irrational! The following exercise helps to demonstrate this point.

Imagine that it's dusk and you're walking along an unfamiliar street. You notice a sudden movement from the corner of your eye. Bang – it grabs your attention. You feel a surge of anxiety. You may also experience physical changes, such as an increase in your heart rate or a leaping feeling in your stomach, and feel an urge to get home as quickly as you can. Alternatively, you may quickly check what made the movement or focus on the road ahead, trying to look as normal or confident as possible. Although 99 per cent of the time you won't be in any danger, your brain isn't rational, and so it works on the principle that potential danger can't be ignored.

Experiences can make the threat system even more sensitive. For example, war survivors often report jumping out of their skin if they hear a car backfire; people who were relentlessly criticised in childhood may become hypersensitive to the slightest hint of criticism later in life; and people who have experienced violence may constantly watch out for signs of anger in others.

We can overestimate threats within us too. People who experience panic attacks can become hypersensitive to signs of an oncoming attack, while people who have suffered with depression may become very sensitive to variations in mood.

Whether the focus of your attention is within you or in your environment, the threat system can come to resemble a supersensitive burglar alarm – going off every time a spider runs across the floor! CFT can help you to recalibrate your threat system at a level that works for you – rather than against you. You do this by developing your compassionate mind, step by step.

Our tendency to over-rule the positive

Overestimating threat is one side of the story. We also overlook or over-rule the positive.

Think back to the walk you were on in the exercise in the preceding section. You may have decided that running was the best option for you. But, while running, you're unlikely to notice (or you may discount) the wonderful things that are around you.

Similarly, you may overlook positive feedback in a report or appraisal because a less favourable comment grabs your attention. Instead of feeling a warm glow from the compliment, your view becomes tainted – you may wonder if the person gave you the positive comment because they feel sorry for you, and assume that they don't actually mean it. Maybe you even wonder if the person has an ulterior motive!

Our tendency for rumination and worry

Ruminating about past events and worrying about the future can regularly trigger our threat system. Consider the following examples to see what I mean.

Imagine shopping for some new clothes. In nine out of ten shops, the staff are extremely warm, friendly and helpful. They encourage you to try on new things and you buy a couple of outfits. In the final shop, two sales assistants briefly look your way and, without even a smile, continue talking. When you ask for a pair of jeans in your size they show very little interest in helping. Again, they continue talking. Despite this, you find a pair of jeans to buy but as you pay, the sales assistant makes no eye contact with you. To cap it all, she short-changes you! You experience an awkward exchange to resolve the situation, with lots of huffing on the sales assistant's part. With no apology, she eventually returns the £10 owed.

Who occupies your mind on the way home? Who do you rant about?

Now, imagine that you're planning a party. How much time do you spend worrying whether people will come? Maybe you worry about the music, food or your outfit? Or perhaps you dwell on whether you can afford the party, have forgotten to invite someone or should have picked a different venue? The list of potential worries can go on and on and on!

WARNING

If we combine our tendency to focus on potential threats with having a mind that spends a lot of time in the future and the past, life can become very difficult indeed. It's a toxic mix that can affect our everyday lives – but one we can choose to address by the development of our compassionate mind.

HUMANS VERSUS ZEBRAS!

Imagine a zeal (yes, that's the group name!) of zebras at a watering hole. Swishing their tails, they drink from the middle pool of water. Suddenly a lion appears from nowhere. The zebras bolt in many directions. Quickly reaching its top speed, the lion manages to bring down one of the young zebras. As it feasts on its kill, what do the other zebras do?

Do they look over thinking 'That could have been me!', 'I need to remember what direction the lion came from so I can avoid it next time' or 'It's all my fault; I should've seen it coming!'? As their hearts race, do they worry they're going to have a heart attack – or even tell themselves off for overreacting?

Fortunately for zebras, they don't entertain such thoughts. Instead they quickly return to a state of rest. They get back to whatever they were doing – something we humans find incredibly difficult to do. Instead, we worry and ruminate, and this prolongs our threat response. Worry and rumination fill our mind and affect us emotionally and physically. This can have a negative impact on our wellbeing.

REMEMBER

Our tendency to criticise ourselves is one of the most common ways in which we trigger our threat system. So, irrespective of what's going on around us, we can have a war zone going on in our own head.

Our tendency to be pulled in different directions

Certain goals come with feelings of interest and excitement, such as going on a date, meeting friends, engaging in a sport or eating a nice meal. Our emotions guide us to move *toward* these things. Other situations, such as a potentially awkward conversation, can result in us feeling wary, anxious or angry. Our emotions may still guide us towards such things (so that we can lock horns!) but, more often than not, they direct us *away* from such negative encounters.

Of course we can feel an urge to simultaneously move towards something (or someone) as well as away from it (or someone)! (You may have felt this way about a potential job interview – feeling excited about the prospect of the new role, but also wanting to run a mile!) These inconsistent or conflicting feelings can be tricky.

One event can result in two very different sets of responses, and these can conflict with each other (hence the term 'mixed emotions'). Despite this being very common, we often worry, get frustrated or criticise ourselves for reacting in these conflicting ways. The following examples explore this idea in more detail.

Imagine that your boss criticises your efforts. What emotions do you feel? Anger may come with thoughts such as, 'How dare he criticise my work?' or 'What does she know anyway?'. You may feel like shouting back or taking your revenge at a later date. Meanwhile, a part of you may feel anxiety and panic, thinking 'My work isn't good enough', and you may want to run away, hand in your notice or cry.

On top of this, the different parts of you can be in conflict. The anxious part may worry that anger will get the better of you, while the angry part may think that anxiety is pathetic.

Now imagine that a colleague is subtly criticising someone else's work. You go along with the conversation, feel slightly swayed by your colleague's argument, and are flattered that they're taking you into their confidence. Later, you begin to feel awkward and anxious about being party to the conversation. Going over it in your head, you begin to feel incensed by some of the things said, but you still feel a sense of connection with them.

You may have noticed that, in the first example, the different reactions seemed to occur simultaneously, while in the second they seemed to switch back and forth.

REMEMBER

Our threat system has been incredibly important to the survival of our species, and the emotions associated with it form an integral part of our everyday lives. Life would actually be quite monotonous without it! That said, it can begin to rule the show and stand in the way of more positive emotions. Our compassionate mind can help us become the referee and also the conductor.

The drive system

In order to survive and reproduce, animals need to be motivated to go out and look for food, shelter and, of course, mates. Our *drive system* coordinates this goal-directed behaviour. When we achieve or acquire our goals, our drive system provides us with a buzz of pleasure. This sensation is produced by the hormone *dopamine*, which is released by the brain.

If the goal is small, we get a relatively small buzz when we achieve it; however, a big goal, such as winning the lottery, may result in a huge 'hit'. It may also result in millions of thoughts about ways to spend the money. We may immediately act on some of these thoughts, seemingly unable to stop ourselves. We may also have difficulty concentrating and sleeping, and feel extremely excited, even euphoric.

REMEMBER

A system that helps us enjoy what we achieve is a good thing, but we can have problems if we're unable to achieve our goals, we set unrealistic ones or we become over-focused on achievement to the detriment of other things. Here are some problems that can arise:

» We may find that ageing, stronger competition, illness or injury can stop us achieving things that previously gave us a buzz. If we have no other means of feeling good about ourselves we may not only lack a buzz of pleasure but we may also experience associated frustration, anxiety and sadness.

» We can overuse our drive system and push ourselves too hard as an antidote to feeling inadequate, threatened and vulnerable. We may set ourselves extremely high standards for our work, house or appearance. When things go well and we achieve our standards we experience positive emotions; however, failing to meet our own standards can quickly lead to feelings of inadequacy, anxiety and vulnerability.

» We may become reliant on the positive responses of others for feelings of self-worth, and spend all our time and effort people-pleasing. This gives us a buzz when we get our desired outcome – but what happens when we are met with indifference or even negative responses from others? If we over-rely on our drive system for positive feelings (rather than utilise our soothing system, which we describe in the next section), we can encounter problems when we fail to get the response from others that we hope for.

» We can lose our sense of connection with others and fail to see the value in other human capacities, capabilities and characteristics if our places of education and work become too achievement-focused. For example, schools that value and reward academic attainment to the detriment of everything else are likely to produce students who make the grades and are competitive, but that are less prepared for adult life. This lack of preparation may also result in emotional struggles if students fail to meet their school's aspirations. Of course, staff and students rarely have much control over their environment – though they suffer the consequences of these surroundings.

» We can 'get into the blue' (to understand this better, refer to the colour-coding that we mentioned in the earlier section, 'Getting to Know the Three Circles') and create a sense of internal 'buzz' through gambling, shopping, theft, perfectionism, weight loss and drug use. These activities can lead to serious problems and may become highly addictive.

>> We may experience *mania* when the drive system becomes 'supercharged', which can result in behaviours that are generally uncharacteristic for us: for example, we may overspend, become promiscuous or be overactive. Mania is often associated with a more talkative and creative version of ourselves that requires less sleep. Although mania is experienced as a positive mood state, agitation and irritability often occur simultaneously. Once mood has returned to normal, individuals often experience feelings of regret and shame, which is associated with their uncharacteristic behaviour. People experiencing mania often feel negative repercussions in their relationships – and sometimes their bank accounts.

The soothing system

Animals tend to enter a state of contentment and peacefulness when they've achieved what they need to and they're in a position of safety. Fledgling birds with full bellies will sit quietly in a state of contentment. The *soothing system* co-ordinates this experience and is associated with chemicals in our brain called *endorphins*. When we find ourselves in this system, or consciously choose to switch it on, the 'activating' states of threat and drive are switched off.

DRIVING OUR DESIRE FOR MORE AND MORE

Many researchers and social commentators are concerned that modern society is over-stimulating the drive system. Marketing campaigns tell us that the latest gadget, hair product, designer label or toothpaste is a 'must have'. We're shown images of happy, gorgeous people with amazing-seeming lives who appear to be made happier by these products, the inference being that if we acquire the product in question, we too can have that lifestyle.

Making the argument even more compelling, campaigns often combine something that triggers our threat system with a solution: for example, 'dull lifeless hair?', 'fine lines and wrinkles?', 'take aim against cavities' and 'you never get a second chance to make a first impression'. This is often referred to as *solution marketing* – pointing out a threat (which stimulates the threat system) and offering a solution (which stimulates the drive system).

Acquiring these 'wonder products' may give us a buzz – even if they don't provide full-bodied hair, a wrinkle-free face and a cavity-free mouth!

The quality and power of our soothing system is strongly associated with the bonds we form with others. In humans, such bonds have evolved over many thousands of years. The first bond we're programmed to make, and potentially the most powerful, is between parent (usually the mother) and infant. This is an 'attachment' bond and it serves to increase the chances of the infant's survival. This bond also brings a sense of connection (often referred to as affiliation) and emotional wellbeing that is beneficial to both parent and infant.

You may have noticed that a baby can become distressed if it's separated from a parent. This response results from the activation of its threat system. Thankfully, the return of a soothing parent quickly restores the baby to a state of contentment.

Likewise, upon being startled a baby is likely to cry, triggering an appropriate response from the parent – they may soothe the child by tone of voice, cuddles and a rocking motion. This is the hallmark of a good attachment.

REMEMBER

Our soothing system has evolved to play a pivotal role in the regulation of our threat and drive systems.

Of course this doesn't suddenly stop when we become adults. When we feel we're cared about and we have good bonds with others, even if we're physically on our own, we're better able to deal with stress. For example, do you seek out others for reassurance or validation when something difficult happens? Is this effect more powerful with the people you're closest to?

DEVELOPING YOUR BRAIN THROUGH EXPERIENCE

Your brain, like your body, undergoes a lot of change and development in order to reach maturity. At birth you have 100 billion or so neurons (brain cells) with approximately 2,500 connections with other neurons. By the age of two or three, each neuron has approximately 15,000 connections. This is a six-fold increase!

Connections that are hardly ever, or never, used disappear, while those that are regularly used proliferate. So, your brain is shaped by your experiences. For example, if your threat system is repeatedly activated, this area is strengthened, and your brain has more capability to watch out for and respond to threats (which can, of course, be very useful if you live in a dangerous environment). If, however you experience more kindness, warmth and caring in your day-to-day life, the associated experience of contentment becomes familiar to you, and your soothing system is strengthened.

The strength of the emotional bonds that we form can have a huge impact on the quality of our lives.

Of course, even if we try, we can't rid a child of all difficulties. However, the way that key people deal with our reactions to threats in our environment is pivotal. If as a child we're soothed and calmed, we realise that distress comes to an end and we discover how to accept the kindness, warmth and caring of others. In time, we then learn to soothe and calm ourselves and also to turn to others. Of course, a number of factors – such as the availability and response of our parents, siblings and friends – can inhibit this discovery process, but active development and engagement with our compassionate mind can be of great assistance.

When I became a first-time parent, a friend said to me, 'Say hello to guilt!' Despite studying child development during my time at university, it was only when I had my second child that I realised how truly different babies can be. Some are easily soothed from birth; others find 'settling' more difficult. Some are easily startled; others sleep through anything! Some are easy to parent; others are more challenging.

In addition, some adults naturally find parenting easy, while others find it difficult. Some find particular stages challenging; others less so. A whole range of factors can affect the bond between parent and child, and this impacts on the soothing systems for both parties.

REMEMBER

If, as an adult, you have difficulty experiencing a sense of contentment or 'getting in the green', it doesn't mean that someone else is at fault. It may be down to the temperament that both you and your parents were born with – which is something you can't choose. It may be due to difficulties your parents had – through no fault of their own – or a whole range of factors beyond anyone's control. It's helpful not to blame but instead to use your compassionate mind to gain insight and then consider helpful options.

Managing Our Emotions: Brain 'Apps'

We're born without shoes on our feet, but do we all walk around barefoot? No, our feet are amazing, but we wear shoes because they protect us, they can assist us in many ways *and* (especially in my case) they can look better!

In a similar way, we're born with a threat-focused brain. This can become even more sensitive if we've had times in our lives when we've indeed been under threat. Maybe we've been undermined, overlooked, ridiculed, hurt or lived in difficult environments. Of course, our threat detection system can be extremely important to us, but sometimes it can cause problems – it can be over-sensitive and prevent us living the life we want to lead. In such circumstances, it can be helpful to consider 'switching our brain apps'. Thankfully, we can do exercises, just as we can work out in a gym, to change our brain!

Apps are now commonplace. They can turn your smartphone into a camera, calculator, Internet connection or gaming system. Within specific applications we interface with our phone differently. We may hold it differently when we use the camera, view it differently when we're reading or playing games, and use specific keys in different ways to interact with apps and other people online.

It can be helpful to think of our compassionate self and compassionate mind as our operating system and our emotional regulation systems as applications for our 'smart brain'. When using the *threat app*, you think, behave and feel in specific ways. The *drive* and *soothing apps* may result in very different emotional experiences.

TIP

Of course, with smartphone apps, we intentionally switch them on and off, but the same isn't necessarily true for our emotional regulation systems. They often do their own thing. For example, a loud bang may trigger your threat system and a hug from a friend may trigger your soothing system, while a trip to a particular high street store may push you into your drive system and lead to more or larger purchases than you set out for.

This book can help you develop ways to switch on your soothing system (or app!) and, in doing so, regulate your drive and threat systems – which is very exciting!

PHYSIOTHERAPY FOR THE BRAIN

Whatever your age, if you want to learn how to play golf, knit, tap dance or speak a new language, new neurons and new connections help make it possible. Of course, learning skills at an early age makes it easier, but you can still pick up new skills and hobbies as you get older. Similarly, you can enhance or maintain your wellbeing as you age. Your efforts change your brain and influence the way your mind works. This is why we often refer to exercises used in CFT as physiotherapy for the brain! Head to Chapter 1 for more on distinctions between CFT and compassionate mind training.

Contemplating Your Own Circle Diagram

Considering how 'developed' your systems are and how they work in relation to each other is useful. This knowledge can help you to understand yourself better, address shame and self-criticism, and consider what it may be helpful for you to focus on.

The following exercises provide a visual way to view your circles (similar to the diagram of the three circles shown earlier in Figure 4-1). We start by considering how things generally are for you, and then consider if your circles are different in specific situations. Examples are provided later in this section to illustrate how others have brought their three circles to life. Finally, in this section you will be asked to consider what events may have led to you feeling the way you do.

On a blank piece of paper, draw out how your circles are generally, relative to each other. Start with the threat system. How big is it? This is the system that is associated with anxiety, anger or disgust. Next, consider your drive system. How big is it? This is the system that gives you a sense of achievement and a buzz. Finally, consider how big your soothing system is. This is the system that creates a sense of contentment and calm.

Include arrows in your diagram to signify the interacting relationships between the three systems. In Chapter 5 we consider how the way we cope with different emotional experiences can throw further light on how your three circles interact.

On a further piece of paper, draw your circles as they relate to different situations: for example, at work, at home and when socialising with friends. Include arrows to signify the interacting relationships between the three systems. Do your circles vary in size in the different situations you've chosen to focus on? Do you find that in certain situations you see a sense of balance between your drive, threat and soothing systems, resulting in three similar-sized circles? Consider your circles carefully – what conditions make a difference to their relative size? Maybe it's the relationships, activities or pressures associated with different environments that make them different?

Some people find that different situations result in little variation in their circles. Others find that their circles vary greatly depending on who they're with, or the place that they're in. These observations offer important insights into the changes you may want to make. The development and application of your compassionate self and compassionate mind can help you with this. For the time being, however, an insight into the difficulties you experience and the reasons for them is important because it undermines your tendency to be self-critical.

To bring the three circles to life, consider the following examples. You'll see how big each person drew their three circles relative to each other, and this will give you some ideas about how to draw your own. Maybe you'll identify with one of the examples, consider yourself a blend or come to realise that your experiences are unique to you and so you represent them in a different way.

EXAMPLE

Chloe described herself as a born worrier. She worried about her school work, what people thought of her and whether she was making herself ill due to stress. On top of this, Chloe gave herself a hard time about almost everything. As a result, she drew a very large circle to represent her threat system.

Chloe coped by avoiding a range of social interactions or events that would trigger her anxiety. Her mood suffered and she lacked any motivation to do anything over and above what she had to do. She never felt a sense of achievement or buzz of pleasure, and so Chloe drew a very small drive system.

Chloe felt unable to ask anyone for help or to let others know how she was feeling because she feared that they wouldn't understand and they'd think she was weird. She had never been able to soothe or reassure herself; therefore, she drew a small soothing circle.

Figure 4-2 shows Chloe's circle diagram.

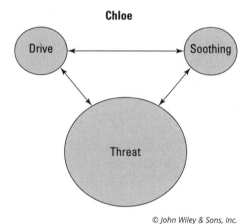

FIGURE 4-2:
Chloe's circles.

Jamie had a difficult childhood and had few memories of being cuddled or reassured by his parents. As a teenager, he recalled indifference or criticism from his mum and dad and, as an only child, for much of his life he felt a loner. Jamie developed a critical way of relating to himself. He drew a small soothing circle and a large threat circle to represent this.

Realising he had a gift for rugby, and a teacher who encouraged him, Jamie threw himself into training and took up any opportunity to play (and get out of his house). He felt a real buzz and a sense of purpose when participating in the sport and, when not playing or training, spent much of his time thinking about it. Jamie drew himself a large drive circle.

When injured, he became extremely frustrated with himself. At such times, difficult thoughts and images popped into his mind more frequently. He was unable to nurture or reassure himself, so he coped by distracting himself with computer games and often returned to training before he was ready. In so doing, he was recruiting his drive rather than his threat system to feel better again.

Figure 4-3 shows Jamie's circle diagram.

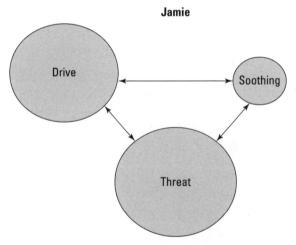

FIGURE 4-3:
Jamie's circles.

© John Wiley & Sons, Inc.

For much of her waking hours, Maxine experienced chronic pain. However, there were times when her pain would subside, even disappear. Because there was so much difference between her pain-laden and pain-free days, she decided to draw herself two circle diagrams.

On a difficult day she was clearly 'in the red' and had no get up and go. Maxine got frustrated with herself, felt sapped of energy and experienced low mood. She drew herself a very large threat circle. At such times she had no drive and found it difficult to show herself any kindness or compassion. She therefore also drew herself a small drive and soothing circle.

On the days when Maxine's pain level was lower – or absent altogether – she drew herself a smaller threat circle. She would then burst into action, getting jobs done and seeing friends. To reflect this, she drew herself an enormous drive system. On such days she was able to see close friends and she related to herself more positively; therefore, her soothing circle was larger than she'd drawn it for her pain-laden days.

Although Maxine felt good at the time, she was unaware that she was pushing herself too hard and, in fact, increasing the possibility that her pain would return with a vengeance.

Figure 4-4 shows Maxine's circle diagrams.

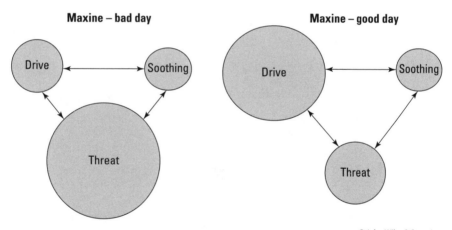

FIGURE 4-4: Maxine's circles: the left-hand figure shows Maxine's bad days, and the right-hand figure shows Maxine's good days.

© John Wiley & Sons, Inc.

Now we return to the diagram you developed to show your life story. This represents how your three circles generally are. Consider the experiences that may have contributed to the size of each of your circles. Maybe you experienced bullying, felt under pressure to do well academically or had a difficult relationship. Maybe you're a perfectionist, an adrenaline junkie or naturally shy. Write these things down in or around your circles in a way that's meaningful to you.

TIP

By understanding how our three circles work and how they can become out of balance, we can begin to address our tendency towards self-criticism and feelings of shame. For many people, circle diagrams illustrate the need to build the soothing system in order to create a sense of balance and, ultimately, wellbeing. I return to these ideas again and again throughout this book.

REMEMBER

Each of our systems, or circles, is important to our survival and wellbeing. The aim is to make them work as well as possible for us!

Chapter 5

Getting to Know Ourselves: Exploring Our Life Stories

One of the biggest blocks to self-compassion is simply not understanding ourselves. When we fail to appreciate the reasons why we feel and behave the way we do, we can become highly critical of ourselves. This sense of disconnection with ourselves can result in anger, anxiety and sadness.

Our lack of personal understanding can also create a sense of disconnection with others, who seem to get along just fine and have everything sorted! We can use this disconnection as a further reason to criticise ourselves and experience shame, as we may believe that others are judging us negatively too.

We begin by making sense of your life and your situation. Exercises help you consider your experiences, influences, worries, fears and concerns. You explore your coping strategies and what you hope to achieve by using them. You also consider whether your coping strategies may cause further issues.

I then provide an example and blank template for you to use, to show how these elements are brought together in a diagram – your 'life story'. The aim of this chapter is to gain an understanding of yourself in order to address any shame and self-criticism you may feel, while opening the door to a compassionate appreciation of your situation and ultimately of yourself.

TIP

Each of the exercises in this chapter contributes to part of your life story, so it's helpful to consider each section before you create your life story diagram. Although the exercises are provided in a particular order, you may prefer to follow a different order, which is fine.

REMEMBER

Putting a spotlight on events, fears, concerns and our struggles is an emotional experience, so it's important to proceed gently.

Recognising Our Experiences and Influences

From the point of conception, our genes (you can think of this as your *nature*) predispose us to a certain temperament. We have the capacity to reach a particular level of academic and emotional intelligence, as well as height! Some of us are also predisposed to carry more weight and experience certain physical health conditions.

However, the likelihood of these attributes becoming a reality is dictated by our experiences (you can think of this as *nurture*). So, the culture we're born into, the type of parents we have, the food we eat, the amount of stimulation we receive, the kind of place we live and the relationships we grow up with all influence the people we become. Head to Chapter 3 for more on your genotype and phenotype.

Use the following exercise to explore these ideas in more detail.

Sit for a while and create a sense of calmness or relaxation in your mind and body. You may do this by simply listening to a piece of music or making yourself comfortable in your favourite chair. Chapter 9 provides additional ways you can use your attention, mindfulness or breathing to create a sense of calm awareness.

If you think the exercises in this chapter are likely to be difficult for you, it may help to develop your compassionate mind and compassionate self first. Head to Chapters 10–14 for more on developing your compassionate mind and cultivating your compassionate self.

1. **Using a blank sheet of paper (or a computer or mobile device, if you prefer), create two headings, *nature* and *nurture*. Under each heading, make a note of the things that have shaped you.** Nature may include how naturally active you are and things you have a talent for or difficulty with. Nurture may include whether you were the youngest of four children or an only child, and where you grew up.

2. **To develop this further, think about your life in five-year chunks.** The following questions are designed to help you:

   • Does anything else come to mind in the time before starting school, in primary, junior school and so on?

   • Did your physical appearance, health or other 'biological' factors particularly influence you?

   Consider your 'tricky' brain by reflecting on the factors outlined in Chapter 3.

   • Consider different environments such as school, home, places of work, and social or sporting clubs. Were there any expectations placed on you or did you place them on yourself?

   • Consider the religious, cultural or societal factors that may have had an effect on you.

3. **Bring to mind the people in your life and your relationships. Have any of these shaped you in any way?** Refer to Chapter 3 for more on the way that relationships can shape you through your 'social mentalities'.

Consider whether any subtle influences apply to you (provided in the nearby sidebar, 'Subtle influences'), and if they do, make a note of them also.

Having competed the exercise, consider how many of your influences were under your control.

Considering your influences in this way helps you realise that much of who you are, how you feel and what you do is not of your choosing. Many of the things we feel shame and self-criticism about are not our fault or of our making.

SUBTLE INFLUENCES

Sometimes you can 'point a big stick' at the things that influence you, while other factors are less obvious. Here are some of the 'small' things that can have a big influence:

- Being around people who are critical
- Being naturally more introverted or shy
- Being shown love and affection dependent on success
- Being stereotyped by those around you
- Being the oldest, youngest or middle child
- Experiencing learning difficulties such as dyslexia, dyspraxia or dyscalculia
- Growing up around people who are seemingly good at everything
- Having a parent who experienced post-natal depression
- Having anxious parents
- Having high expectations placed upon you
- Lacking experiences outside of your immediate family
- Looking 'different' from other people
- Noticing how your friends and family apply certain stereotypes to themselves and others
- Receiving too much attention from others

Collectively, your subtle and not-so-subtle influences interact with each other and create the person you are today. It's both sobering and miraculous. Taking time to let this realisation sink in can be incredibly moving. Awakening to all of this, we begin to have choice: the choice to make helpful changes that impact positively on our own and other people's wellbeing (instead of living on automatic pilot!).

Remember: In exactly the same way, when we're affected by others it's important to remember that they're the product of their influences too.

Exploring Your Worries, Fears and Concerns

Most people have worries, fears or concerns. These can then drive or influence our attention, behaviour, emotions, how our body feels and the types of thoughts that occupy our mind (head to Chapter 4 for more information on the threat system and the negative impacts of such worries, fears and concerns).

Worries, fears and concerns fall into the following two categories:

>> Worries, fears and concerns relating to or about our *external world*. These may include what people may think or feel about us and how they may behave, such as isolating us, attacking us verbally or physically, or aligning with others against us. These are linked to the experience of external shame (head to Chapter 1 for more on external shame).

>> Worries, fears and concerns relating to or about our *internal world*. These may include what we think about ourselves, thoughts and images that pop into our heads, bodily sensations, or our emotions. These are linked to the experience of internal shame (head to Chapter 1 for more on internal shame).

In the following exercise, you consider how worries, fears and concerns affect you.

On the same sheet of paper (or the same page on your computer or mobile device) that you used for the exercise in the preceding section (if you have room!), make a note of any worries, fears and concerns that you have. (Alternatively, use a separate sheet of paper – but make sure that you can refer to your notes from the previous exercise.) Consider the worries, fears and concerns that you have and write these down. Maybe you're concerned about the judgement of others, being left out or feeling alone. Maybe you're concerned that something is wrong with your emotions – you may even be worried *about* the concerns you have.

To develop this further, look to each of the influences you noted down in the previous exercise and consider if they're associated with any worries, fears and concerns. Some may be linked to an experience of internal shame, others may be linked to external shame, and some may relate to both internal and external shame.

Having considered your worries, fears and concerns in the context of your influences, you may be able to see some links between them and so identify reasons why you're the person you are today.

TIP

If you find it difficult to identify any worries, fears or concerns, consider doing this exercise again when you're feeling sad, anxious or angry. Maybe when you feel strong emotions, you fear always being that way; or you're concerned that your emotions may impact negatively on your relationships, you'll end up rejected by others and feel like an outsider, or your emotions will get the better of you.

As a consequence of evolution, most of us are programmed to be wary of heights, things that move erratically, confined spaces and the dark. This programming has been advantageous for the success of our species.

Because group living and co-operation have been important to our survival and protection, we're also primed to be wary of what we call *social threats*. These involve concerns that we're being negatively evaluated or that others feel anger towards or disgust in response to us. We can spend a lot of time monitoring and reacting to potential threats from others. It's therefore not surprising that what underpins many of our concerns and fears is the threat of social isolation.

Getting to Grips with Our Coping Strategies

We all try to get by the best we can and in order to do so we develop a range of coping strategies designed to help us. Evolutionary science refers to these as protective and safety strategies. While some strategies appear to be intentional choices, others seem more automatic.

Here are some examples of common coping strategies you may have used at some point in your life:

>> Apologising continually

>> Avoiding anything out of your comfort zone

>> Avoiding awkward or anxiety-provoking situations

>> Becoming/doing what others seem to want

>> Causing yourself pain

>> Checking yourself in a mirror, that you've turned things off, or that you've locked doors and windows

>> Covering up with excessive makeup

>> Criticising or bullying yourself

>> Deferring to or over-relying on others

- » Doing certain things only with 'safe' people
- » Doing excessive levels of exercise
- » Engaging in an excessive 'post-mortem' after an event
- » Engaging in excessive cleaning or washing
- » Keeping a lid on your emotions
- » Keeping people at arm's length
- » Making do/settling for things that aren't ideal
- » Over-controlling your diet
- » Over-eating
- » Over-preparing or over-planning
- » Over-thinking/excessively monitoring yourself or the situation
- » Pushing yourself over and above what is needed
- » Putting on a happy or brave face/wearing a social mask
- » Saying yes all the time
- » Seeking reassurance
- » Using alcohol/drugs (prescribed, over the counter or illegal/recreational)

Of course, given particular circumstances we may do some of these things, some of the time, without any negative consequences. For example, in a new country you may explore your environment by initially only going out with people you know. You may be tempted to go on a crash diet before a big event or check windows and doors over and over for months after a burglary. But problems occur when we use such coping strategies to excess. They can also prevent us finding out positive things about ourselves and other people. For example, if we continue to only go out with 'safe' people, it's likely to impact on our confidence and may prevent us from meeting new people. Always wearing excessive makeup may prevent us from realising that we're approached more often when wearing less makeup, and perpetually using drugs may have all manner of negative outcomes.

With your worries, fears and concerns in mind, consider what you do, or have done, in order to cope or 'get by' in the world, making a note of each on the sheet of paper you used for the preceding exercises in this chapter (if you have room – alternatively, you may be using a computer or mobile device). Looking at the preceding list of common coping strategies as a helpful prompt may help.

YOU DON'T HAVE TO DEMOLISH YOUR OLD HOUSE BEFORE BUILDING A NEW ONE!

Well-meaning people can often advise us to cut down on our drinking, start saying no, drop our guard or stop being so hard on ourselves. Of course, this can be sensible advice, but it's difficult to make changes, and doing so can be very anxiety-provoking.

Here's where the analogy of house building comes in. Imagine you have a house (your coping strategy) in which you're getting by, maybe you're even doing quite well, but in the long term you realise it has limitations and you want to move.

Why not build a new house (develop a new coping strategy) first, maybe even a neighbourhood of houses (strategies) and *then,* when ready, make the move? Your old house will still be there if the need arises, but you now have plenty of different options!

Understanding Our Intentions

When we engage in certain coping strategies, we're aiming to achieve desirable outcomes. We refer to these outcomes as *intended consequences.*

Here are some examples of common intended consequences that you may have worked towards as you coped in different situations in your life:

» Avoid conflict

» Avoid control or decrease anxiety

» Avoid criticism

» Avoid disappointment

» Avoid 'failure'

» Avoid rejection

» Avoid shame/uncomfortable emotions

» Be more prepared for other people's reactions

» Calm others down

» Feel a sense of pride

» Generate a buzz

- >> Give you more confidence
- >> Help you respond quickly
- >> Improve mood
- >> Increase the likelihood of escape
- >> Increase the likelihood of success
- >> Keep others safe
- >> Keep people happy
- >> Keep yourself in check
- >> Keep yourself safe
- >> Make things more predictable
- >> Make you feel more attractive
- >> Make you less noticeable
- >> Prevent negative things happening
- >> Provide a sense of wellbeing
- >> Punish yourself for something
- >> Stop you feeling other things
- >> Stop you thinking of other things

Consider the preceding list of intended consequences. Do many of these apply to you? If so, make a note of them on the sheet of paper (or computer screen/mobile device) that you used for the preceding exercises in this chapter. If space doesn't allow this, use another, making sure that you can review all the information you've written on these exercises at the same time.

Thinking in turn about each one of your coping strategies (that you identified in the preceding section) and seeing if these follow through to any of the intended consequences can be helpful.

TIP

Don't restrict yourself to the list in this section or any other list when you're considering your own coping strategies or their intended consequences – these lists are simply meant to act as prompts to get the ball rolling. You know your motivations better than any list! Listen to yourself.

Considering the Unintended Consequences

As you work your way through this chapter, you start to build up a list of your coping strategies, and to understand why you choose to cope in these ways (if you haven't done this yet, flip back to 'Getting to Grips with Our Coping Strategies' and 'Understanding Our Intentions' and take a look at these exercises). You also consider your own fears and influences. In this section, you consider the *unintended consequences* or *drawbacks* associated with the things that you do in order to cope with events in your life. For example, you may be self-critical due to the wish for self-improvement, but this often results in low mood; avoiding a range of situations may prevent us feeling anxious, but it also restricts our lives; and going along with others to avoid conflict may mean that you're a festering ball of resentment! Unfortunately, sometimes our actions, although intended to be helpful, lead to unexpected negative outcomes. These may be in the short-term, long-term or both.

Here are some examples of common unintended consequences that you may experience in different situations in your life:

>> Addiction

>> Awkwardness

>> Being taken for granted

- » Conflict
- » Eating problems
- » Exhaustion
- » Feeling stuck/trapped
- » Guilt
- » Hangovers
- » Increased anxiety
- » Inability to 'enjoy the moment'
- » Injury/scars
- » Isolation
- » Lack of flexibility
- » Lack of opportunity to develop your own skills/confidence
- » Lack of opportunity to gain a sense of achievement
- » Lack of true acceptance/validation from others
- » Low mood
- » Nobody knowing the true you
- » Not feeling as though you know yourself
- » Over-reliance on certain people
- » Over-thinking/excessively monitoring yourself or the situation
- » Regret
- » Resentment
- » Self-criticism
- » Shame
- » Unmet needs
- » Wariness from others
- » Wariness of others

Consider each of the coping strategies you generated in the exercises in the earlier section, 'Getting to Grips with Our Coping Strategies'. Do any of them 'bite you on the bum' – in other words, do they lead to unintended consequences? Review the preceding list of common unintended consequences for inspiration (but don't be restricted to items on the list).

Using the same sheet of paper from the preceding exercises in this chapter (or another sheet if you don't have room), make a note of any unintended consequences associated with your coping strategies.

You may find it useful to review your notes from all the exercises you've completed so far from this chapter (I suggest that you complete each of these in turn) as you consider the unintended consequences of your thoughts, feelings and behaviours.

It may be worth gently considering the unintended impact on others also. For example, spending time checking everything you do, with the aim of keeping yourself and others safe, may mean you spend less time with your partner or children, while taking control of everything may mean that others don't develop their abilities and confidence.

Certain behaviours, emotions and thoughts may appear in multiple sections of your life story. For example, self-criticism may be a coping strategy, but it may also be an unintended consequence of certain behaviours, while lack of opportunities may be recorded as both an influence and an unintended consequence. The sense it makes to you is important, not which or how many categories particular experiences fall into.

Your life story can provide an understanding of how difficulties developed and why they remain. For example, some of our coping strategies and unintended consequences impact on our relationships which, in turn, result in additional worries, fears and concerns. Many maintenance or feedback cycles can maintain our difficulties, thus creating a vicious cycle. Sad and frustrating, isn't it?

We look at your own life story in more detail in the later section, 'Developing Your Own Life Story'.

Developing an Account of Your Experiences

The following example illustrates how information gained from each of the exercises in this chapter can be drawn together by means of a diagrammatic *life story*. (As with the other examples in this book, Jennifer is not a real person but an amalgamation of the stories of several people.) The aim of this process is to address shame and self-criticism by making sense of ourselves. This then paves the way for a compassionate view of and relationship with ourselves.

First, you look at a description of the key experiences in Jennifer's life. You then see a life story diagram based on these.

EXAMPLE

Jennifer was the oldest of three children. Her younger brother was eight years her junior and her younger sister was ten years younger than her. With her parents both working long hours, Jennifer had a lot of responsibility for looking after her younger siblings.

Jennifer's mum was preoccupied with what other people thought of her. She would spend what seemed like hours getting ready to go out and spent more than she could afford on her clothes, hair and makeup. She also suffered from panic attacks, which seemed to be triggered by crowds, unplanned visitors and spiders.

As a young child Jennifer turned to her father when she was worried or upset, but he wasn't around that much. She recalled happy memories of holidays before her siblings came along, but as money became tighter and family life got busier, such times became less frequent.

At nine years old, Jennifer began puberty. She recalled being extremely self-conscious of her changing body. She began to avoid exercise, hating to change in front of other children, and slowly began to gain weight. A group of older girls teased her and twanged her bra most break times; this was followed by almost three years of relentless bullying. Her friendship with Alison, who lived close by and attended the same school, was incredibly important during those years. With bright red hair and freckles, Alison knew what it was like to be bullied too. It was around the same time that Jennifer's younger siblings arrived on the scene. The difficulties she was having seemed to go unnoticed by her parents, and Jennifer didn't want to worry her parents by speaking to them about it.

When Jennifer was 14, her mum enrolled at a local slimming club. 'I think you should come with me,' her mum said. 'Let's get our pretty little daughter back.' This comment confirmed to Jennifer that she was indeed fat and ugly.

Setting her mind to weight loss, Jennifer quickly achieved her 'ideal weight', but despite this her attention was now firmly grasped by what other people thought of her, what she thought of herself and her weight. At around the same time, her friend Alison moved over 200 miles away. They tried to keep in contact but, with very different lives, their friendship faded. This was a huge loss to Jennifer. Struggling to fit in with the other girls around her, she felt increasing levels of anxiety. Jennifer felt like an outsider, constantly judged by both herself and others. She continued with school but hated much of her time there.

Keen to leave school, Jennifer started working at a local salon at 16 and trained as a hairdresser. Being in front of mirrors all day, she made sure that her hair and makeup was as 'perfect' as she could get it. Secretly, though, Jennifer hated the person who looked back at her. She was highly critical of herself: she felt she was overweight (though the scales didn't support this) and a 'vacant shell' of a person. She chatted and joked with the other staff but never let them get too close, fearful that they would turn on her or see her for the fake she was. As Jennifer's brother and sister grew up, they began to suggest meeting up socially but Jennifer declined, saying she was too busy. In reality, Jennifer feared that they too would discover her to be a vacant shell. All of this pretence and avoidance was exhausting.

Jennifer's mood began to suffer and her sense of shame increased. She felt resentful of other people and couldn't see any way out of her situation.

Figure 5-1 shows the 'life story' that Jennifer developed. The first box has a range of different influences and experiences that span Jennifer's life to date. Some of the concerns, coping strategies and unintended consequences appear to be a direct consequence of her life experiences, while others seem to be the result of things she did to try to deal with certain problems. In addition, it can be argued that some of the unintended consequences can themselves be classed as experiences (and so can therefore be placed in the first box).

TIP

What's important in any life story diagram is to put the elements together in a way that makes sense to you, and to give a comprehensive account of how problems have developed and how they're maintained.

REMEMBER

No life story ever gives a complete account of someone's life and circumstances, but Figure 5-1 provides an idea of the factors that shaped Jennifer, the worries, fears and concerns she developed, how she coped, what she hoped to achieve (and at times did) but also the unintended consequences. Her life story also indicates how such unintended consequences resulted in her feeling weird and even more of an outsider.

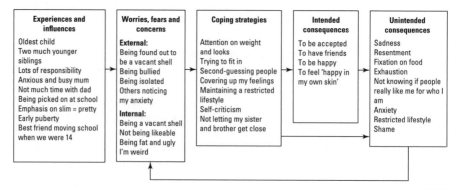

FIGURE 5-1:
Jennifer's
life story.

Credit TBC

Developing Your Own Life Story

In this section you develop your own life story. This may go some way towards addressing the shame and self-criticism that you may experience. Understanding the influences that have shaped you, and appreciating the ways in which you cope but also the problems that this may bring, opens the door to a more compassionate way of relating to yourself.

Using the information that you collected in each of the exercises in this chapter, use the blank diagram in Figure 5-2 to develop your own life story. As you fill in the different boxes, you may become aware of issues that you need to think about more. For example, you may have reflected in the earlier exercises on one way of coping, but you may not have noted its potential drawbacks. Or you may have remembered an early life experience but not reflected on the key concerns or fears that you associate with it. Take your time to reflect on and consider such things.

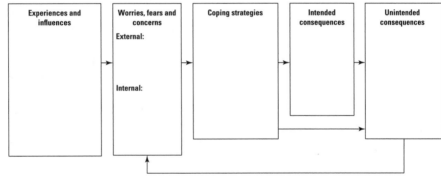

Credit TBC

FIGURE 5-2: A template for your life story diagram.

REMEMBER

Sometimes you may feel disloyal to friends and family if you write down how they may have impacted your life in a negative way. In addition, you may fear what other people would think if they saw your life mapped out in this way and as things appear to you at this present time. It's helpful to remember that this exercise is for you alone and not something that will be scrutinised by others. It's hoped that this process will improve your life and that of others, so it's a compassionate act to engage with it.

TIP

You may want to use your notebook or journal to experiment with alternative ways of putting together the information that you've collected. The additional space may allow you to play around with the content.

The next exercise will help you consider your life story on an intellectual level, considering if it makes sense and accounts for the difficulties you may experience both in relation to the way they developed and the vicious cycles that may maintain them.

Stand back and consider the following questions:

>> Does your life story explain why you're in the situation you find yourself in right now?

>> If your life story didn't apply to you, but instead applied to someone you cared about, would it make sense?

>> Is your life story believable?

If you answer 'no' to any of these questions, consider why this is. Maybe you've become self-critical and this is, in itself, an important realisation and one to emphasise more in your life story.

Alternatively, you may have missed an important piece of information. It may help to speak to someone who has your best interests at heart; maybe someone who knew you at key points in your life and who you can discuss this with.

TIP

If you still find that you're being self-critical or undermining yourself because of some aspect of your life story, make a note of this so that you can come back to it later. Your life story is the focus of a self-compassion exercise in Chapter 12 and a compassionate writing exercise in Chapter 14. Chair work (Chapter 17) and cultivating compassionate thoughts (Chapter 13) are also likely to be of benefit to you if you remain self-critical and undermining of yourself due to aspects of your life story.

Alternatively, consider seeking the input of a professional, who may be able to help you consider your life story further.

Taking Your Life Story from Thought to Feeling

Thinking about your life story is very different to *feeling* it. The first approach involves using a pragmatic and intellectualising frame of mind (which we look at in the preceding section); the second involves allowing yourself to emotionally connect with your story. Both are important. It's almost impossible to do one and not the other, but here we attempt to develop your emotional connection with your life story.

Find a place that is, as far as possible, free from distractions: somewhere you can be for 15–20 minutes. Allow your breathing to slow slightly as you relax your body and settle your mind. (For more on how to settle your mind and body, head to Chapter 9.) Evoke your compassionate mind, embodying your compassionate self (head to Chapter 10 for specific exercises).

Begin by recalling that we're all a combination of our biology (nature) and our experiences (nurture) (as we explore in the earlier section, 'Recognising Our Experiences and Influences'). At every point in life, we're doing our best to get by in a difficult world. Unfortunately, the things that we do to cope can sometimes have unintended consequences in terms of our wellbeing (and potentially the wellbeing of others).

Hindsight means that we may look back on specific situations and judge ourselves harshly, or think that we chose the easier rather than the more helpful option in a given situation – or else that we simply got things wrong. This may result in self-criticism and self-recrimination.

Holding all of this, gently in mind, allow an emotional connection with your life story, in the same way you would do if it were the life story of someone you cared about.

REMEMBER

Turning back time and recalling all the reasons that you act in certain ways at particular points is impossible. What's important now is to attempt to understand yourself both intellectually and, most importantly, emotionally.

Chapter 6

Considering Your Beliefs about Compassion

A number of different beliefs may interfere with your ability to open your mind to compassion and let compassion into your life. Imagine that you were brought up with the idea that being compassionate towards yourself was indulgent or selfish. Maybe you were told that you didn't deserve compassion or simply weren't shown it. What then? It's likely that you may now struggle with self-compassion and also with those who show it to you.

This chapter explores the beliefs many people hold in more detail. First, I consider the important point that positive emotions can be challenging in unexpected ways (life's never simple, is it!). I then guide you through an evaluation of your own beliefs about compassion, before breaking down these misconceptions to explore some healthier perspectives.

Feeling Positive Isn't Always Easy

We know and accept that 'negative' emotions are difficult and we can struggle with them. We generally don't like feeling low, anxious, angry or disgusted, even though these emotions are part of the human condition and incredibly important to us.

It may be surprising to realise that many of us struggle with 'positive' emotions too. Imagine that you've been depressed or anxious for six months or longer. One day you wake up and notice a sense of lightness, happiness and contentment. What pops into your mind then? For many it's the worry that you may be setting yourself up for a fall or kidding yourself, and all too soon your happiness will be taken away. You may then fall into a low mood, or feel anxious again.

Now imagine that, having yearned for a warm and tender relationship, someone begins to direct such qualities towards you. They're sensitive to your needs and motivated out of care for your wellbeing. Because of your previous experiences, this may turn out to be extremely threatening, despite the fact that this is exactly what you've been yearning for. So, instead of feeling warmth and a sense of connection with the person, you feel anxious and isolated. Something that 'should' be a positive experience turns into a very difficult one.

The nearby sidebar 'Fear of compassion: It doesn't seem fair!' explores the 'Catch-22' nature of the difficulties many people face. In other words, your experiences lead to difficulties that can set up a vicious cycle and require a considerable amount of energy to overcome.

FEAR OF COMPASSION: IT DOESN'T SEEM FAIR!

Imagine that, having been deprived of an essential nutrient, you're now in physical pain day after day. Now, imagine that the nutrient becomes available, but taking it makes you feel really ill, maybe even worse. It just wouldn't seem fair, would it?

Unfortunately, many people find themselves in this situation with respect to compassion. For one reason or another they're deprived of it (maybe from those in their environment, maybe from themselves) but the antidote to their distress (being shown compassion, or showing themselves compassion) is toxic to them.

One solution is to find a way to live with the pain, but this is a lonely path to walk. We run the risk of exhaustion and can feel overwhelmed. Another, more helpful, way is to slowly and steadily open up to the beneficial effects of compassion – without blowing a fuse!

Your threat system can trigger a range of difficult thoughts, feelings and physical sensations (as you see in Chapter 4), and the reason for this is largely based on your experiences – the ones that you explore in Chapter 5.

Evaluating Your Beliefs about Compassion

Because you're working to develop your compassionate mind and compassionate self, you may find it helpful to check out whether you hold any beliefs about compassion that may hold you back. (In Chapter 7 we explore why we may have difficult physical reactions too, and how those around us can also make our compassionate journey difficult.)

Identify the beliefs that you hold about compassion (for others, for yourself and from others) using the following list of statements. *Note:* Many of the statements are similar – read each statement slowly and carefully to ensure that you note the variation throughout the list.

Place a tick beside each statement that you agree with:

>> If I'm compassionate towards other people it means that I pity them.

>> If others are compassionate towards me it means that they pity me.

>> If I'm compassionate towards myself it means that I pity myself.

>> Compassion is the same as wallowing.

>> Compassion is all about being soft and fluffy.

>> Having compassion for others means I am being weak.

>> Having compassion for others means they must be weak.

>> If I accept compassion from others it is a weakness.

>> Being compassionate towards myself is weak.

>> If I practise compassion it means that I will never have negative thoughts again.

>> If I practise compassion it means that I will never have difficult emotions again.

>> Self-compassion is about being selfish or self-centred.

>> I don't deserve compassion from others.

>> I don't deserve to show myself compassion.

>> Some people don't deserve compassion.

>> Practising self-compassion means putting my needs first to the detriment of the needs of others.

- ≫ If others are compassionate towards me, it means that they are letting me off the hook for something.

- ≫ If I'm compassionate to others, it means that I'm letting them off the hook for something.

- ≫ If I'm compassionate towards myself, it means that I'm letting myself off the hook for something.

- ≫ Feeling compassion for others will be too hard and overwhelming.

- ≫ Feeling compassion from others will be too hard and overwhelming.

- ≫ Feeling compassion for myself will be too hard and overwhelming.

- ≫ Feeling compassion will set me up for a fall.

- ≫ If I feel compassion *for* others, my guard will be lowered and they will take advantage of me.

- ≫ If I allow myself to experience compassion *from* others, they will take advantage of me.

- ≫ If I allow myself to feel self-compassion, others will take advantage of me.

ONE SET OF RULES FOR OTHERS, ANOTHER SET FOR OURSELVES?

Imagine that a friend messes up at work. You may be motivated to check how they're doing. If they seem to be feeling down, anxious or angry you may offer to talk it through with them, offer some reassurance, maybe disclose something similar that you once did – or perhaps bring their attention back to all the things they've done well. You may offer to meet up with them outside of work, or make them aware that you're still thinking of them via a message or email a day or so later. In simple terms, you're sensitive to how they're feeling and what they may need.

Now imagine that you find yourself in the same situation. How easy is it for you to be sensitive to your own distress: to be validating, reassuring and supportive? How easy is it for you to do something that helps you to move forward? How easy is it for you to accept support and reassurance from those around you?

You probably find it hard to apply the same rules to yourself. At the same time, you may find that it's very easy to beat yourself up and ruminate on your 'mistake'. The compassionate approach you show others may feel a million miles away from how you treat yourself.

TIP

It may help to discuss each of the statements with someone else.

Use a blank sheet of paper to make a note of any patterns you notice. Do the statements you've ticked centre around one or more of the following:

>> Compassion for others?

>> Compassion from others?

>> Self-compassion?

You may find that you've put ticks against a range of different statements. Becoming aware of your beliefs provides you with an opportunity to gently question whether they're indeed correct or not.

REMEMBER

Many of us have no problem with being compassionate to others, but accepting compassion from others and practising self-compassion can be a different matter altogether. Check out the nearby sidebar 'One set of rules for others, another set for ourselves?' for more on this.

Breaking Down Your Beliefs about Compassion

While trying out the exercise in the preceding section, you may have realised that a number of common beliefs about compassion hold some weight for you. You may have also noted that you especially struggle with a certain aspect of compassion, be it compassion from others, compassion for others or compassion towards yourself (if you haven't tried this exercise yet, it may help to turn back to this section before reading on).

In this section, you look at some of the beliefs you considered in the preceding exercise to see if they hold any water. Many of the items combine a number of beliefs under the same heading. For example, we look at the belief that compassion is associated with weakness as a whole instead of dealing with it in relation to compassion for others, from others or self compassion. This is because compassion doesn't change – it's the same regardless of where it's directed. I also provide an alternative way of looking at these beliefs, to help you reconsider any unhelpful perspectives.

REMEMBER

The views that we hold can have a big impact on the development of our compassionate mind and compassionate self. It's helpful to gently explore them. If blocks remain for you, it may be helpful to discuss your views and concerns with someone you trust. Alternatively, it can help to suspend your views for a little time and give new ideas 'a go'. You never know, you may discover something.

VIEWING PITY ACROSS CULTURES

Chapter 2 outlines how we define compassion within Compassion Focused Therapy (CFT). It's also important to recognise that different people and different cultures view the concept of pity in different ways. For example, Michelangelo's *Pietà* is a work of art depicting the mother of Christ holding her dead son's body. When many Italians speak of the sculpture, they reflect that this is the depiction of ultimate love and compassion. Within Italian culture, the word *pietà* has no negative connotations.

Compassion means . . . wallowing in pity?

Pity can be a very evocative word. For many it means looking down, or being looked down on, from a position of superiority. Using this definition, we fail to acknowledge our own or another person's strength and resilience. Pity in this sense can also give the impression that the individual is defined solely by the situation they find themselves in rather than their difficulty just being part of them.

Compassion (be it for others, from others or for ourselves) is absolutely not about pity. As you find in Chapter 2, compassion comes with a sense of common humanity. From this position we acknowledge the strength and resilience in ourselves and others.

And what about wallowing – in pity or, indeed, any other emotion? *Wallowing* is commonly understood to be the act of indulging ourselves in the pleasure of an activity. As you discover in Chapter 2, the second psychology of compassion is being motivated 'to prevent and alleviate distress'. With our wise, compassionate mind we may realise that it's helpful to stay with our strong emotions and allow ourselves to be consumed by them for a time. This decision isn't based on pleasure or enjoyment but the realisation that it's helpful, if not essential, to go through this process. Alternatively, our compassionate mind may motivate us to do something more active to address our difficulties. Both options take strength and courage and are by no means passive.

TIP

From the outside looking in, a grieving person may appear to be wallowing in their sorrow. However, truly allowing yourself to feel a sense of overwhelming loss is extremely difficult. Many people will talk of the need to 'surrender' to these feelings. This takes strength and courage, but the pain ultimately leads to acceptance and a reconnection with others.

Compassion is . . . weak, soft and fluffy?

Being sensitive to the distress that we, and others, may feel and being motivated to alleviate or prevent it is not a sign of weakness.

TRUE STRENGTH PROGRAM

United States psychologist Russel Kolts developed the True Strength Program for individuals experiencing difficulties with anger. With CFT at its core, the programme successfully challenges some of the assumptions about compassion for others, from others and for ourselves, and participants are encouraged to develop their compassionate minds and compassionate selves as an act of strength and courage. In doing so, they move towards an alleviation of their own suffering and that of others.

Of course, at times we all turn away from our own pain and that of others. We deny it, ignore it or minimise it. This is often how we cope. But when we face pain and suffering, we do so with great strength, courage and commitment.

Compassion involves 'doing' – and what we do to prevent or alleviate suffering can vary. It may involve courageously speaking up for yourself despite an overwhelming urge to remain quiet, or letting people see the true you despite a fear of rejection. In one situation it may be the act of listening and bearing witness to someone's pain, and in another it may be directing an individual towards something or someone who may have a helpful solution.

REMEMBER

Compassion can be soft and gentle, but to define it only as this would be wrong, as it also takes great strength and courage. It has a backbone of steel!

Compassion means . . . no more negative thoughts or difficult emotions?

When people first begin to practise CFT, they may feel they're failing because they still experience strong emotions, or even feel more of them. However, compassion involves opening ourselves up to strong emotions rather than suppressing, denying or dissociating ourselves from them. It involves being aware of any negative thoughts that occupy our mind – thoughts that may relate to other people, our life or ourselves in general. We then use our compassionate mind to do something, or appropriately do nothing, about these negative thoughts and strong emotions.

If life was free of any disappointment, pain, suffering, upset, need or conflict, maybe we wouldn't have any negative thoughts or emotions and maybe no need for compassion – but life just isn't like that.

REMEMBER

We practise compassion *because* we have negative thoughts and difficult emotions.

Self-compassion is . . . selfish and self-centred?

People are often surprised to find that self-compassion often brings with it a greater capacity to truly 'be there' for others. This is because you gain a mind that's supportive rather than in conflict with itself – a mind that's freed up from internal wrangling! When you experience the calmer waters of self-compassion, you're better able to explore, try new things, take risks, broach difficult situations, reach out to others and see things from different perspectives.

Compassion is . . . undeserved?

If you feel you don't deserve compassion, you may judge yourself or your actions negatively and experience shame. This belief may be the product of how others have treated you in the past, or a view you have formed about yourself.

In Chapter 5 you focus on your life story – this involves developing an understanding of the experiences and influences that have helped to shape you. Emotionally connecting with the reality that your genetic make-up, life experiences and living environment is not of your choosing can help you to see that we're all deserving of compassion.

You can also think of your own sense of being undeserving as a fear, block or barrier that you can overcome as you develop your compassionate mind and compassionate self. The following exercises help you to get started. The first will help you identify if it's self compassion or compassion from others (or both) that you believe you don't deserve. Honing down what aspect is difficult for you may give you some insight into how this belief developed and whether you still believe this to be the case. The second takes a look specifically at compassion from others and helps you explore this in more detail.

Think about these two scenarios:

» Consider whether you believe that you don't deserve to show yourself compassion *or* whether you believe you don't deserve to experience compassion from others. You may have considered this during the exercise in the earlier section, 'Evaluating Your Beliefs about Compassion'. Although one belief often comes with the other, this may vary. Considering whether you believe you deserve to show yourself compassion or receive it from others may help you to be more specific about what your personal block is and to consider why this is the case. (Chapter 5 helps you to explore your experiences and may help you consider where such difficulties originate from.)

» Consider this: if you believe that you don't deserve compassion from others, does this vary for different people in your life? If this is the case, consider why this is. For example, you may find that you can experience compassion from people you know well but that, when it comes to compassion shown by people who know you less well, you think 'they don't really know me, and if they did they wouldn't show me compassion'.

You may find that you experience compassion in different ways when it's shown to you by older or younger people, males or females, friends or relatives. It may then be helpful to consider why this is and to look at your earlier life experiences for clues. It may help to consider this insight in the context of your life story (refer to Chapter 5 for more on your life story).

TIP

In CFT, compassion is broken down into six attributes. Head to Chapter 2 to familiarise yourself with these. It may be that you struggle with one attribute and believe that you're undeserving of that aspect of compassion but not others. For example, you may struggle specifically with sympathy or distress sensitivity from others.

Ask yourself, 'What attributes of compassion do I deserve to show myself?' Empathy, non-judgement, sympathy, sensitivity, tolerance of distress or care for well-being, for example? If you still believe you don't deserve compassion, consider why you may struggle with specific attributes. Insight itself can be liberating.

REMEMBER

You can repeat the above exercises in relation to many of the beliefs outlined in this section. For example, you can ask which specific attribute of compassion is 'weak', which attribute would set you up for a fall, and so on.

TIP

If you still believe that you don't deserve compassion, Chapters 12 and 14 can help enhance your compassionate understanding and feelings towards yourself.

REMEMBER

People can feel like they deserve to give themselves a hard time, maybe for something they have or haven't done or related to experiences they've had. If you think this applies to you, it may be worthwhile revisiting Chapter 1 to explore the impact self-criticism can have.

The following example may help you to understand the value of exploring any negative beliefs you may hold about deserving compassion.

EXAMPLE

Chloe often felt socially isolated and this affected her mood. She became frustrated with herself and self-critical because, although she had people around her, she struggled to feel a sense of connection with them. After careful consideration, Chloe realised that she didn't have any problems experiencing compassion from male friends and relatives. She believed she was deserving of their compassion (or at least that she hadn't done anything that made her undeserving). However, Chloe also realised that she found it difficult to experience compassion from her female relatives, and some of her female friends. Realising that, at some level, she believed she didn't deserve compassion from these people gave Chloe something to ponder. She wondered if this accounted for why she often kept people at arm's length. Later, she reflected that this had something to do with some of the family rules she grew up with.

TIP

If feeling undeserving of compassion is really tripping you up, or you feel you deserve to punish yourself or give yourself a hard time, you can try two more things. First, speak to someone you know who has your best interests at heart. Open up to them about your experiences and difficulties and ask whether they think you should punish yourself and give yourself a hard time. Ask if they think you deserve to be compassionate towards yourself.

A second option is to speak to someone who is removed from your current situation, such as a professional therapist; your GP may be able to recommend someone who can help you explore this further.

What about other people – do you sometimes feel that others don't deserve compassion? This can be very tricky, especially if you're thinking about someone who is responsible for causing you, or other people, distress, and who you may feel anger towards. Within CFT, the therapeutic stance is that everyone deserves compassion, no matter what they have or haven't done. A therapist develops understanding of a given situation, but doesn't judge. Nothing a person says will change their position. This perspective is imperative to addressing an individual's shame and self-criticism, because it allows individuals to open up and ultimately helps them develop their own compassionate mind.

REMEMBER

I don't advocate that you *should* develop compassion for someone who has hurt you. The aim of CFT is to first and foremost develop your self-compassion, and from this stable base it's your choice whether you begin to consider others with compassion.

Self-compassion is . . . always putting my needs above other people's?

Sometimes it's helpful to put other people's needs before our own. Parenting is the perfect example! Imagine that you've been invited to a party, but it clashes with something really important in your child's life that you can't miss. You may try to rejig things (if you think the party would be good!), but if the clash remains you reluctantly send your apologies, knowing that you've made the right decision.

But things become tricky when we perpetually put the needs of others first. Our wellbeing can suffer and we may feel a sense of anger and resentment. We may feel taken for granted and uncared for – and then beat ourselves up about it. Compassion is about striking a balance between focusing on our own needs and focusing on the needs of others – it's not healthy to consider our own needs as an afterthought.

DO WE NEED COMPASSION?

Rather than considering if people deserve compassion, it can be helpful to reflect on whether people need it. The case of Maajid Nawaz may help us consider this. Following the horrific death of Lee Rigby, a Royal Fusilier who was murdered by Michael Adebolajo and Michael Adebowale, in London in 2013, Maajid wrote a courageous and thought-provoking article in *The Daily Telegraph*. Entitled 'I was a radical Islamist who hated all of you', he spoke about how he, a young, middle-class, educated and popular individual, had been radicalised. He spoke of how, while in prison, his hatred towards others was eventually challenged and turned around by the kindness of strangers: kindness that was given by those who knew his history and did not judge him for it.

Since then, Maajid advocates engagement through conversations at a grass-roots level to help prevent other young men and women following his path.

Judgement, marginalisation, and being spat on and sworn at is likely to have fuelled his views. Even a neutral response from people ignoring or denying his views is likely to have left his hatred unchecked. In my eyes, compassion from others seems to have been integral to the change in him. He *needed* compassion. And if other people are more likely to take responsibility for their actions (or inactions) through compassion, they need it too.

If this is hard to stomach, and I can understand if it is, it can be helpful to think about what society needs. It *needs* less hatred and loss. Compassion is a potential solution.

TIP

If you think that the needs of others are more important than your own, experiment by trying to create some middle ground. What can you begin to do that won't, as far as you can see it, have a negative impact on others? Alternatively, consider practising self-compassion for the sake of others; maybe by developing self-compassion, you'll be more content and less anxious or frustrated, and this may have a positive impact on the people around you. Experiment and see what helps.

REMEMBER

People often find that they're better able to be the friend, parent, partner, son or daughter they want to be if they practise self-compassion.

Compassion means . . . abdicating responsibility?

Key to a compassionate perspective is developing and understanding ourselves and why we are the way we are. From this stance, we move away from self-criticism and shame. However, this doesn't mean that we relinquish responsibility or excuse our own actions. In fact, when we practise compassion we're more likely to put ourselves *on* the hook and to take responsibility for the things we do. The nearby sidebar, 'Placing myself on the hook – compassionately' looks at an example from my own life, where I used my compassionate mind to work through a challenging situation in a self-compassionate way.

REMEMBER

Taking a compassionate stance involves being sensitive to the difficulties we and others face and then being motivated to do something about it. This requires a commitment to changing things for the better where we can.

The following example looks at taking responsibility using the compassionate mind.

EXAMPLE

When John became emotional around other people he tended to quickly switch to sarcasm. Sometimes this was directed towards himself in a self-deprecating way, but mostly it was directed at others. It didn't matter if the emotion he felt was anxiety, anger or despondency. His witty retorts seemed to exacerbate difficult situations and keep others at arm's length. He felt quite isolated and at times angry towards others who seemed to intentionally wind him up, or say things to upset or worry him.

EXAMPLE

PLACING MYSELF ON THE HOOK – COMPASSIONATELY

As a trainer in CFT I'm observed by the audience but, from time to time, also by other Compassionate Mind Foundation trainers. (The Compassionate Mind Foundation is a charity that runs training events for individuals and groups who want to learn how to use CFT in both their personal lives and at work.) This may be because they're co-facilitating the event with me. At other times, it's in an attempt to maintain consistency across our trainers and their events, and it give us an opportunity to reflect on the training experience and ultimately to learn from each other. Despite me knowing the rationale for this, in the early days I certainly found it daunting to have the likes of Paul Gilbert or Deborah Lee in the audience! They are heroes of mine, and no matter how warm and supportive they were, I worried that I'd mess up and that they would think I wasn't up to the job.

At one particular introductory training course I was 10 weeks into my first pregnancy, and very ill with it. Paul Gilbert was leading the training and I was assisting. Throughout the training, Paul would, every so often, suggest that I went home because, in his words, I 'looked dreadful' (which obviously helped!). He was happy to continue without me. But I continued because I wanted to stay with the group until the end, and also to learn from Paul.

On the third and final day, just before the last break, I fielded a difficult question from the audience. My response didn't appear to answer the person's question. I became anxious and defensive and ended up in a 'reference-off' about a certain subject (whereby the delegate would quote one reference and I would respond with another). I realised that my threat system had taken over (head to Chapter 4 to find out more). As this went on, I looked around the room and saw that the audience seemed to range from disengaged (and desperate for their coffee break) to agitated or embarrassed.

At the break I went to the toilets and dissolved into floods of tears. I beat myself up about what a mess I'd made, and I was also angry towards the delegate for not letting the point drop. Listening to my self-critic, I considered taking up Paul's offer of going home. If I'd done this, I may have avoided everything CFT-related for some time, maybe focusing on other things instead. Later, I may have blamed my pregnancy or the delegate for the difficult situation I found myself in. This was the Mary of old – and this part of me felt very familiar.

After a few minutes, I paused and considered what would be helpful. I engaged in my soothing rhythm breathing (which you discover more about in Chapter 9), evoked my compassionate mind (head to Chapter 10) and thought through the situation. With my compassionate mind I reflected that I hadn't answered the question in the best way possible, I'd become anxious and therefore defensive, and maybe I hadn't appreciated the delegate's viewpoint. I also reflected that maybe I needed to read a bit more about the specific area raised, as maybe I didn't know it as well as I could. I brought to mind that the delegate was at the training because they wanted to learn and wanted to discover new things to help their clients. I considered that it's understandable for questions to be posed if a person disagrees with something. Maybe they became anxious and defensive too, and this made the interaction even more difficult.

With this viewpoint in mind, I returned to the workshop (a bit puffy-eyed). Paul facilitated the penultimate segment and then, after a bit of breathing time, I facilitated the feedback section at the end. Among other things, I was able to reflect with the group on the discussion that had taken place, both the content and the activation of my 'threat system'. I felt as though I was able to both face and repair it for all involved.

After the training course had finished, I asked Paul for feedback regarding how I had handled the situation and I was able to take his words and the emotional tone of his feedback on board. I left having learnt a lot from the experience. I went on to read some of the papers Paul had suggested to me to enhance both my understanding and my training of others.

In simple terms, my self-critic would have put the other person 'on the hook' or blamed my 'pregnant' self. This may have felt okay, but would I have learnt anything from it? By engaging with my compassionate mind I was able to take an appropriate level of responsibility for the situation and do something enriching about it.

Having worked to develop his compassionate mind, John spent some time considering a number of social situations from the perspective of the other party. He saw his role in both the development and maintenance of his difficulties. Facing up to this was difficult for John, but he was hopeful that by doing so things would change for the better. Instead of being self-critical about it, he began to understand why he did what he did. His actions were, in fact, understandable given some of the difficulties he'd faced, and he was able to recognise this too. With this new perspective, he was able to take responsibility for some of his difficulties and also for developing some ideas about changes he could make.

REMEMBER

Looking at our behaviour with a compassionate mind allows us to notice if we're contributing, or not, to the difficulties we experience. With emotional warmth rather than blame or self-criticism, we can support ourselves to make positive changes.

Compassion is . . . too hard and overwhelming?

Compassion isn't all hearts and flowers, skipping and hopping. It involves being sensitive to and engaging with the distress others or we may feel, and being motivated to do something about it.

When we tune into our own distress and that of other people, we can feel strong emotions. Memories and images may pop into our minds and we may have a range of difficult thoughts.

For this reason, CFT suggests that you build up your emotional resources (think of it like the training you would do before climbing a mountain!). Attention training (Chapter 8), soothing rhythm breathing (Chapter 9), compassion for others (Chapter 10), letting compassion in (Chapter 11) and self-compassion (Chapter 12) are just some of the exercises designed to help you face and experience the emotions that arise.

REMEMBER

If engaging with compassion from or for others, or for yourself, begins to feel too overwhelming, consider the following advice:

>> Go at a pace that's comfortable for you. It can be helpful to allow a bit of time for your emotions to settle, so take a break if you need to.

>> Start gradually. Remember, if you were learning to swim, you'd enter at the shallow end. Approach the exercises in this book in a similar way. For example, it may help to initially only engage with compassionate exercises for 30 seconds each, and then to slowly build this up over time.

>> Engage in compassionate exercises at a time when you feel you have the resources and support to do it or when life is relatively stable and free of stress.

>> Schedule in some pleasurable activities around reading this book, such as spending time with good friends, taking some time for yourself, going for walks or engaging in other fun and healthy experiences.

>> Speak to your GP about psychological therapy if you feel that you need the support of a professional.

TIP

We can all feel that we don't know what to do to assist other people or ourselves. We may feel inadequate and unskilled. (This is particularly true for therapists, whose role is to assist individuals to alleviate their distress.) This can be very painful. At such times, it can be important to remember that 'being with' and 'staying with' our own pain, or that of someone else, can be everything we or another person needs in that moment.

REMEMBER

Human beings are amazingly resilient and can survive much hardship – especially if they have others around to assist and bear witness.

Compassion . . . sets me up for a fall?

As we considered in the earlier section, 'Feeling Positive Isn't Always Easy', people can sometimes become wary of positive emotions. Fear can be triggered by experiences of compassion, connectedness and safeness. Alternatively, it may be joy and happiness, calmness, or relaxation that are difficult. We go on to look at the reasons why individuals may develop such difficulties in Chapter 7.

Individuals may believe that positive experiences precipitate something negative happening and, if caught unawares, that they will be unprepared and therefore the negative impact will be greater. In addition, some believe that feeling good attracts negative things as some form of 'payback'. This may be related to thoughts of being 'undeserving' (refer to the earlier section, 'Compassion is . . . undeserved?') or arise as part of any superstitious beliefs that an individual grows up with.

REMEMBER

Working on your compassionate mind and compassionate self doesn't trigger negative life events occurring. The presence of compassion in your life can actually decrease your tendency for conflict, disappointment and lost opportunities.

TIP

Self-compassion can actually be the best way of preparing yourself for the difficulties and setbacks that life inevitably brings. Self-compassion builds your ability to cope with hard situations, and it's through coping with setbacks that confidence in your ability to cope increases. If your fear of 'falling' gets in the way of you experiencing positive feelings, it may be helpful just to think, 'I'll give it a go' – you'll quickly experience the benefits.

THE WEATHER ANALOGY

I love the North of England where I grew up, but November to March, and even the months either side, can be cold, wet and grey. Imagine that it's mid-January and, after weeks of awful weather, you wake up on a Saturday morning and it's a clear, crisp, sunny winter's day. What do you do? Do you think 'tomorrow will be bad so I may as well just stay indoors', or do you do something outside and appreciate the sun and the clear skies while they last? It's likely that you decide to get outside. However, when we sustain a period of anxiety or low mood, a 'good day' may be something we're wary of. Thoughts such as 'don't get too excited', 'this won't last' and even 'there must be something wrong because this isn't usual' may pop into our heads.

I playfully share this analogy with my clients, when I think I know them well enough and they won't think that I'm belittling their experiences. We then reflect on the need to work out a way to enjoy the good days. Begin to relish the good days, because the bad days will come around again – this is part of the British climate and part of being a human being.

Compassion means . . . people will take advantage of me?

Thanks to the human brain's basic 'better safe than sorry' default setting, and perhaps some difficult life experiences, our threat system often ends up running the show (refer to Chapter 4). Living this way isn't very efficient and – bottom line – it's difficult to live like this, too.

Compassion can actually make our threat system run more efficiently; it makes us wiser and helps us decide when we need to put our guard up and when we don't. This means that we're better able to detect when someone's taking advantage of us and more skilled to deal with such situations in order to resolve them. For example, your compassionate mind and compassionate self can help you to notice patterns occurring in relationships, such as the colleague who repeatedly fails to pull their weight or the relative who relies on you for chores that they can do themselves. Your compassionate mind and compassionate self can then give you the strength, courage and skills to have a difficult conversation, support you if the conversation doesn't go the way you hope, and help you decide what to do next.

Chapter 7

Facing Barriers to Compassion

Beliefs about compassion can interfere with the development of our compassionate mind and compassionate self (Chapter 6 explores this in more detail). Our emotional reactions, maybe resulting from trauma or difficult life events, can also impact on our experience of compassion, and so too can the responses of others.

In this chapter, we look at how the brain works when we experience positive and negative emotions, and we consider the way that the brain can be conditioned to pair up our emotions. We also discover how to address our own emotional barriers, as well as how to deal with resistance to positive change that may, perhaps unintentionally, come from others in our lives. Finally, we draw together what we've discovered in this chapter and in Chapter 6, and look at ways to negotiate these barriers to achieve positive outcomes.

Understanding Difficult Emotional Reactions

Our emotional state has a huge bearing on what occupies our mind. It makes sense that if we're feeling happy, we're more likely to think about something positive in the future or recall something nice that happened in the past. If we're feeling anxious, we're more likely to imagine difficult things ahead and remember the things that didn't go to plan.

The reverse of this is true also. What we bring our attention to, be it in the future or the past, can trigger an emotional change in us. Bringing our attention to an argument may set off a cascade of anxious or angry thoughts. Focusing on a cherished memory may result in us thinking about other happy memories. (Head to Chapter 8 for a more in-depth look at attention.)

In the following sections, I consider why our emotional reactions may not always follow this simple pattern (good leading to good; negative leading to negative). I also explore why positive emotions may trigger negative emotions and what you can do about it.

Weighing up how positive emotions can trigger negative emotions

Why is it that the seemingly positive emotional experience of compassion can trigger negative emotions and difficult memories that we then need to work through?

Two key factors can help you to understand this experience:

>> Compassion involves being sensitive to our own distress and the distress of others. Feeling compassion can therefore be a very moving, yet healing and enriching, experience.

>> Our brains can seemingly 'pair' certain emotions with each other, so that the experience of one emotion can trigger another.

The following examples help to illustrate the importance of these two factors. Each of the examples illustrates how use of your compassionate mind to consider early life experiences can be extremely moving – compassion is paired with sadness and sorrow.

Marta and Neil's examples also illustrate how emotions can become wired together. If a desire for closeness with a parent is met with a negative reaction, this is likely to play out in adulthood.

EXAMPLE

As mum to two very young children, Helen held it together following the death of her sister. She threw herself into her work and family life. Four years on she found that she was increasingly 'edgy', regularly snapping at her children and family, and she often felt overwhelmed.

Helen decided that things needed to change and, following a friend's recommendation, she began to read about Compassion Focused Therapy (CFT) one evening after the children had gone to bed. Looking at her life story from the perspective of her compassionate mind, Helen connected with the immense sense of loss she felt about losing her sister. She began to cry and cried herself to sleep that evening.

Helen's compassionate mind allowed her to be sensitive to the distress that lay beneath her tension and agitation. It put her in contact with her loss. Although this was painful in the short term, allowing herself to grieve and tolerate her distress was a turning point for Helen. She began to work through her feelings and slowly she began to feel as though she was regaining the person she had been before her sister's death.

Later, when talking to a friend, she reflected that she hadn't expected to feel worse before she felt better, but now realised that this was exactly what she needed to do.

EXAMPLE

Marta repeatedly found that as relationships became more 'serious', she backed off. After the breakdown of yet another relationship, she felt isolated, her mood suffered and she wondered what was wrong with her. Approaching her late 30s, Marta decided to seek therapy with a CFT therapist in order to address this.

Marta was surprised to find that she felt physically sick when beginning to work on compassionate imagery (see Chapters 11 and 12 for more on this). This experience was also tinged with a sense of anger at times.

In order to try to understand this, Marta reviewed her life story (you discover more about life stories in Chapter 5). She reflected that her parents had often been unpredictable in their responses to her. This was especially true at key times in her life. Sometimes they were comforting, but at other times they were dismissive or even punishing. Bringing her attention to this, Marta felt a sense of sadness. This sadness can be seen as a result of a sensitivity to her distress. Marta's compassionate mind allowed her to reflect how difficult this must have been for her when she was a child.

Using her compassionate mind, she recalled a number of significant memories. For example, one day she'd come home from school upset because girls had been bullying her, but instead of giving the comfort she sought, her mum had told her that she must have done something wrong and that she needed to go back in to school and work out what it was. Marta's desire for compassion and closeness to her mum was then paired with a sense of panic that she had done something wrong and a tinge of anger that at some level this wasn't fair.

It seemed to make sense to Marta why developing images and experiences of compassion in her mind could evoke an anxious knot in her stomach and feelings of anger and frustration. Marta began to understand that this was due to childhood experiences where all of these emotions seemed to come together and become fused. Noticing this, and gradually working through and accepting such emotions, was pivotal to Marta's continuing journey to develop her compassionate mind and compassionate self.

EXAMPLE

Anger always seemed to get the better of Neil. At times it gave him a sense of control, but it also meant that he lost job after job due to confrontations or simply from walking out. He also struggled with relationships, and although he initially felt drawn towards someone, this was quickly followed by a feeling of nothingness or overwhelming panic.

It took four or five sessions of CFT for Neil to develop a trusting relationship with his therapist. As time passed, he felt increasingly able and prepared to look towards his past for answers as to why he was so angry. With sadness, Neil recalled that when he was upset as a child, and in need of a hug, he was ignored, rejected or even humiliated by his parents. His relationship with them was very strained and, with a deep-seated sense of anger, he began to get into trouble at school.

Neil considered that this difficult relationship may account for the fact that, as an adult, when he felt drawn towards others, he simultaneously experienced a sense of anger and frustration. At other times his emotions appeared to be 'switched off', and he felt nothing. Positive experiences and emotions seemed to trigger difficult ones.

Recognising the link between his early experiences and those in his current life was a big breakthrough for Neil. He became less critical of himself and, like Marta (refer to the preceding example), decided to continue to develop his compassion-ate mind and compassionate self. When Neil noticed strong emotions he 'allowed them to be' rather than pushed them away. Repeatedly noticing and fostering a calmer frame of mind, he was able to gently increase his ability to experience compassion for himself and closeness to others.

Conditioning the brain

Russian psychologist Ivan Pavlov's concept *of classical conditioning* helps us under-stand why certain stimuli (or events) can trigger what initially seem like unusual responses (remember how Pavlov trained dogs to salivate upon the presence of a sound rather than the presence of their dinner!). Neuroscience research (which studies the nervous system from many different disciplines) has furthered our understanding and helps account for why our emotions can seemingly become paired with each other.

The phrase 'neurons that fire together, wire together' encapsulates this very simply.

As a child, if you're punished for feeling anger, you're likely to become anxious about showing anger again. Any personal experience of anger may then be quickly followed by a feeling of anxiety – that someone will notice the anger and punish you. Over time, this association becomes quicker and quicker and makes it likely that your future emotional experience of anger will be paired almost simultaneously with anxiety. Subsequent experiences of anger can then act as a trigger for anxiety, or the emotions may 'show up' at the same time.

For some, the triggering emotion can seem to be missing altogether. Situations that are likely to produce anger may produce anxiety instead, bypassing the experience of anger entirely. Likewise, situations likely to produce sadness may trigger anger. The following examples help to illustrate this.

Nadine had suffered abuse at the hands of her father when she was young. As an adult, she was extremely anxious, suffering from panic and health concerns, and she had difficulty sleeping.

Upon arriving at her first CFT therapy session, Nadine mentioned that she had used the bus, because her car had been written off one night while it was parked on the street. It transpired that the driver had fled the scene and not reported the incident. Nadine talked anxiously about the situation and expressed a range of concerns about her ability to buy another car (or not), and how this would impact on her life. She told herself off about where she'd parked and wondered if the incident was some kind of 'payback' or bad karma. When asked if she felt anger, Nadine looked vacantly at her therapist. 'Anger at myself, maybe', she responded, but she didn't feel any anger towards the other driver.

Hugh was bullied at school. It was worse when the bullies saw he was upset, so Hugh learned to keep his guard up and retaliate. He kept his feelings of hurt and upset at bay because he felt it was dangerous to show these feelings to the children who bullied him.

Later, as an adult, whether after the loss of his job, his marriage breakdown or his son's diagnosis of cancer, Hugh felt no degree of sadness. Instead he kept his guard up, he confided in no one, and he felt extreme anger.

These examples help illustrate that while our reactions to events may seem odd, when we understand them in the context of our experiences, they make sense. Chapter 5 can help you consider why you may have seemingly unusual emotional responses to events. The nearby sidebar 'Triggering traumatic memories' provides a further example of how we may have been 'conditioned'.

TRIGGERING TRAUMATIC MEMORIES

TIP

When in the midst of trauma, many people dissociate. They describe 'tripping out', 'blowing a fuse', 'switching off' or 'going on automatic pilot'. Things seem unreal and emotions seem to be held at bay. As with the examples provided in the section 'Conditioning the brain', this response can be confusing, because instead of feeling strong emotions we feel nothing.

This reaction is an in-built mechanism to help us cope with trauma. Bringing the trauma to mind after the event can trigger exactly the same reaction and, although designed to help us, it doesn't allow us to naturally work through the memories or the associated emotions. As such, we can get stuck.

By building our compassionate mind, we can approach and work through traumatic memories gently, and from a safe place, in order to ensure that we don't trigger difficult reactions. In so doing, we slowly pair the traumatic memory with feelings of compassion rather than feelings of nothingness or being overwhelmed.

Our task is to first and foremost understand our emotions and reactions and then consider learning a new way of relating to ourselves and others.

Identifying your emotional barriers

Overcoming emotional barriers takes time and we return to this concept many times in this book. For example, Chapter 9 can help you to develop your soothing rhythm breathing as a foundation for stabilising your mind. This approach can then help you to dip in and out of strong emotions. Chapters 11 and 12 use imagery to help you to allow compassion in from others and to develop self-compassion, respectively. Such practices can help you to tolerate strong emotions with strength, courage and wisdom. I outline compassionate letter writing and chair work in Chapters 14 and 17 respectively, which can help you explore and relate compassionately to the different parts of you. All these practices (and many others in this book) can be used to help you work through strong emotions and calm your mind.

You may also have started work on overcoming emotional barriers while developing your life story in Chapter 5 and reviewing the beliefs that challenge you in Chapter 6.

Addressing your own emotional barriers

I wish I could offer a quick fix to help you overcome your emotional barriers, but it's a personal and unique journey for each of us, and it takes time. The following exercise starts this process by helping you identify the emotional barriers that you may have and begin to explore the feelings they're associated with.

Find a place that is, as far as possible, free from distractions – somewhere you can be for about 15 minutes. Sit in a relaxed, open posture with strength and alertness to your spine. Soften your facial expression, slightly relaxing your jaw. It's helpful to close your eyes, but you may prefer to settle your gaze on a low fixed point.

You may use soothing rhythm breathing, a mindfulness practice (for both, see Chapter 9) or another form of exercise to create a sense of calm awareness in your mind and body before you start this exercise.

When you feel ready to begin, take the following steps:

1. **Gently consider if anger, sadness, anxiety or any other emotion is difficult for you.** As Neil and Marta did in the earlier section, 'Weighing up how positive emotions can trigger negative emotions', consider if this difficulty relates to any of your experiences at home, school, work or in other environments.

   Remind yourself that our brains are tricky (refer to Chapter 3) – our emotions can become 'wired' in a way that's problematic for our wellbeing. Understanding ourselves, our emotions and our reactions can be a powerful antidote to the self-criticism and frustration that we may experience, especially when change is slow and obstacles stand in our way.

2. **Gradually and gently allow yourself to sit with some of the thoughts, images, physical sensations and feelings that you experience.** If your emotions begin to feel overwhelming and you wish to reduce them, use your soothing rhythm breathing, mindfulness, imagery or other exercises that increase your sense of control and calm your mind and body.

TIP

   If you haven't already practiced soothing rhythm breathing, mindfulness or other CFT exercises, simply consider getting up and moving around, having a stretch or taking a few calming breaths before you re-engage with the exercise.

If you find this exercise difficult, it may help to develop your compassionate mind and compassionate self first. Head to Chapters 10–14 for more on developing your compassionate mind and compassionate self.

TIP

If you find it difficult to work through strong emotions and emotional memories, talking to your GP may be a good starting point because they can direct you to further sources of help. We all benefit from the input of someone else from time to time. Seeking the help or advice of others can be valuable, and isn't shameful at all. In fact, it can be the most compassionate thing to do.

Overcoming Barriers Created by Others

It is human nature to be wary of change, yet change is what we attempt to make when we embark on CFT. However, the development of our compassionate mind and compassionate self can become even harder to manage if other people resist the changes we're trying to make.

The following examples illustrate how Charlotte, Ken and Michelle's best efforts were blocked by others.

EXAMPLE

Charlotte was painfully shy and found that she avoided a whole range of situations for fear that she may be judged by others. Having worked to develop a sense of inner support, strength and courage, Charlotte began putting herself forward for things she'd never have dreamed of before. When she first volunteered to chair a meeting, everyone looked shocked. Her boss took her to one side and asked, 'Are you sure you're ready to do this – maybe build up to it?' This show of concern made Charlotte doubt her readiness.

As she chaired the meeting the following week, it seemed that some people were just smugly watching and waiting for her to mess up. She found it difficult to keep the meeting to time because people didn't listen to her attempts to move the discussion along (no matter how she did it). They also tended to talk over her or to interject.

So, Charlotte found she had an additional barrier to overcome. Not only did she have to work to develop her compassionate mind and compassionate self, she also had to negotiate the reactions of others.

EXAMPLE

Ken had a large circle of friends, and on a one-to-one basis had no problem with any of them. However, he didn't speak much when they were out in a large group because he felt self-conscious, as though everyone was watching and judging his contributions. On nights out, four or five key friends would take up much of the air space, and their conversation was fast and furious, resembling a doubles tennis match. Ken wanted to join in and had things to say, but his anxiety got the better of him.

Having built up his confidence in many other ways, he decided to take action to try to overcome his anxiety and become part of the group. One night, he felt confident enough to interject with a witty remark. He was shot down in flames and the conversation quickly moved on. Again, when a lull in conversation occurred he tried to initiate a discussion, but the conversation was hijacked by others. It was as if his friends were used to the roles each of them played, and resisted Ken being any different from usual.

Ken was reserved for the rest of the night. He later decided to try and build up his confidence in smaller groups and also to take up some opportunities to make new friendships.

TIP

Sometimes it's helpful for us to develop the strength, courage and commitment to change ourselves (whether it be how we relate to ourselves or others) but sometimes it can be helpful to consider whether we actually need to change our environment.

EXAMPLE

Michelle's mum and dad were always arguing, and she worried that they were going to separate. Night after night she struggled to sleep due to their shouting and her worrying. She hung out with a group of girls at school. They played pranks on other kids, were disruptive in class, failed to do homework and saw detentions as 'badges of honour'. Michelle felt part of the group and it distracted her from the things that were going on at home.

One day her teacher asked to see her for a one-to-one chat and spoke about her concerns for Michelle if she continued on this path. Over the following term they met regularly to talk about how things were and what she truly wanted for herself and her future. Her tutor directed her towards some reading and she made good use of some of the exercises, especially those that helped her understand herself and what she wanted for her future.

Michelle tried to share some of her thoughts with the other girls but they didn't want to know, they even ridiculed her for them. She tried to work in class but they constantly disrupted her. Every step Michelle took seemed to be undermined or resisted by her 'friends'.

Realising that her sessions with her teacher were never going to replace peer friendships, Michelle decided to join some after-school clubs. She realised that other girls may be wary of her, and they themselves may resist her wish for friendship, but she thought it was worth trying. Over the following weeks she spent less time with her old 'gang' and more time with others.

TIP

In Chapters 15 and 16, I focus on ideas to help you take action and express your-self. These ideas can be extremely helpful when those in your environment seem to resist the changes you attempt to make.

Negotiating Your Barriers

In this chapter, and in Chapter 6, we explore some of the challenging views, emotional consequences and obstructive reactions of others that can act as barriers to enhancing our wellbeing. In this section, we aim to draw your findings together and look at how you can negotiate your barriers.

On a blank sheet of paper (or on a computer screen or mobile device), make notes on the following points:

1. **Identify any challenging views that may be holding you back.** Consider your experiences of:

- Compassion for others

- Compassion from others

- Self-compassion

You may have already identified and addressed these views as you read Chapter 6. If not, you may want to refer to that chapter for more information on challenging these views.

2. **Consider if you experience strong emotional reactions to events, or times when your emotions don't seem to match the situation you find yourself in or you simply switch off emotionally.**

Refer to the earlier section, 'Understanding Difficult Emotional Reactions' for more information. (***Note:*** It will help to refer back to this as you work through any of the CFT exercises in this book in order that you can understand some of the emotional experiences you have.)

3. **Think about the reactions of others.** These may be reactions you predict or ones you've experienced. Explore your thoughts and feelings in relation to these reactions.

Head to Chapter 13 if you wish to explore the thoughts you have and Chapters 15 and 16 for ideas about how to overcome the barriers others may pose.

Refer to the earlier section, 'Overcoming Barriers Created by Others' for more information on how other people can impact your experiences.

4. **Although beliefs, emotional reactions and the reactions of others may pose barriers to the development of your compassionate mind and compassionate self – and are a key focus of many CFT exercises – are there any changes that you can think of right now that it may be helpful to make?**

Changes it may be helpful to make may include:

- Asking a friend or relative for their views
- Seeking advice from your GP
- Scheduling some time to sit and reflect on the difficulties you've experienced
- Giving things a go, despite having reservations
- Gently allowing yourself to feel angry, anxious or sad about something that has recently happened (and exploring how it feels; Chapter 17 provides a range of exercises to help you with this)

5. **If you've identified some potential changes, are there any potential drawbacks that may be associated with them? Consider each in turn.**

For example, asking someone's views may risk them becoming concerned about you, seeking advice from your GP may result in an awkward conversation and an unhelpful outcome, and giving things a go may risk disappointment, as Ken found in the preceding section.

6. **Turn your attention to any positives that may result from each of the changes you make.** Write down what the positive outcomes may be.

For example, you may find out more information, you may become emotionally calmer, you may make new friends or you may change relationships for the better.

7. **While being sensitive to the distress you may feel, and motivated to prevent and alleviate it, spend some time responding to and completing the following statement.** Do so in relation to each change you're considering making.

Taking into account the potential drawbacks associated with making a change, and the potential benefits, it may be helpful for me to:

By identifying and exploring your own personal barriers, and considering changes it may be helpful to make (while weighing up the potential risks and benefits), it is hoped that you now understand yourself better. It is also hoped that this enhances your motivation to develop your compassionate mind and compassionate self and prepares you for the changes you wish to make.

TIP

Many things can stand in our way as we work to develop our compassionate mind and compassionate self. Some barriers are firmly within us; some are in the hands of other people. Some are clear from a long distance; others seem to catch us unawares. Some seem easy to negotiate; others are more problematic. When we become aware of a barrier, we're given an opportunity to grow and move ourselves to a deeper level of understanding. This deeper understanding is good for everyone!

REMEMBER

If (having worked through the exercise in this section, and read through this chapter and Chapter 6) you don't identify any challenging views or barriers to contend with and overcome, don't feel ashamed! It doesn't mean that you're insensitive, that you 'haven't lived' or that you 'don't get it'. Neither does it mean that you lack reflection or personal insight. It just means that, be it through personal factors or experiences, you may have an easier route to developing your compassionate mind and compassionate self than you expected – which is good news indeed.

3 Developing Our Compassionate Mind

IN THIS PART . . .

Discover the impact our attention has on us.

Prepare for compassionate practices by exploring mindfulness and soothing rhythm breathing, as well as other approaches.

Explore the benefits and challenges of extending compassion to others.

Experience the benefits of receiving compassion from others.

Develop self-compassion.

Chapter 8

Directing Our Attention

W e're often 'called to attention'. It can happen at school, work, a train station or an airport. But many of us don't appreciate that we can consciously direct our attention in a way that's helpful to us.

Neither do we realise that we can affect how we feel by combining attention with an emotional tone of our choice. Compassionate attention combines focusing on things with our compassionate mind. It may help to think of attention as a spotlight, while compassion is the torch we choose to use. With practice, this can become a beneficial means of enhancing our wellbeing.

In this chapter, we begin by considering how we direct our attention and what catches our attention (and how this can activate our threat system). We then begin to train our attention by combining it with compassion. We also take a brief look at open field awareness, which goes beyond the single focus attention that we explore for most of this chapter.

TIP

You can try the exercises in this chapter anywhere; all you need is your imagination. However, to enhance your experience it helps to try them in a place that is, as far as possible, free from distractions – somewhere you can be undisturbed for about 15 minutes. To prepare for each exercise, sit in a relaxed, open posture with strength and alertness to your spine. Soften your facial expression, slightly relaxing your jaw. It's helpful to close your eyes, but you may prefer to settle your gaze on a low fixed point. You may use soothing rhythm breathing, a mindfulness practice (both outlined in Chapter 9) or another form of exercise to create a sense of calm awareness in your mind and body.

Because the exercises in this chapter often involve bringing your attention to images in your mind and combining these images with a warm emotional tone, they're a form of compassionate imagery. In this chapter we use such exercises to illustrate the power of attention and what we choose to focus it on. Head to Chapters 10–12 for more on compassionate imagery.

Delving Deeper into Attention

Single focus attention involves focusing our attention on a single point, such as an event or experience. Here we use single focus attention to explore the impact our attention has on us.

We start by considering what attention is in more detail: the focus of your attention, and how it can affect you both physically and emotionally. You can then begin to realise why it's useful to train your attention to focus on things that are helpful to you.

Attention as a spotlight

Imagine entering a dark room, armed with a spotlight. As the light catches a large object you stop for a moment and focus on it. You then move the light to pictures on the walls, ornaments adorning the surfaces and objects on the floor. As light illuminates one part of the room, other parts fall into darkness. The room, and its contents, are continually present, but you experience only certain aspects at any one time.

TIP

Thinking of attention as the spotlight of the mind can be helpful. When we consciously bring our attention to one thing, we take it away from others. Certain things come into focus while others fall into the background.

Attention and physiology

Our attention not only has an impact on what we see – it can also have a powerful effect on our physical sensations.

This exercise explores how consciously moving your attention can affect the sensations you experience. When you're sitting comfortably and you feel ready to begin, follow these steps:

1. **Close your eyes, and bring your attention to the sensations associated with your left foot.** Explore these sensations for a minute or so.

2. **Bring your attention to your right foot.** Maybe you find yourself focusing on your toes, the sole of your foot, and the contact your foot has with the floor or your shoe. Explore these sensations for a minute or so.

3. **Bring your attention to the fingertips of your right hand.** Explore the sensations in your fingertips.

4. **Rub your fingertips against your thumb and experience the sensations associated with this movement.** Imagine that you're doing this for the first time, and experience this sensation anew for about a minute.

5. **Repeat Steps 3 and 4 with your left hand.** Approach this hand in the same way that you considered your right hand – as if for the first time.

What did you notice? You may have experienced heightened sensations in each area as you brought your attention to it. Other sensations may have gone into 'darkness'.

Interesting, isn't it? We can consciously move our attention and, in doing so, experience different sensations in the part of our body that we're focusing on.

Attention and emotions

By intentionally choosing the focus of our attention, we can influence our emotional state.

This exercise explores how consciously moving your attention can affect your emotions. When you're ready to begin, follow these steps:

1. **Close your eyes and bring to mind a time you recall really laughing, maybe with family or a friend, maybe watching a film or TV programme. Re-familiarise yourself with the memory for a short time. What do you notice?** Maybe a warm expression comes to your face, or a smile as you remember the situation. You may also find that you re-experience feelings of happiness.

2. **Now, for a short time, move your attention away from the happy memory and focus on your breathing. Experience a sense of slowing down.** Alternatively, you may prefer to focus your attention on the sounds around you.

3. **Bring your attention to a situation that you have found difficult recently.** Make sure that it's something that you feel comfortable revisiting. Maybe you think about a situation that made you slightly anxious or sad.

   Stay with this experience for a short time. What do you notice? Maybe a slight furrowing of your brow or a heaviness in your body? You may find that you re-experience feelings of anxiety or sadness.

4. **Return your focus to your breathing, and experience a sense of slowing down.** Alternatively, you may prefer to focus your attention on the sounds around you.

5. **Bring your attention to an enjoyable day out or a holiday.** Allow this experience to sink in.

By intentionally calling to mind different situations, we can evoke different emotional states. This has important implications for our wellbeing, because we can choose what it's helpful for us to focus on and move away from areas of difficulty.

REMEMBER

Once our threat system is activated, it can be difficult to move our attention away from the activating situation, memory or worry. In the previous exercise, you may have found it difficult to move your attention away from the difficult situation – the experiences evoked are 'sticky' and persistent. Thankfully, with practice it will become easier and easier to step out of your threat system and into your soothing system (or 'out of the red and into the green'). (You can find out more about the threat system and the soothing system in Chapter 4.)

Catching Our Attention

In the following sections, we find out why certain things catch a lot of our attention, and we consider the potential consequences created by this diversion of attention.

Many of us tell ourselves to 'get a grip' and to think, behave and feel more rationally. However, in the following sections we discover that humans are born to be irrational. We're wired to attend to potentially 'dangerous' situations rapidly. Understanding ourselves in this way is important as it can help to decrease or even eliminate the shame and self-criticism we may feel due to the way we think, feel or behave.

The sensitivity of our threat system

Our mind has a 'better safe than sorry' default factory setting (refer to Chapter 4 for more on how we often overestimate the threats around us). As such, our attention is easily caught by perceived threats. The spotlight's focus (refer to the earlier section, 'Attention as a spotlight') is therefore not equally divided between all the different things in our environment. Instead, the spotlight is drawn, like a magnet, to potential threats. As a consequence, we often simply miss neutral as well as positive things in our environment.

Consider how this plays out in everyday life.

Imagine that you're one of a hundred party guests. Some people you know, many you don't. Partygoers are laughing, smiling and being generally open and welcoming towards you.

Now imagine that from the corner of your eye you see someone who is seemingly scrutinising you in a negative way. Where does your attention become focused? With the 99 welcoming guests or with the one who seems to be judging you?

Your attention is easily caught by the guest who may be a threat to you. It's likely that you'll repeatedly check to see if they're still looking at you, as though your attention is 'hooked' on them.

Considering the consequences

If our attention is grabbed and our threat system is activated, it can mean that a genuine threat is on the horizon. However, it may be an over-reaction and we may not actually be in any danger at all, whether physically or emotionally. However, we still experience the repercussions in the same way, regardless of the reality of the threat.

In the following exercise, we return to the scenario in the preceding section – you're at a party of 100 guests, and you notice that someone seems to be scrutinising you negatively from afar. The exercise considers the consequences of this perceived negative scrutiny.

At the party, your attention is drawn to the one guest who seems to be negatively disposed towards you. Consider the following questions to see if any of these ring true for you:

>> **What happens physiologically?** Maybe an increase in your heart rate, a feeling of tension in your body, the sensation of butterflies in your stomach or a sense of hotness in your face and body?

>> **What emotions do you experience?** Maybe you experience feelings of anxiety, a lowering of mood or a build-up of anger (towards yourself or others)?

>> **Do you try to understand your possible relationship with this person?** Maybe you begin to interrogate your memory to see if you recall the person from somewhere. Have you offended them in the past? Have they offended you? Are they linked with someone else you know?

>> **Do you begin to scrutinise yourself?** You may wonder about your clothes or body shape, or whether people can see that you feel uncomfortable or anxious.

>> **Are you motivated to move away from the guest or closer to nearby friends?** Maybe you can shrug the negative attention off and stay around your friends. Alternatively, you may find that you can no longer appreciate the company of your friends and engage in their conversations.

>> **Do you take direct action?** You may choose to address the situation head on by smiling in the direction of the guest you're concerned about, or even go up to them to introduce yourself. Or, you may simply remain aware of this person throughout the evening.

Whatever happens, the 'threat' may repeatedly draw your attention while you're at the party. And, as if that hadn't disrupted your evening enough, you may also find that you mull over the situation, and its effect on you, in the hours and days after the event.

Consider another situation. This time, we look at a work scenario.

Imagine that you receive a report or appraisal. It outlines your many skills and achievements. It also includes a couple of suggestions in relation to things that you may find it helpful to work on over the coming year. What's your attention drawn to? What's going round in your head an hour, a day or a week after – the positives, or the areas the appraiser suggests it would be helpful for you to work on?

TIP

In the absence of perceived threats in our environment, a whole range of 'internal' experiences can grab our attention too. These may include thoughts and images that pop into our mind without invitation, bodily sensations, and feelings. These internal experiences can be difficult in their own right but they can also set off a cascade of worries similar to the ones outlined in the preceding exercise. The nearby sidebar 'Internal attention grabbers!' provides information about just some of the internal experiences that can grab our attention and are associated with mental health difficulties. *Note:* Many of these internal attention grabbers are commonly experienced by the general population. However, the severity, intensity and duration of them may result in a particular diagnosis.

INTERNAL ATTENTION GRABBERS!

Certain mental health difficulties are associated with particular internal attention grabbers. Here are a few:

Mental health difficulty	Internal attention grabbers
Generalised anxiety and obsessive compulsive disorder	Worrying thoughts and images that come to mind
Depression	Negative thoughts and images
Panic, health anxiety and eating-related difficulties	Physical sensations and related worries
Trauma	Re-experiencing events in your mind
Psychosis	Hallucinations
Mania	Racing thoughts and ideas

So things we perceive as 'threatening' easily catch our attention. Threats take up the foreground while the neutral or positive things take a back seat. As a consequence, our minds can become a playground for negative thoughts, images and experiences.

THREAT SYSTEM – FRIEND OR FOE?

In Chapter 4 we discover that our threat system is incredibly important and, at times, that it alerts us to real danger. It also alerts us to subtle threats, such as the way another person may be viewing us. This can allow us to react in a helpful way – to adapt or change our behaviour. As such, our threat system can be classed as a friend to us.

However, our threat system can become over sensitised and, left unchecked, this sensitivity can prove problematic for our wellbeing. For example, it can continually bring to mind things that haven't gone so well for us, or concerns that we may have for the future. It can draw our attention to bodily experiences or tell us that other people are judging us. In this way, our threat system may be seen as a foe.

Taking both aspects of our threat system into account, it's helpful to warmly understand why our threat system is being triggered and then to consciously do something that is helpful. This may involve listening to our threat system and what it's alerting us to, *or* calming it down. You can calm your threat system with the help of exercises found throughout this book, especially in Part 3.

Directing Our Compassionate Attention

Our attention is not fixed in place. What we attend to can have a great bearing on the thoughts and images that occupy our mind, how we feel physically, what we're motivated to do and the emotions we feel. So where is it helpful to direct our attention? When we consciously direct our focus to the things that are helpful to us we call this *compassionate attention*. This is one of the skills of your compassionate mind.

In the following sections, we explore how to direct, train and move our attention in a compassionate way.

Practising compassionate attention

When we practice compassionate attention, we do so with a sense of care for our own or another person's wellbeing. Try the next exercise and explore the experiences you have when you alternate between bringing your attention to things you should be grateful for and thinking about a positive thing that has happened over the last month.

When you feel ready to begin the exercise:

1. **Focus on the positive things in your life that you know you should feel grateful for.** Do this for a minute or so. Having done this, gently allow the experience to fade from your mind and refocus your attention on your breathing or maybe the sounds around you.

2. **Now, with a sense of emotional warmth, bring your attention to something positive that you've experienced over the last month.** This may be a time when you've enjoyed someone's company, shared a joke, appreciated a view or felt a sense of calm contentment. Do this for a minute or so. Having done this, take a few soothing breaths. Allow yourself a bit of time to experience a sense of slowing down.

3. **After a while, gently allow your attention to focus back to the things that you identified in Step 1.** Do this for a minute or so.

4. **Gently and warmly return your attention to the positive experience that you identified in Step 2.** Allow yourself a little time to reconnect with the physiological and emotional experiences this evokes.

Notice a difference? Hopefully, you discover that compassionate attention (practised in Steps 2 and 4) comes with a sense of warmth and gentleness. This is in contrast to Steps 1 and 3, where you're forcing yourself to think about something you should feel grateful for.

Practising compassionate attention is very different from telling ourselves to 'think positive!'. When we tell ourselves to 'look on the bright side' and 'consider how lucky we are', this often undermines us and brings with it a sense of self-criticism and threat.

Compassionate attention doesn't always involve focusing on positive things. It can involve bringing our attention to things that are painful, including things that it's helpful for us to experience, process or work through. These painful things can be internal (such as our feelings and physical sensations) or external (such as the pain and suffering of someone else).

Training our compassionate attention

With practice it becomes easier to consciously move and focus your compassionate attention on things that are likely to enhance your wellbeing. This is one of the six skills of your compassionate mind. Chapter 2 provides a description of all six skills.

We begin to develop this skill by engaging in exercises associated with feelings of warmth and connectedness.

Allow at least 10 seconds for each step of this exercise in order to let the experience 'sink in'. Practise these steps at intervals throughout the day. (In Chapter 9, we continue to develop our compassionate attention by practising mindfulness to further train our attention.)

Follow these steps when you feel ready to begin:

1. **Gently bring your attention to things that you feel a sense of gratitude for.**

2. **Gently bring your attention to things that you're looking forward to.** Such events may be associated with experiences such as joy, relaxation, connectedness and excitement.

3. **Gently bring your attention to memories of connection with others.** These memories may involve a range of different experiences such as joy, excitement, being soothed, feeling safe and contentment.

Engaging with these simple exercises can help improve your wellbeing. They create a sense of warmth and connection with others and they have a positive effect on your physiology and emotions. In time, your attention will naturally be drawn to and settle on things that give you a greater sense of wellbeing.

Moving our compassionate attention to manage social situations

Our threat-focused mind can become fixated on certain things. We may focus on our heart rate or breathing. In addition, we may monitor signs of anxiety such as a shaking hand, our voice or the perceived redness of our face.

We also often monitor other people, and scrutinise their reactions to us. This can lead to further anxiety! (The earlier section 'Catching Our Attention' explores how this happens and these consequences in more detail.)

REMEMBER

One way of addressing the negative social comparison voice in our head is to focus on a sense of common humanity and connectedness with others. I provide an exercise in Chapter 1 to help you do this.

To help manage the consequences of our threat system being activated, it can be helpful to move our attention towards things that are helpful to us. We call this *compassionate* attention because we notice our distress and do something about it.

TIP

Consider the following suggestions to help you guide your attention and therefore turn down, or even switch off, your threat system:

>> Next time you're feeling anxious while in conversation (for example, because you're worrying the person is judging you), gently move your attention from your worrying thoughts by calmly taking a soothing breath and directing your attention to the colour of the other person's eyes or listening with curiosity to their accent.

>> If you find that you're focusing on and worrying about an ache or pain, an unusual sensation, your heart rate, or any other physical sensation, give your

mind a break by taking a calming breath and gently moving your attention to the noises, smells and sights around you. Chapter 9 introduces breathing exercises that can assist you with this.

By switching your attention from something you perceive as threatening to a neutral or calming focus, you'll feel more physically and emotionally relaxed and replace threatening thoughts with curious ones.

REMEMBER

Although we can intentionally move our attention, it can be quickly caught by other things. When we become aware that our attention has moved, it's helpful to see it as an opportunity to choose where to redirect it.

Moving our attention doesn't mean saying goodbye to difficult emotions. We develop our compassionate mind out of care for our own wellbeing *because* we feel difficult emotions. As we begin to notice where our attention is and become familiar with the exercises in this chapter, we can begin to have increased choice with regard to what is helpful for us. This may involve attending to certain things and moving our attention from others.

Looking Beyond the Spotlight: Open Field Awareness

This chapter explores *single focus attention* – how we use our attention like a spotlight, moving it from one thing to another. It also brings your awareness to the type of torch it can be helpful to use and suggests that a compassionate torch, rather than a threat-focused torch, is important for your wellbeing.

In this section, we take a look at open field awareness. If single focus attention is a spotlight, *open field awareness* is our panoramic view. When we use our compassionate attention to practise open field awareness, we experience a warm sense of connection and relationship with our environment.

To give you a brief flavour of this relationship, try the following exercises:

>> Close your eyes and imagine that you're looking out to sea. Broaden your attention to take in the full experience and a sense of connectedness with the wider environment. Engage in this exercise for a minute or so.

>> Close your eyes and imagine that you're having a warm drink while sitting in a café. Broaden your attention to take in the range of different experiences while simultaneously feeling a sense of connectedness with the other people around you. Engage in this practice for a minute or so.

TIP

As you broaden your attention to the scene, you're likely to gradually develop a feeling of expansiveness. From time to time, your attention may narrow down to one aspect of the experience. When you notice that this has happened, gently broaden your attention once more.

This next exercise practises open field awareness 'in situ' rather than using your imagination.

While out and about one day, use the moment to broaden your experience and take in everything around you. This is open field awareness. Begin by taking in a beautiful view or a wide expanse of sky. Expand your awareness to the full visual scene, the sounds you hear and the experience of the air or wind on your skin.

As you become more familiar and comfortable with this exercise, practise it in more complex environments, such as while you're walking, exercising or even waiting in a queue.

TIP

Some people find open field awareness relatively easy, while others find it more difficult. In Chapters 10–12 you use a range of imagery exercises and explore additional types of single focus attention and open field awareness.

In the meantime, you may find it helpful to continue to practise the exercises covered in this chapter. With time, you become aware of your mind being 'hooked' by things that are unhelpful to your wellbeing and better able to direct your attention in a way that is beneficial to you.

Chapter 9

Preparing for Compassion

P reparation is key to many things. We prepare surfaces before painting, soil before sowing and our bodies before exercising. Preparation can make things easier and make it more likely that we achieve the things we aim for. In the same way, before engaging in compassionate practices, we need to stabilise our body and mind. We do this by developing a helpful posture and facial expression. We also use soothing rhythm breathing and mindfulness.

Regular mindfulness practice brings an increased awareness of what influences us, such as our thoughts, emotions, environment and physical sensations. This moment–by–moment awareness allows us to choose what's helpful for us to focus on, experience or do, rather than simply live our lives on automatic pilot.

In this chapter, we look at a number of ways in which you can build a solid foundation for the compassionate practices provided in other chapters. We also introduce the practice of mindfulness, and how mindfulness can help you to prepare your mind for compassion.

Focusing on Your Body

Our emotions can often be observed in our body posture. For example, if you're angry, you may raise your chin slightly, put your shoulders back and stand square-on to someone. In contrast, when you feel sad your head may go down, your shoulders curve inwards and you may avoid eye contact.

But have you ever considered that you can intentionally change your emotional state by adjusting your posture? Amy Cuddy, an American social psychologist and associate professor at Harvard Business School, has demonstrated that simply changing your posture for two minutes can impact on your cortisol and testosterone levels. She found that individuals practicing certain postures before interviews were more likely to perform better.

Compassion Focused Therapy (CFT) therefore uses this understanding about the impact of body posture on emotional states to increase the effectiveness of the exercises we use. By adjusting our posture, we're better able to develop our compassionate mind.

TIP

Start out by engaging with these exercises within the safety and security of your own home (assuming you can find a stress-free place without any disruptions or distractions). You can always experiment by trying different locations or maybe different times of the day to see what works for you. As you become more and more able to access the capacity for inner soothing, the location becomes less important and you'll be able to use it in a wider range of situations. You can then practise them at any time: while waiting for a bus, sitting on the train, lying in bed or even taking a bath.

REMEMBER

A number of therapies encourage individuals to 'lean into the discomfort' associated with certain exercises or continue until difficulties are overcome. Although this can be hugely beneficial, CFT advocates that if focusing your attention on your body or breathing makes you feel panicky or anxious, it may be helpful to turn your attention to those exercises that don't, at least in the initial phases of your practice.

TIP

Closing your eyes or lowering your gaze obviously makes reading difficult! It may help to make your own recording of the exercise instructions (for this chapter and for any of the exercises in this book), using a calm, quiet voice. You may wish to change the wording slightly to suit you. As you become more familiar with the exercises it's likely that you'll be able to practise them from memory.

In the following sections, we look at exercises around posture, facial expressions and tone of voice, and breathing, and we return to these topics throughout the book.

The more time we spend noticing how our posture, breathing, facial expression and tone of voice affect us, the more we can help ourselves slow down and develop a helpful frame of mind. Our body then begins to remember how this feels and, with practice, it can become easier and quicker to access our capacity for inner soothing.

Developing a helpful posture

Our compassionate mind has strength and courage; it's also sensitive to our own and other peoples' distress. As such, it's helpful to develop a posture that embodies your compassionate mind's strength and courage. In CFT we refer to the embodiment of your compassionate mind as your compassionate self. Head to Chapter 1 for more on this.

Your posture can have a big impact on how you feel. To briefly experience the impact of your posture, try this exercise:

1. **Stand up, if you're not standing already.**

2. **Place your feet together, heel to heel, toe to toe. Close your eyes and imagine that someone pushes you from one side.**

   You may feel a little vulnerable to toppling over – and if someone was really pushing you, maybe you would.

3. **Adjust your posture and stand with your feet hip-distance apart, your knees ever-so-slightly bent (so your knees are relaxed). Close your eyes and feel your weight going down through your body to the ground. Once again, imagine that someone pushes you from one side.**

   Now, you're likely to experience a greater sense of stability and a decreased likelihood of toppling over.

Comparing these two postures highlights the important role that posture has to play in the development of your compassionate mind and its embodiment as the compassionate self.

The following exercise assists you with developing a helpful posture. As you become more familiar with the exercises in this chapter and begin to practice them regularly, you may want to consider positions such as laying down (or return to standing, as with the preceding exercise); however, here we begin by developing a helpful posture from a sitting position.

If sitting is difficult for you, explore other positions that help you explore the impact of your posture. The useful thing is to find something that's helpful to you.

The goal for this exercise is to explore a sense of alertness and strength in your body, together with a feeling of inner stillness. This is different from relaxation. When you're relaxed, your muscles lose tone and you may experience them as being floppy. It also helps you compare the impact of different postures.

1. **Find a comfortable chair that allows you to sit with your back upright and your shoulders slightly back.**

2. **Sit with your feet flat on the ground, hip-distance apart, shoulders more or less in line with your hips.**

3. **Open your chest by gently bringing your shoulders back.** As your chest expands, you may feel a sense of alertness in your spine and calmness in your body, and perhaps experience a feeling of strength and dignity.

4. **Take a few moments to explore how this feels, and make slight adjustments until you've created a posture that's helpful to you.**

5. **Time to explore a contrasting posture. Allow your body to slump, your chest bowed in slightly.** Explore the impact of this posture on you.

6. **Take a few moments to return to the posture you found helpful in Step 4.**

You should now have an idea of a posture that brings with it a sense of alertness, strength and inner stillness. You can return to this posture in subsequent exercises.

TIP

Divers provide a good example of achieving a sense of stillness combined with alertness and strength. Before diving, they stand on the edge of the board or platform and calm themselves by creating a feeling of inner stillness. When ready, they dive. I'm not suggesting that you visit a diving board later today, but it can be helpful to imagine creating such a feeling of stillness that comes with strength and alertness. (If the diving example fills you with anxiety, it may be helpful to imagine yourself in another way, perhaps as a strong mountain – we're not all confident divers!)

Exploring helpful facial expressions and tones of voice

We can use our bodies and muscles in many ways to deliberately try to create physical and emotional states that are helpful to us. Sometimes when we intentionally 'create' a friendly face or tone of voice, we can directly alter the feelings in our bodies. It may or may not be a dramatic change, but every little bit helps!

In this exercise we explore the impact facial expressions have on us.

1. **Sit comfortably in your chair and engage with your soothing rhythm breathing for a minute or so.** (See the next section for more on this.)

2. **Adopt a neutral facial expression: one that neither conveys warmth nor negativity.** Do this for couple of minutes.

3. **Create a friendly face, with a gentle smile.** You may do this by imagining that you're with somebody you really like being with – someone you have a sense of affection for. Hold this friendly expression for a while. Gently consider how this facial expression affects your mind and body.

4. **Return to your neutral expression and experience its impact on you.** Gently consider how this experience contrasts with the feelings you experienced in Step 3.

5. **Return to your friendly facial expression again (from Step 3), and experience its impact on you.**

We're all different, so we experience things in different ways. However, the previous exercise illustrates that, just as your emotions and bodily sensations can affect your facial expression, the reverse is also true. By consciously changing your facial expression, you can significantly affect your mind and body. Although you can't see your facial expression, you can feel it.

In the next exercise, we consider how your tone of voice can impact upon the meaning of any statement.

Explore the importance of your tone of voice using this exercise:

1. **Use the statement 'everybody wants to be happy' and say it in your mind as if you were talking to someone you felt contempt for.**

2. **Now say the same statement with a sense of anger and frustration.**

3. **Finally say it in a warm and gentle way.**

You can easily see how tone of voice changes the meaning of a statement we make to someone else. This is also true for how we speak to ourselves. It's not just what we think – it's the emotional tone of what we say to ourselves that can be helpful or hurtful.

Try the following exercise to explore the impact of your tone of voice in more depth:

1. **Sit comfortably in your chair, in the helpful posture that you worked on in the earlier section, 'Developing a helpful posture'.**

2. **Slow down your breathing for a short time.** It may be helpful to engage with your soothing rhythm breathing (head to the next section 'Introducing soothing rhythm breathing' for more on this).

3. **Say 'hello' followed by your name using a neutral tone of voice. Do this with each out-breath.** Maintain a neutral facial expression. Explore how you experience this in your mind and body for 15 seconds or so.

4. **Now say 'hello' followed by your name using a friendly tone of voice. Do this with each out-breath.** This time maintain a friendly facial expression. Explore how you experience this in your mind and body for 15 seconds or so.

5. **Repeat Steps 3 and 4.**

What did you notice? You may have noticed that you get quite a different feeling depending on whether you use a neutral voice and maintain a neutral facial expression, or a friendly tone of voice and a friendly facial expression.

REMEMBER

We react to our own internal voice tone in exactly the same way as we react to someone else's voice. In other words, if someone speaks to us using a warm tone of voice, it may affect us in a positive way. If they speak with indifference, anger or disdain, it may instead have a negative impact.

A friendly facial expression and tone of voice can create a sense of inner warmth. This can be enhanced by simply bringing your attention to your body and directly evoking a feeling of inner warmth – as though your whole body is gently smiling.

TIP

Some people find it difficult to direct a friendly tone of voice towards themselves because they believe that they don't deserve it or it simply makes them feel uncomfortable. We explore these difficulties in more detail in Chapters 6 and 7.

Introducing soothing rhythm breathing

We can bring a sense of soothing to our minds and bodies by simply focusing on and adjusting our breathing. CFT advocates that we bring a warm emotional tone to our breathing and refers to this as *soothing rhythm breathing*. It's a means by which we can step out of our threat system and into our soothing system (refer to Chapter 4 and also the nearby sidebar 'Understanding the body's arousal systems' for more information). Breathing in this way can prepare us for a range of different exercises (as you find throughout this book).

In this exercise, you utilise the helpful posture that you developed in the preceding section to help you explore and discover a breathing rhythm that is soothing to you (your soothing rhythm breathing).

1. **Sitting in the same type of chair as you used in the exercise in the preceding section, place your feet flat on the ground, hip-distance apart, shoulders more or less in line with your hips. Open your chest by gently bringing your shoulders back.** Feel your chest expand.

2. **Gently close your eyes or look towards the floor while allowing your gaze to be unfocused.**

3. **Focus on your breathing – slow down and deepen your breathing to find a rhythm that's soothing to you.** Notice the sensation of slowing down: maybe your focus is on the gentle rise and fall of your belly; maybe the expansion and contraction of your rib cage; maybe the sense of air coming in and out of your nose or mouth.

4. **Explore whether it's helpful to slow down and deepen your breathing with the aid of counting. Count 'in 2, 3 – out 2, 3'. Try counting for a little longer and deeper ('in 2, 3, 4 – out 2, 3, 4') and then longer and deeper again (in 2, 3, 4, 5 – out 2, 3, 4, 5).** Does this help to soothe you, and slow your breathing down further?

   Try this for 30 seconds or longer. If you find it helpful, you can continue counting if you want – but you don't have to. Whether you choose to count or not, we will refer to the breathing pattern you find soothing as your soothing rhythm breathing.

   The rhythm of breathing you find soothing to you will differ day to day, hour to hour, situation to situation. Key to the practice is finding a rhythm that is soothing to you at that moment in time.

   TIP

5. **Engage with your soothing rhythm breathing for five minutes or so, creating a feeling of inner slowing with each out-breath.**

   Notice how your body feels, creating an experience that's soothing and calming to it.

6. **Become aware of the weight of your body resting on the chair and the floor underneath you.** Notice how your body feels slightly heavier in the chair now that you've slowed your breathing rhythm. Allow yourself to feel held and supported, while staying alert and maintaining your helpful body posture. You may also become aware of the stability in your body that results from the slowing and deepening of your breathing.

7. **If you notice that your mind has wandered, which it may well do, gently guide your attention back to your breathing.** As you return your attention to your breathing each time, notice the feeling of your body slowing down.

8. **Bring a sense of warmth in your facial expression and soften your jaw, maybe bringing a gentle smile to your face, and once again engage with your soothing rhythm breathing.** Do this for five minutes or so, continuing to breathe deeper and slower than you do in your everyday life. Try to stay alert and focused on your practice.

9. **When you're ready, widen your awareness to the room you're in, the noises that surround you and the chair that's supporting you.**

UNDERSTANDING THE BODY'S AROUSAL SYSTEMS

When we're charging around or experiencing threat-based emotions such as anxiety or anger, we're in a state that's referred to as *sympathetic arousal*. In this state, our breathing becomes shallower and quicker.

When we're no longer in the drive or threat system (refer to Chapter 4 for more on these systems) the body switches to what's called a 'rest and digest' mode, or *parasympathetic arousal*. In CFT, we refer to this as the soothing system. In this state our breathing is slower and deeper, and we feel calmer and more at ease. By deliberately slowing our breath we have a chance of bringing more calming, soothing parasympathetic activity to our bodies.

Training our minds and bodies to become more in-tune with our parasympathetic system can be very helpful for wellbeing and great preparation for cultivating our compassionate mind and its embodiment as the compassionate self.

Sitting in a helpful posture while engaging in your soothing rhythm breathing will help you to switch out of the red or blue and into the green (head to Chapter 4 for more on your three circles and, more specifically, your threat (red), drive (blue) and soothing (green) systems). The more you practice this, the easier it will become. From this foundation you can then build your compassionate mind and embody your compassionate self.

Welcoming Mindfulness into Your Life

In the previous sections, we focus on our body, looking at how our posture, breathing, facial expressions and tone of voice can influence us emotionally. In this section, we turn our attention to our minds by looking at how mindfulness can help to prepare us for compassion.

In Chapter 3, we look at the challenges we face and how our evolved brain is almost always on the go. We spend a lot of our waking hours thinking about the past and future. We also think about other people's minds – what they make of us and how we compare to them. Although we may focus on the positive aspects of our future and the past, we're more likely to focus on the negatives. Going over and over difficult times or predicting future difficulties can be very stressful. We may feel locked into painful thoughts, feelings and memories.

WE'RE ALL HUMAN

The Dalai Lama once gave an example of how he used to love to fix watches when he was an adolescent. One day he was fixing a beautiful watch but dropped a screw into the mechanism, and in his frustration he took a hammer and smashed the watch! What's interesting is that his moment of frustration meant he did exactly the opposite of his true intent – which was of course to fix a beautiful watch.

In essence, mindfulness offers a way of noticing what our minds are up to and directing our attention to where it's likely to be helpful. *Mindfulness* involves bringing our attention (refer to Chapter 8) to the present moment. We do this with a sense of curiosity and non-judgement. Mindfulness practices calm our mind and body and, in so doing, we become more aware of whatever occurs in our mind and body, moment to moment.

You can experiment with a broad range of mindfulness practices (we look at some of these in the later section, 'Exploring mindfulness exercises'). Some involve learning to be more fully aware of an activity in the present moment, such as mindful eating and walking. Others are based on *observation* – becoming mindfully more aware of how our mind is operating and then beginning to take control over it, leading to a wiser control over our emotions, behaviours, thoughts and physical experiences.

REMEMBER

Mindfulness isn't about getting rid of things that occur in the mind. It's about becoming familiar with the workings of our mind, understanding our true intentions and developing acceptance. For example, in CFT we hope to develop a compassionate awareness that parts of ourselves are often angry, anxious or upset. Mindfulness of these emotions is a really useful step to understanding how our tricky brains can get up to all kinds of things that make our true intention difficult to maintain (Chapter 3 looks at your tricky brain in more detail).

With mindfulness, we focus only on the present moment. We don't focus on the moment to come or the moment that's just gone. Even though our consciousness exists in the here and now, many people don't live in the here and now – they live in their thoughts about tomorrow or regrets about yesterday. Mindfulness is about living where we exist – which is now.

The practice of mindfulness involves bringing our attention to the present moment with curiosity, without judgement and with acceptance of what we observe. It helps us to:

>> Slow things down.

>> Be in the present moment (instead of lost in our thoughts, ruminations or memories).

>> Become more aware of what's going on in our (tricky!) minds and bodies. (Head to Chapter 3 for more on your tricky brain.)

>> Make and implement choices about what we pay attention to, instead of letting our threat or drive systems monopolise us. (Head to Chapter 4 for further information regarding our threat and drive systems.)

The following sections delve deeper into mindfulness, looking at how it can help you to develop your compassionate mind, what kind of exercises you can practise to develop your ability to be mindful, and how mindfulness can help you to manage difficult emotions.

Developing your compassionate mind with mindfulness

REMEMBER

The development of compassion is helped by mindfulness practices because mindfulness allows us to observe, without judgement, the different motivations, emotions, thoughts and feelings occurring within us.

In Chapter 3, we discuss how evolution provided us with the amazing ability to think about the past, present and future. This has been hugely important for our survival. However, this ability also means that we can find ourselves dwelling on past situations (how a night out went, what we did last holiday or where we left our keys!) and predicting events in the future (what we'll have for tea, what time we'll get home or what an approaching interview will be like). In other words, our minds can be focused everywhere but the present. We can be constantly pulled away from our moment-to-moment experiences, and this can have a powerful impact on our wellbeing.

To complicate things further, competing thoughts, feelings and urges can also fill our minds and can prove problematic. For example, desperate to make friends, we may accept an invitation to a party but feel the urge to cancel out of fear and a feeling that it won't go well.

REMEMBER

Mindfulness helps us to stand back and become aware of our urges, thoughts, feelings and bodily sensations without judgement. By learning to hold and focus our attention, we create a space in which we can choose how to act – and this may include doing nothing at all. When we learn to intentionally hold our attention, we can begin to hold ourselves in compassionate states of mind. From this standpoint, we can then be more consciously aware of what's helpful to ourselves and others and consider the best way to act.

Imagine that you're at a busy train station setting out on a journey. Experience yourself as part of the flow of people moving from the entrance, to the trains and then onward to your destination.

THE ORIGINS OF MINDFULNESS

Mindfulness is the translation of 'Sati', which is an Indian word meaning awareness, attention and remembering. Its origins lie in ancient eastern cultures. Awareness involves being conscious of your experiences. Without this, nothing would exist. Attention relates to developing a focused awareness that allows you to attend to that which you choose. Remembering involves reminding oneself to pay attention to experiences moment to moment – because we only exist in the present moment; the past is gone and we can only visit the future in our imagination.

In recent times, mindfulness has been developed in the West as a practice to promote wellbeing. The therapeutic use of mindfulness has been developed by Dr Jon Kabat-Zinn and has since been found to be of help to a wide range of individuals, from those who consider themselves to be psychologically 'well' to those who identify themselves as suffering from anxiety and depression, among other difficulties.

Now suppose you were able to stop and stand somewhere, maybe on a balcony overlooking the station, and simply observe the flow of people on the trains. You're no longer part of the flow but have become an observer. In a similar way, the practice of mindfulness moves us from being part of a situation to observing it.

Exploring mindfulness exercises

In the following sections, we look at some of the many mindfulness practices that aim to help focus, stabilise or ground our minds.

Practicing mindfulness helps you become accustomed to noticing when your mind has wandered and learning to gently refocus your attention. This skill will be of great benefit in Chapters 10–12 as you engage in a range of compassionate exercises.

As you work through each exercise, consider applying the techniques that I introduced in the earlier section, 'Focusing on Your Body':

>> Adjust your body to find a helpful posture that brings with it a sense of stability and inner stillness

>> Adjust your facial expression in order to experience an enhanced feeling of inner warmth

>> Engage your soothing rhythm breathing (if this is helpful to you)

The first exercise, in the upcoming section 'Say hello to your observing mind', highlights the value of applying the above techniques when practising mindfulness.

REMEMBER

Approach each exercise with a sense of warmth and curiosity. When you become aware that your mind has wandered, without judgement gently return your attention to the focus of the exercise.

TIP

Engage with each mindfulness exercise whenever you have a fleeting free moment. You may be surprised to find just how helpful even brief opportunities to practise can be.

Say hello to your observing mind

In this exercise, we become more familiar with your mind. Developing an awareness of its ability to focus *and* its tendency to wander brings us another step closer to training it.

Begin to develop your observing mind:

1. **Sit quietly in a chair and adjust your body to find your helpful posture. See if you can sense stability and inner stillness in your body and a sense of slowing down – but don't worry if you can't at this point.**

   Check out the earlier section 'Developing a helpful posture' if you need a reminder.

2. **Adjust your facial expression in order to experience an enhanced feeling of inner warmth. Engage with your soothing rhythm breathing.**

   Refer to the earlier sections 'Exploring helpful facial expressions and tones of voice' and 'Introducing soothing rhythm breathing' if you need to.

3. **Hold yourself here for a minute or so and notice what happens to your mind.**

   Notice how it so easily wanders away from the focus of your breath. Each time you notice that your mind has wandered, bring it back to your breath.

TIP

In the preceding exercise, you shift from engaging with the contents of your mind to becoming an observer of it, just like when you moved to the balcony at the railway station and observed what was going on below (refer to the earlier section, 'Developing your compassionate mind with mindfulness' for more on the railway station exercise). Notice and wake up to the reality that your mind has wandered and then gently return it to the exercise.

If you notice that you're criticising yourself or getting frustrated, gently disengage yourself from these negative feelings and 'move to the balcony' once more.

REMEMBER

Our brains have a 'mind of their own' and you can't control yours absolutely. If your mind wanders, recognise this without judgement and move on – your brain can't help it, but with training it can improve!

Listen and become mindful of sound

Actively listening to sounds is, at least initially, one of the most universally appreciated forms of mindfulness. Sounds, by their nature, come and go and capture our attention. They're external to us – and this can help if you find focusing on your body or breathing difficult. Being mindful of sounds keeps us anchored in the present moment, rather than everywhere but. By developing a conscious awareness of what our mind focuses on, how it wanders and how this can affect us, we begin to become aware of our choices. Do we allow our evolved brain to rule the show or do we consciously train it in a way that's helpful to us?

For five minutes or so, allow yourself to experience the sounds around you by actively listening. Experience them as they come and go without the need to interpret or make sense of them. Explore how listening feels. Experience listening as if you're experiencing the sensory qualities of sound for the first time – with what's sometimes called a *beginner's mind*.

TIP

If you have things on your mind that make it difficult for you to focus, jot these things down on a piece of paper. Attempt to leave them on the paper while you engage in the exercise. With time, you'll begin to see such distractions as the mind simply wandering, as it does, but while you're getting started, writing them down can help.

It's often interesting how different you feel after a mindfulness practice and how you experience the things you've written differently. You may feel a greater sense of calmness, connectivity to your environment or a sense of expansive awareness. It's also likely that you become more aware of the things that grab your attention and experience a greater sense of perspective about your worries and concerns.

Experience mindfulness of the body

Focusing your attention on your body is a great way to take your attention away from all the 'noise' that your mind creates. Worries and rumination are just some of the experiences that your mind can become over-focused on if left to its own devices.

For five minutes or so, allow yourself to experience the sensations in your own body. Notice your breath slowly moving in and out. Notice the rise and fall of your belly. Become aware of the sensations your breath brings with it. Notice your ribcage expanding then contracting. Bring your attention to the temperature of your body and the warmth in your chest. Notice how your body feels supported. Move your attention round your body, from place to place, and notice how it feels.

Sometimes your body will feel tense or you may be aware of pain or discomfort. If this is the case, just notice it and then move your attention to another part of your body.

The next time you're having a slight argument with somebody or you're having a good time, bring your attention to how your body feels and observe how your body is responding to the situation.

TIP

It may be that you're extremely aware of how your body feels in different emotional states, and you may not want to focus in on your body's sensations. However, it can be helpful to be mindful and to observe these sensations, rather than to dwell on them or become overly focused on them to the detriment of other things you may prefer to be thinking about. Remember the train station analogy (from the earlier section 'Developing your compassionate mind with mindfulness') and move to your own personal balcony!

Focus mindfully on a visual point

For many reasons, you may find it difficult to close your eyes during a mindfulness practice. While some people simply don't like it, others find that closing the eyes results in difficult images popping into the mind. Equally, practicing mindfulness while focusing on a visual anchor point may give you more versatility. For example, you can practice this exercise while sat at a bus stop, in a meeting or in a café.

EXPLORING THE POWER OF THE HUMAN MIND

Some of the strongest ways to illustrate the power of the mind involve sexual imagery. For example, imagine an erotic scenario (whatever works for you!). When you begin to notice a feeling of arousal, stop – and then refocus your mind on something else, such as doing the washing up or going to the post office to post a parcel. Notice how your body changes. This change can happen quite quickly! Now, return to your erotic imagery and observe what happens in your body once more. You can probably see that what we bring our attention to, and become mindful of, has a big impact on how we feel emotionally and physically.

This exercise is also a fun way for us to realise just how powerful imagery is and how different exercises bring different changes to the body. If you don't find this example helpful, imagine a situation such as a holiday or sport that really excites you and then once again switch your attention to something mundane or even slightly anxiety-provoking.

For five minutes or so, fix your gaze on a *visual anchor point* – something that you can see, a metre or two away from you – something that's on the floor or low down so that you're less aware of visual distractions around you. (If nothing obvious lies before you, feel free to place something suitable on the ground.) Observe the anchor point's shape, edges, colour and texture.

While your eyes are open, additional sources of distraction may exist. This is perfectly normal. If you become distracted once again, the trick is to become mindful that your attention has wandered and bring it back to the exercise.

TIP

If you previously found focusing on your breathing or body difficult, it may be helpful to combine those exercises with mindfulness of a visual (or tactile, which I look at in the next section) anchor point.

If you're uncomfortable about doing exercises with your eyes closed, this is a good exercise to begin with. Later, you may feel more confident about closing your eyes during an exercise if you know that you can open them, at any time, to see a visual anchor point of your choosing.

Focus mindfully on a tactile object

Touch is a powerful sensory experience. Mindfully focusing your attention on the smooth surface of a pebble or the intricacies of the charms on a bracelet can bring your awareness into the present moment.

For five minutes or so, bring your attention to a *tactile anchor point* – something that you can touch. This may be something like a stone, a keyring, a piece of jewellery, a purse or a wallet. Notice how it feels, experience its weight, and notice the temperature of the object and how it feels when you manipulate it in your hands.

You may find it helpful to pick a different object each time you practise. Alternatively, you may practise with the same, or a similar, object each time. The importance lies not in what you choose to use but whether your choice is helpful to you in your practice.

REMEMBER

Pick anchor points (visual or tactile) that you don't associate with difficult emotions, otherwise these emotions may interfere with the exercise.

Walk the mindful walk

Here we combine a physical activity with mindfulness – mindfulness on the move. While some find this more complex than a sitting mindfulness practice, others find it much easier. The exercise helps to focus your attention and bring your awareness into the present moment – instead of everywhere but.

MINDFULNESS CAN BE BOTH DIFFICULT AND EASY

Our busy brains and the complexity of modern life mean that inbuilt obstacles to mindfulness practice exist. We may fail to prioritise our own wellbeing or fall into the trap of striving 'to get it right'. We tend to do things with a sense of urgency or maybe while thinking about multiple other things, and it's therefore easy to let a whole day or even week go by without any awareness of the present moment or conscious attention to that which we may find helpful.

However, mindfulness is something that can be easily practised, doesn't need special equipment and requires only time and motivation. It can be practised while going for a walk, sitting quietly, while in a busy place or even while washing your hands.

For 15 minutes or so, walk outdoors and become mindful of what's around you. Bring your awareness to the sky, the patterns created in the clouds and the colours around you. Notice buildings and trees and bring your sensory awareness to them; notice what it's like to actually move your body, walking one foot in front of the other. Notice the air on your skin and the smells in the air.

TIP

Although this exercise involves broadening your awareness to different sensory experiences, it can be helpful to focus on *one* specific element of your experience, such as the sensation of walking or things you can see.

During mindful walking, you may be disrupted by bumping into people you know. We simply can't remain undisturbed all the time! Where appropriate, respond to the situation and then return to the exercise.

TIP

Mindful walking is very different from walking to get somewhere or to achieve an exercise goal. However, you can combine this practice with something you need to do and get just as much benefit from the exercise (physical and mindful!). For example, set off extra early for your walk to work and allow yourself to walk mindfully without having to check the time. Mindful dog walking is also an option (as long as your dog is generally well-behaved!).

Becoming mindful of difficult emotions

REMEMBER

For some, intense emotions arise when they practise mindfulness, as though the process clears a space into which emotions that have been hidden, bottled up or suppressed, move.

If your emotions are manageable, attempt to view them with curiosity and non-judgement and return to the exercise.

TIP

Anchoring practices can help if you want strong emotions to subside a little. The visual and tactile anchor exercises described in the earlier sections, 'Focus mindfully on a visual point' and 'Focus mindfully on a tactile object' are examples of such practices. Whether you notice strong emotions in your everyday life or during the exercises I provide in this book, you may choose to reduce them by refocusing your mind on an object, be it in a visual or tactile manner. Gaining a degree of control of your emotions can be extremely helpful. In so doing, you may feel more comfortable with emotions such as anger, anxiety and sadness, armed with the knowledge that you have some degree of control over them.

REMEMBER

If emotions feel too intense, making your exercise difficult to return to, allow yourself to sit with the emotion for a while and experience it. Strong emotions can feel frightening and uncomfortable, but they do subside. Often, allowing ourselves to experience intense emotions such as sadness and anger, and then feeling them fade away, can actually be a healing process.

If your emotions remain intense and you feel that you need to try a different approach, it may be helpful to move onto some of the exercises in Chapters 10–12. These exercises can increase your sense of personal resilience and help you to deal with difficult emotions. Alternatively, it may help to speak with a therapist about your concerns and, together, develop a plan for how you can work through them.

Developing Your Mindfulness Practice

TIP

Everyone's different. Finding exercises that are helpful can take time and curiosity. Once you discover ones that are beneficial to you, it's helpful to engage in these regularly and deepen your experience. We refer to this as 'self-practice'.

Mindfulness practices have been found by many to be hugely beneficial in their own right. If you wish to pursue mindfulness practice further, you may want to read one of the many excellent books available, such as *Mindfulness For Dummies* by Shamash Alidina (Wiley) and *Mindfulness: A Practical Guide to Finding Peace in a Frantic World* by Mark Williams and Danny Penman (Piatkus).

REMEMBER

You can practise mindfulness for long or short intervals; inside or outside; as part of another activity or as an activity in its own right; in a busy or peaceful place; and by day or by night.

If you have any difficulties with the mindfulness exercises in this book or elsewhere, consider discussing your concerns with a compassion focused therapist.

TIP

When you have a feel for what mindfulness is, you can begin to play around with how you introduce it to other areas of your life as well. Here are some examples:

>> **Slow down your eating behaviour.** Begin by slowing your breathing. Notice the shape and colours of your food. Notice the textures and allow yourself to take in any smells that are associated with your food. Notice the sensation of smell. When you put the food in your mouth, explore its textures and tastes.

Practise the same type of exercise as you drink a warm or cool drink. Allow yourself to become fully aware of the different sensory experiences associated with drinking.

>> **Wash your hands mindfully.** It may help to wash your hands with something that you've chosen due to its texture (silky or granulated), smell or colour.

>> **Choose a piece of music to practise mindfulness of sound.** It may be helpful to choose a piece that's calming and soothing.

>> **Keep reminders around you.** Placing sticky notes on the fridge, drinking from a specific mug or putting a pebble in your pocket can remind you to bring your mindfulness practice into your everyday life.

>> **'Buddy up' with someone.** Send each other text messages to remind each other to engage in mindfulness practices.

TIP

In Chapter 8 you become more familiar with your ability to move your attention; in this chapter, you become mindful of the focus of your attention, so you can then begin to intentionally combine and infuse this focus with compassion. It may be helpful to see attention as your spotlight (refer to Chapter 8 for more on this), mindfulness as the process by which you intentionally and non-judgementally observe, and compassion as the torch or perspective that you choose to use.

Chapter 10

Practising Compassion for Others

Compassion can be expressed in three ways: the compassion we experience *from* others, the compassion we experience *for* others and the compassion we experience for ourselves.

Together these three elements are referred to as compassionate 'flow'. In other words, compassion flows from us to others, from others to us and we then show compassion to ourselves.

Our tricky brains (refer to Chapters 1 and 3), life experiences and hectic lifestyles mean we're often drawn away from what we truly want to focus on and what we want to do. We can quickly find ourselves living on automatic pilot.

Consider which 'version' of you that you want to cultivate. This may be your angry, anxious, sad or compassionate self (head to Chapter 17 for more on the different 'versions' of ourselves). What are your personal motivations? If you're motivated to be in tune with your own and other people's distress and to prevent or alleviate this distress, and you want to know more about how to develop your compassionate self so that you can help others, this is the chapter for you.

In this chapter, we focus on compassion for others. We consider the qualities of your compassionate self, how to develop your compassionate self and how you can use your compassionate self to assist others. Together, we refer to these exercises as 'compassionate self cultivation' (a concept I introduce in Chapter 1).

Experiencing Compassion for Other People and Creating Positive Outcomes

The benefits of practising compassion for people are often two-fold: we assist someone else and as a direct result we feel a sense of purpose. Both parties are likely to feel emotional warmth and an enhanced sense of connection with each other. Practising compassion for others can assist us in everyday situations, such as when we come face to face with someone we don't like – it can help us to feel more at peace and less wound up by others and can even help us develop compassion for those parts of ourselves that we don't like.

Compassion Focused Therapy (CFT) recommends that we also practice compassion for those individuals that we don't know 'from afar'.

But what about practising compassion for those who you don't understand and maybe don't even like? This is much more difficult, and you may ask, 'What's the point in that?'

You may be surprised to realise that it can be helpful for you to practise compassion for people who you can't understand or don't like. The two-fold benefits I mentioned at the beginning of this section haven't changed: you may help someone and in addition feel a sense of purpose.

The two key reasons for practising compassion for people that you don't like so much, or that you just can't figure out, are:

>> **We're all more similar than different.** You're this version of yourself, today, due to a mixture of many factors that were not of your choosing, just like other people. This sense of commonality awakens us to the struggles many people experience and helps us to become motivated to understand and address them.

Everyone wishes to be happy and free of suffering. No one wishes to feel inadequate, angry, afraid or lonely. We all wish for good health, a sense of purpose and meaningful connections with others, but our genes, tricky brains (Chapter 3), societal influences and life experiences mean that we're easily drawn into different views and behaviours that can be problematic for ourselves and others.

>> **We can better understand ourselves by better understanding others.** If we intellectually and emotionally understand the struggles and darker sides of other people, and practise compassion for them, it can help us recognise and work through our own difficulties – the parts of us we often don't like to think about.

Maybe the people you don't like and don't understand are friends and allies you are yet to discover!

TIP

Identifying the Qualities and Attributes of Your Compassionate Self

You may already have an intuitive sense of what your compassionate self (or you at your compassionate best) is like. You can think of your *compassionate self* as the embodiment of your compassionate mind. In other words, your compassionate mind provides you with compassionate attention and thoughts, but your compassionate self walks, talks and engages in courageous acts.

Before we explore the physicality of your compassionate self, you may find it helpful to consider its qualities.

Write down the qualities you'd hope your compassionate self would have. Maybe you include qualities such as kindness, patience, warmth, sensitivity and friendliness?

In Chapter 2, we explore how compassion feels in the mind and body by focusing our attention on someone or something in distress. It may be useful to re-engage with this exercise or to review any notes that you made at the time.

TIP

Take a look at the compassionate attributes outlined in Chapter 2. Perhaps you missed something important that you can add to your list?

Missing an important attribute from your list may suggest that this exercise is difficult for you. Alternatively, it may be something that is so second nature to you that you don't recognise it!

TIP

If you find that certain attributes create more difficulty for you than others, it may be helpful to consider why this is or head to Chapters 6 and 7 for more on common barriers to compassion.

Your list is probably full of compassionate qualities and attributes by now, but there may be a few qualities that you haven't considered. The following sections delve deeper into the qualities of compassionate wisdom and the value of strength, courage and commitment when developing your compassionate self.

REMEMBER

Don't worry if you look at your list of 'want-to-have' qualities and feel you have a lot of qualities to work on – that's what this book is for! The later section, 'Cultivating Your Compassionate Self', explores how you can build on your compassionate qualities.

Compassionate wisdom

Compassionate wisdom comes from the realisation that we're all shaped by our biology and by experiences that we have little control over. None of us designed our tricky brains (refer to Chapter 3) or bodies, nor the society and culture into which we were born. It's from this perspective that compassionate wisdom emerges. Compassionate wisdom allows us to stand back and see ourselves in the flow of life.

Compassionate wisdom allows us to stop and make helpful choices. We appreciate the problems associated with self-criticism and the benefits of developing a supportive relationship with ourselves.

REMEMBER

With compassionate wisdom, we awaken to impermanence: the fact that everything is transient and in constant flux, nothing lasts and everything evolves. From this perspective, we see difficulties and the sources of upset, as well as contentment and the circumstances that support it, as constantly changing. We see things in context and appreciate our ability to change things that are changeable in a helpful way.

Compassionate strength, courage and commitment

Compassion involves turning towards and engaging with distress – your own and other people's. It also involves taking action. This may mean staying with your own emotional pain or that of someone else. It may mean intervening and letting your voice be heard despite the anxiety you may feel when doing so. Compassionate acts take great strength and courage.

Despite our best intentions, at times our efforts are thwarted. We may attempt to intervene during an argument, yet our voice isn't heard and we're ignored. At times we get things wrong, for ourselves and other people. For example, we ask if someone requires our help, but this is taken as a criticism. This is where compassionate commitment comes to the fore. We don't simply give up; we consider what may help, adjust our behaviour and try again. This example demonstrates our compassionate self in action.

Cultivating Your Compassionate Self

In the past you may have decided to become fitter or to learn a new sport. If you invested your time and energy, you'll have noticed changes to your body or improvements in your skill level. In the same way, you can decide to cultivate a certain aspect of yourself: you can cultivate your compassionate self, or 'you at your best'. Time and effort will show its rewards.

You do this by first focusing on the experience of compassion in your mind – we refer to this as your compassionate mind and the exercises as compassionate mind training. Attention to your posture and physicality helps to expand this experience from one of the mind to one of the mind and body. We refer to this full mind and body experience as your compassionate self and the exercises as compassionate self cultivation.

In the later section, 'Showing Compassion for Others', you use your compassionate self to relate to a number of individuals. In Chapters 15 and 16, you focus on your compassionate self in action.

TIP

Preparation can make all the difference during an exercise, enhancing your experience. Use your soothing rhythm breathing or a mindfulness exercise, and allow a gentle smile to soften your face (refer to Chapter 9 for more on preparing yourself for compassion exercises), to create a sense of calm awareness in your mind and body.

In this exercise, you explore your compassionate mind by intentionally exploring a range of qualities. You will then be asked to experience these qualities in your body. This is your compassionate self.

1. **Find a place that is, as far as possible, free from distractions. Sit with a relaxed, open posture, with strength and alertness to your spine.** It's helpful if you close your eyes, but you may prefer to settle your gaze on a low fixed point.

2. **Bring to mind the qualities and attributes that you wrote down on the list that you produced in the earlier section, 'Identifying the Qualities and Attributes of Your Compassionate Self' and allow yourself to feel them. If you don't immediately experience these qualities and attributes, begin by imagining how they'd feel.** For example, you may not feel a sense of strength, but imagine how it may feel to be strong. Spend a few moments on each.

3. **Explore how each of the qualities and attributes feels in your body.** It may help to adjust your posture to assist you further, or to recall a time when you experienced compassion for someone and to then consider how your body felt at the time.

4. **Turn your attention to the quality of wisdom.** Consider that we did not ask to be born, nor did we choose the time or place of our birth, our family, culture or tricky brain (refer to Chapter 3). Acknowledge that complex factors have shaped us and continually influence us.

5. **Explore a sense of inner strength. It may help to feel an alertness in your spine, a slight raise of your chin and relaxation in your shoulders. This may be the strength to bear your own or someone else's pain. Alternatively, it may be the strength to set boundaries or intervene when compassionate action is required.** Allow yourself to feel expansive, solid and grounded. (Chapter 9 provides more detail about the quality of inner strength and practices that can help.)

6. **As you embody your compassionate self, feel a sense of courage and a commitment to be helpful.** For a few moments, explore this feeling in your mind and body.

7. **Become aware of the physicality of your compassionate self.** Experience its qualities as you embody it. Allow a gentle smile or warm facial expression to appear on your face. Adjust your posture to find a position that enhances the experience. It may help to feel a greater sense of alertness to your spine and an expansion in your chest.

8. **Consider what tone of voice you'd use if your compassionate self was to speak.** How would you walk, move and interact with other people?

9. **Consider playfully getting up and moving around as your compassionate self.** If you feel comfortable and ready enough to do this, engage in this experience for a while before you come to the end of the exercise. You may feel as though you're acting the part or you may feel that this is part of you – a part that comes to the fore in your life from time to time.

For much of our lives we allow our compassionate self to be triggered by external events, maybe when we see someone we care for in distress or relate to a person or animal who is sick or injured. In CFT, we intentionally choose to cultivate and switch on this part of ourselves because it's helpful to do so – for both ourselves and others.

TIP

Choose a pebble or semi-precious stone that you can use when you're working on developing your compassionate self. Place it in your pocket, wallet or purse. When you unintentionally come across it, use this trigger to focus some time cultivating your compassionate self.

You can also use other helpful triggers or routines to remind you to cultivate and embody your compassionate self. You may decide to inhabit your compassionate self when you wake up each morning, when you go on specific walks, when you eat or drink, or even when you're in difficult meetings!

WARNING

Exercises that work to develop your compassionate self can reveal personal blocks. For example, you may think 'What's the point in doing this?'; you may become self-critical and think 'I'm just kidding myself'; or you may meet resistance from others. When you become aware of a block, gently consider why this may be difficult for you and consider ways to overcome it. Chapters 6 and 7 consider a range of personal blocks to compassion and provide ideas for how to overcome them.

TIP

If you find inhabiting your compassionate self, or being 'you at your best', difficult, imagine yourself into the role – just like an actor transforms into someone who's depressed, super-confident or anxious. Bring to mind what a compassionate voice sounds like, what a helpful posture looks like, what sort of facial expression a compassionate person may have, and so on, and imagine that you inhabit these elements.

Take pleasure in your intention to cultivate your compassionate self. With practice, you'll eventually find that it feels more natural and a part of you.

Showing Compassion for Others

After you feel you've sufficiently developed and practised your compassionate self (refer to the preceding section), you can focus your compassionate self on developing your compassion for others.

You begin by focusing the attention of your compassionate self on those you love. It's a good starting point as it's likely that you'll find this relatively easy. You then progress through a range of exercises that may be increasingly challenging. As your compassionate self builds, so too will your ability to engage with these exercises.

TIP

In Chapter 12, and throughout Part 4 of this book, you use your compassionate self to assist you.

In the following sections, we look at differing scenarios in order to cultivate your compassionate self and focus it on others.

Begin each exercise by evoking your compassionate self (using the exercise in the preceding section).

Compassion for someone you love

First up, we consider practising compassion for others in the easiest way – we look at practising compassion for someone you love.

Bring to mind a person (or an animal) whom you love and have a relatively uncomplicated relationship with. Hold them in your mind's eye (imagine them in detail) and bring warmth to your facial expression as you do so. Focus on your compassionate feelings for them. It may help to imagine a warm light or a colour emanating from you to them.

After you've experienced this for a while, use a warm tone of voice to name them in your mind.

Say the following phrases (if these phrases don't work for you, consider adapting them to suit you). It's helpful to say these phrases on your out-breath. At the end of each phrase, insert their name:

> May you be well . . .
>
> May you be happy . . .
>
> May you be free of suffering . . .

Turn your attention to feelings of joy, and the feeling of sharing an enhanced sense of connection with your loved one.

When you feel ready, allow the image of your loved one to fade from your mind's eye. Spend a few moments tuning into the feelings that have arisen in you, noticing in particular how and where you feel them in your body.

TIP

At the end of this exercise, it can help to ask yourself what you can do for your loved one that may be of benefit to them. You may have noticed that the exercise provided you with some ideas of things you can do for or with them, or maybe things you may change, which are motivated by compassion. You may simply feel motivated to engage with them in a slightly different way.

Engaging with this exercise further develops your compassionate mind and compassionate self. Directing compassion to others is likely to bring with it an enhanced compassion for and connection with the person upon whom you focus the exercise.

Compassion for someone similar to you

Practising compassion for someone similar to you can help you develop compassion for the aspects of yourself that you struggle with. The following exercise explores this further.

Consider something that you struggle with. Maybe your confidence, appearance, emotions or relationships. Alternatively, you may bring to mind experiences that you've had that are associated with shame or self-criticism.

Now bring to mind someone who struggles in a similar way to you. They may be someone you know, someone in the public eye or a pure product of your imagination. Focus on your compassionate feelings for them and allow warmth to develop in your facial expression.

With a warm tone of voice, name them in your mind and use the phrases that you used in the preceding section. Say each phrase, adding the person's name (if appropriate) at the end of each phrase.

Consider if your compassionate self may have additional things to say to this person. Perhaps 'I know you worry and I hope you find some peace', 'I hope your mood improves' or 'May you find a sense of contentment'.

When ready, allow the image to fade in your mind's eye. It can help to make some notes of any additional phrases your compassionate self said in order to emphasise and remember them. These additional phrases may apply to other situations and other people.

REMEMBER

Practising compassion for those similar to you may highlight blocks and obstacles that you need to overcome. For example, you may find that when you bring someone to mind who struggles in a similar way, critical thoughts pop into your mind. Such insights are incredibly important and provide you with something to work on. For example, you may want to consider their difficulties in the context of their life story (refer to Chapter 5). Overcoming some of your blocks towards others will help you to overcome obstacles to being compassionate towards yourself (self-compassion). Be gentle and consider blocks from the perspective of your compassionate self.

TIP

This book is written with many people in mind. Some struggle in a similar way to you, others differently. What unites us all is a wish to be well, happy and free of suffering. With this in mind, you may want to consider the other readers of this book from the perspective of your compassionate self, following the format outlined in this section.

Compassion for your self-critic

We can relate to ourselves in a positive or negative manner. We can be our own best friend or our own worst critic. It's like having different characters in our heads. We refer to this negative and undermining character as our *self-critic*. It's usually angry or disappointed with us and our efforts, and it goes on and on about the things we've done or should have done. With a negative tone of voice, it can tell us we're stupid, pathetic, ugly, fat or a waste of space. Chapter 1 looks at your self-critic in greater depth and gets you more familiar with it.

Although your self-critic is part of you, it can be helpful to practise compassion for it – as though it is separate from you. This can help you to gain distance from your self-critic, to consider its motivation, and to ultimately develop a healthier relationship with it. In this first exercise you're asked to think about your self-critic in a specific situation – a time when you recall being self-critical. We do this first because it's easier to generate a sense of your self-critic when it's linked to a specific situation.

REMEMBER Compassion for your self-critic is also a form of self-compassion.

Begin by bringing to mind a time when you've been critical of yourself. Slowly and gently begin to see your self-critic in your mind's eye, noticing its posture, facial expression, feelings and so forth (head to Chapter 1 for more on this).

Evoke your compassionate self, reminding yourself of the compassionate qualities you hold. From this viewpoint, and using these qualities, experience compassion for your self-critic.

Consider what lies behind its barrage of negativity and what its needs are. Experience a connection with it. Maybe it wants you to be happy and free of suffering, but it goes about things in an unhelpful way?

With a warm tone of voice, relate to your self-critic using the phrases that you used in the earlier section, 'Compassion for someone you love', to focus your compassion. Say each phrase holding an image of your self-critic in mind. You may choose to name your self-critic, referring to it as 'critic', 'blob', 'bully' or 'gremlin'.

Imagine compassion flowing from you to your self-critic. If this proves difficult, focus your intention on being compassionate to your self-critic.

Using a warm tone of voice, consider whether there are any additional statements your compassionate self is motivated to say to your self-critic. It may help to jot down additional statements in order to emphasise and remember the things you wish your self-critic to know.

Allow the image to fade from your mind's eye.

TIP

As you've been focusing your attention on part of you that can be associated with strong emotions, engage with an exercise that brings with it a sense of calm and inner warmth before getting up and stretching your body. This helpful exercise may be a mindfulness practice or your soothing rhythm breathing, for example (refer to Chapter 9 for some options).

REMEMBER

We don't actually have a self-critic living in our minds. Our self-critic represents a sequence of patterns in our brain and is associated with our threat response (refer to Chapter 4 for more information on the threat system). So, fighting it simply triggers the very same system. Relating to our self-critic compassionately calms down our threat system, allowing us to gain a sense of calm and wellbeing.

Your compassionate self is aware that fighting or criticising your self-critic brings with it further problems – you're fighting fire with fire. In contrast, realising what lies behind your self-critic (usually fear) and developing compassion for it is like throwing a blanket around it.

TIP

Practicing compassion for your self-critic 'in general' when it's not related to a specific situation can be more difficult than the preceding exercise, therefore I suggest that you do the following exercise having practiced the preceding one first. (It doesn't matter if you go from one straight into the other or whether you practice it on a later occasion.)

Repeat the preceding exercise, bringing to mind your self-critic in a more general way and not linking it to a specific event. Hold your self-critic in your mind and explore your compassion for it.

TIP

Before you re-read notes or statements written from your compassionate self's perspective, engage in an exercise to evoke your compassionate self once more (refer to the earlier section, 'Cultivating Your Compassionate Self' for a suitable exercise). Doing this means that the things you've written will have more salience and are more likely to 'sink in', creating lasting change.

Compassion for the people we overlook or dislike

We have a tendency to favour those we love, reject those we don't like and ignore those that fall in between. This is perfectly normal and a consequence of our evolution.

However, our mind and compassionate self allows us to reflect and choose whether it's helpful for us to do this. As we widen our circle of compassion, we can consciously choose to bring our attention to those we may normally ignore and, in so doing, we may discover a wider sense of connection to others. We may then decide to turn our attention to those we don't like and begin to consider their motivations, fears, concerns and wishes, practising compassion for them when we're ready.

Focusing on those you overlook, try the exercise in the earlier section, 'Compassion for someone you love'. Begin by focusing generally on those you overlook, rather than on individuals.

When you're ready to take this exercise to the next level, be specific about the individuals for whom you're practising compassion. Maybe they're individuals who you regularly come into contact with, such as a person working in your local store, a colleague or an acquaintance.

TIP

If you struggle at first, consider this analogy. When you begin to use free weights in the gym, you're unlikely to start by attempting to lift heavy weights – and if you do, you're likely to quickly experience failure. Instead, you slowly increase the weights that you lift, noticing when you experience some difficulty and proceeding to the next level when you feel ready to negotiate the next step. In the same way, you develop your compassionate self step by step.

When you feel ready, engage in the next exercise and use your compassionate self to experience compassion for people you don't like.

Consider people who you don't like, beginning with someone it's relatively easy to feel some compassion for – maybe initially focus on someone who causes you a small degree of irritation, later moving on to someone who arouses stronger feelings.

Use the phrases provided in the earlier section 'Compassion for someone you love' and progress at a pace that's comfortable for you.

Compassion for someone who you dislike, especially if they've caused you harm, can be extremely difficult, so engage in these exercises as and when you feel ready. It may be helpful to focus on developing self-compassion (turn to Chapter 12) first and to return to these exercises when you feel strong enough to do so.

TIP

When difficult emotions arise, engage in a mindfulness practice, practise your soothing rhythm breathing, or find your compassionate place (outlined in Chapter 11). Alternatively, you may wish to seek the support and advice of someone who has your best interests at heart – or a professional.

It can help to let go of strong negative emotions towards other people by compassionately considering what factors may have influenced them. This doesn't mean that they're not responsible for the things that have happened, it just means that you're choosing to live in a way that's helpful for you.

Focus on your intention and gently notice any strong reactions you have. Appreciate that your reactions are there for a reason and, instead of acting on or running away from them, gently recognise them, hold them in mind and be compassionate towards them. Chapter 17 provides further ways to explore and work through any strong emotions that you may have.

Compassion without boundaries

In this exercise, you open your mind to all living beings. You do this to help develop and strengthen your compassionate self. If you practice compassion without boundaries, inhabiting your compassionate self becomes more familiar and automatic. You can then inhabit this version of yourself more readily in all aspects of your everyday life.

Having evoked your compassionate self, bring to mind the people who you're close to and imagine them surrounding you. After a while, consider the people who you're fond of but that you have less connection with, and imagine them also surrounding you, but in a wider ring encircling your nearest and dearest.

Consider the people with whom you experience some degree of difficulty in your life, for whatever reason, and blend them into your image, occupying an even wider ring.

Continue to widen the circle, adding those who live in your town or city that you have limited contact with, those with whom you have no contact, and those who live in your country and on your continent. Finally, imagine all living beings everywhere and send them your wish of happiness and a life free of suffering.

Experience your heartfelt wish and your expansive sense of compassion as it flows from you. You may perceive it as a wave, a colour or a light.

Feel the sense of connection and interdependence that this compassionate wish grants you, appreciating and feeling grateful for the many ways that we're all linked and that we depend upon each other.

When you feel ready, allow the image to fade from your mind and sit for a while, tuning into the feelings that arose in you during the exercise.

You may choose to use the phrases provided in the earlier 'Compassion for someone you love' section.

Chapter 11

Allowing Compassion In

Compassion has three dimensions; together, these are referred to as *compassionate flow*. The three dimensions are:

>> The experience of compassion from others (the focus of this chapter)

>> Compassion for ourselves – *self-compassion* (the focus of Chapter 12)

>> The compassion we extend to others (the focus of Chapter 10)

Compassion Focused Therapy (CFT) suggests that each dimension is important and that balance between them is key. Consider if you were compassionate to others and could feel self-compassion, yet you were unable to let in compassion *from* others? What if you could feel self-compassion and were able to receive compassion from others, but you were unable to experience compassion *for* anyone else? Finally, what if you were able to experience compassion for and receive it from others, but you had a *self-critical* mind?

Of course, finding yourself in such a situation isn't your fault, but when you become aware of such difficulties with an area of compassion, it's helpful to do something about it and address the imbalance.

In this chapter, we explore the challenges of accepting compassion *from* others and use relationships, memories and novel images to assist us. We also look at how welcoming compassion from others can help to develop our compassionate mind and compassionate self.

Responding to Compassion from Others

An act of compassion from others may involve them cleaning and dressing a wound, stepping in when we're being bullied or allowing us time to talk things through. We can hugely benefit from such actions in a very practical way, but we can also benefit from experiencing the human connection that often comes along with such interactions.

TIP

Explore this concept further by trying the following exercise.

Imagine losing your footing and falling awkwardly in a busy street. Aware of those around, you feel a flash of shame. A passer–by quickly offers their help. Consider how the following scenarios may affect you differently:

>> **Scenario 1:** You quickly get up, declining the person's offer of help and, holding back your tears, move to a bench, where you sit for a while until the pain subsides.

>> **Scenario 2:** You have fleeting eye contact with the passer-by and accept their offer of help in a pragmatic manner. The person walks with you to the bench and, making little eye contact, you hold back your tears. You thank them for their time. Once again you sit for a while until the pain subsides.

>> **Scenario 3:** You make eye contact with the person and recognise their wish to help. You thank them and walk to the bench together. You allow your tears to be seen. You both sit, initially in silence, and after a short while you begin to speak, maybe eventually smiling as you talk about the fall.

Now consider the following questions:

>> Which situation is likely to lead to a more helpful experience for you?

>> Which situation is likely to lead to a more meaningful experience for the passer-by?

While each scenario provides you with a reasonable way to deal with a difficult situation, different consequences may follow:

>> In Scenario 1, the passer-by may feel slightly awkward following their attempt to intervene. Alternatively, they may simply continue with their day, not giving you much thought. You, on the other hand, will experience the pain, discomfort and shame on your own.

>> In Scenario 2, the passer-by is likely to feel positive about their ability to be of assistance to you. In addition, you're likely to appreciate their intervention, be it fleeting.

>> In Scenario 3, both you and the passer-by are likely to feel much more positive about the human connection you shared. Of course, you may prefer to avoid the situation and may feel slightly awkward, but these feelings can be balanced by a sense of connection and an experience of compassion.

Compassionate acts from others are important, but our ability to fully experience and appreciate them is central to human connection and wellbeing.

TIP

CFT helps us become aware of the options open to us and to choose those that promote wellbeing. As such, one of the questions we ask ourselves and others is 'What is helpful?'. Sometimes what's 'helpful' feels positive, be it a listening ear, the warmth of a hug or an offer of support. At other times, actions that are helpful to us may feel uncomfortable, even negative. For example, if you let your guard down you may feel vulnerable with others, which can be very difficult. However, in the long run such actions are likely to be helpful and meaningful. In other words, they're likely to result in a greater sense of connection with others and address any shame and self-criticism we may feel.

TIP

If, while engaging in any of the exercises, you became aware of some form of personal block or resistance to compassion (from others), gently reflect on what beliefs or experiences may account for this. Blocks may come with an urge to avoid the person showing compassion. We may 'squirm' uncomfortably or discount their act of compassion, assuming that they wouldn't be that way if they truly knew us, or maybe that they have an ulterior motive. Such difficulties with receiving compassion from others can be the product of events in our past or our current situation.

TIP

It may help to review your life story (Chapter 5) and consider why compassion from others may be tricky for you. Chapters 6 and 7 explore your beliefs about and emotional responses towards receiving compassion, and consider the blocks placed in your way by other people. You may choose to discuss this with someone, use it as the focus of a compassionate letter (see Chapter 14 for more on compassionate writing) or simply observe the difficulty you have with warmth and non-judgement.

REMEMBER

Shame and fear of negative reactions and judgements by others can block our ability to connect with and experience compassion from people. So too can the views and judgements we have and make of ourselves, so consider these carefully.

Discovering the Power of Compassionate Imagery

Compassionate imagery involves using your imagination to create images that help you to experience compassion. This may be compassion for others, or the experience of receiving compassion from others or from ourselves. Compassionate imagery stimulates particular brain systems that can be helpful to us.

While some compassionate imagery exercises activate our soothing system (refer to Chapter 4 for more detail about this system), others can provide us with the motivation, strength and courage to face difficult situations. We explore these exercises later in this section.

The following exercise powerfully demonstrates the effect that our imagination and imagery can have on us. Take time to really think yourself into the scenarios, slowly answering the questions in each part of the exercise as fully as you can before you move onto the next part.

Some of the images that occupy our minds are clear, while others are fragmented and hazy. Some are of real places, people and events, while others are totally imaginary or synthetic. Many bring different emotions, physical sensations and thoughts. Our imaginations can be amazingly weird and wonderful!

1. **What happens when you're hungry and you see an amazing plate of your very favourite food?**

Your mouth may begin to water and you may feel sensations in your belly as your stomach acids get going.

2. **Imagine that you're just as hungry but there's no food to be had. What happens if you *imagine* the amazing plate of food?**

Your imagination actually triggers your body to produce saliva and stomach acid!

If you hear your stomach rumbling, you know why! You may not have had the original plate of lovely food in front of you for this exercise, but just imagining how you would feel is enough to cause a physical reaction to the image.

If hunger hasn't sent you running to the shops, consider this next set of questions.

1. **What happens when you're in the presence of someone you find sexually attractive?**

You may experience a sense of arousal.

2. **What about if you instead simply imagine them in your mind – what happens then?**

Your body responds in exactly the same way – in fact, imagery can be even more powerful as you can create an *ideal* image – you're not worrying about your lumps and bumps, or theirs for that matter!

REMEMBER

Our brain doesn't discriminate between the real and the imagined. Both real and imaginary images can create powerful reactions within us.

In the next exercise, you think about two experiences that are closely linked with your general wellbeing.

1. **What happens when someone is critical and undermining of you and your efforts?** Maybe you can think of a time when this has happened. Explore how you felt at the time.

   You may feel threatened. You may feel angry, upset or anxious and, if so, you'll experience these emotions in your body. Maybe your muscles tense, or you experience a heaviness in your body or a churning in your stomach.

2. **What happens when you're critical and undermining of your own efforts?** It may help to think about a time when you've been self-critical and explore how you felt at the time. The experience may be associated with a mental image of a bully, or a stern part of you. Alternatively, your self-critic may embody a sense of disappointment or disapproval. Head to Chapter 1 to explore your self-critic further.

   At some level you may tell yourself that self-criticism is helpful, but when you address yourself in this way you actually trigger your threat system and you're likely to feel angry, upset or anxious.

3. **What happens when, following a setback or disappointment, someone notices that you're upset, anxious or angry, and they relate to you with kindness, validation, warmth and understanding? How does their compassion make you feel?** If you can think of a time when someone has related to you in this way, bring it to mind and remember how it made you feel.

   You may feel cared for and supported. This support can help reduce difficult feelings and provide you with the strength and courage that you need to face a similar situation again, or help you to put things in perspective for next time.

4. **Finally, what happens if you use your imagination to generate inner support and encouragement?** You may imagine, for example, an older, wiser and more compassionate version of you who's able to provide support and encouragement.

   Such imagery will have a powerful effect on how you feel physically, your emotional state, what you focus on and what you then do. You're more likely to be equipped to deal with the situation in a more helpful way.

REMEMBER

Self-compassion involves practicing this kind of supportive and encouraging relationship for ourselves, and this is the focus of Chapter 12.

In the following sections, we consider some helpful hints to allow you to utilise compassionate imagery, before delving into using compassionate imagery in different scenarios.

Engaging with compassionate imagery

Some people take to compassionate imagery like a duck to water, while others struggle – but you won't know until you try, so dip your toe in and give it a go!

For those who struggle to create images in their minds, it can help to initially consider an image to steer your mind towards. Photos, drawings or paintings can be useful starting points. From here, you can then adapt your compassionate image to suit your needs and preferences.

If you do find it difficult to get started, keep these basic principles in mind:

1. Develop your *intention* to allow compassion in. In other words, if you're motivated and can see a rationale for letting compassion in, you'll eventually find a way. Proceed with curiosity and gentleness.

2. The point of the exercises is to *experience* (or *re-experience*) compassion from others. As such, don't be dismayed if your mind doesn't create the most amazing image. Focus instead on how you feel. The creation of a warm light in your mind may be more powerful for creating an experience of compassion than a detailed image in human form.

If your compassionate place or ideal compassionate image is a real place or person (see the later sections, 'Visiting your compassionate place' and 'Cultivating a compassionate ideal' for more on these), gently consider if there are any negative connotations that may come along with these images. Real people can let us down, and places can be associated with positive as well as negative memories. Consider picking aspects of people or places and blend them to create an idealised image and experience.

TIP

You may like to try blending compassionate images together. For example, you may imagine a colour surrounding you or a channel of warm light flowing in and out of your body while you're in your compassionate place. (Check out the later sections, 'Visiting your compassionate place' and 'Finding your compassionate colour or light' for more on these types of compassionate image.)

Music and smells can enhance emotional experiences, so consider engaging with a specific piece of music or smell before, during and/or after an exercise.

If you settle on a particular image or experience, allow it a sense of fluidity and an ability to change over time. This way you won't tire of it and it can adapt to your needs.

Your mind will wander during these exercises. Your attention may be caught by sounds or bodily sensations. You may begin to worry or start self-monitoring, asking yourself, 'Am I doing this right?' or 'Is this a good image for me?' This is perfectly normal. When you become aware that your mind has wandered, bring it warmly and without judgement back to the focus of the exercise. Chapters 8 and 9 provide more information on focusing our attention and our mind's tendency to wander.

Using compassionate imagery to experience compassion from others

The following sections explore exercises that use memories, relationships and fantasy to help you experience or re-experience compassion from others in different scenarios. Allow 15 minutes or so for each exercise, and really explore and experience the sensation of letting compassion in.

Prepare for each exercise by finding a place that is, as far as possible, free from distractions. Sit in a relaxed, open posture with strength and alertness to your spine. You may find it helpful to close your eyes, but if not you can settle your gaze on a low fixed point. This may be part of a pattern on the carpet, a leaf on the ground or something you've placed on the floor. If your eyes are open, allow your gaze to soften and your sight to become hazy.

Start each exercise by using your soothing rhythm breathing or a mindfulness practice to create a sense of calm awareness in your mind and body. Chapter 9 provides more information on mindfulness and soothing rhythm breathing.

As you start each exercise, bring a warm expression to your face or a slight smile to your mouth in order to enhance the experience.

After you complete each exercise, you may find it helpful to sit for a while and allow the experience to gently fade from your mind and body, or to write some notes.

Re-experiencing compassion from others

Experiencing compassion from others can have a powerful effect on us. This may be physical, emotional or more practical in nature (that is, we may benefit from someone carrying our bags or fixing our car). In this exercise, you recall a time when you were able to feel someone else's compassion for you. As you become more experienced with this exercise, you may choose to recall a time when someone was compassionate but, at the time, you were unable to feel it. Maybe you discounted the person's intention, were overwhelmed by other emotions or simply didn't appreciate their sensitivity to your distress and motivation to do something about it.

1. **Recall a specific occasion when someone showed you compassion.** Maybe it was at a difficult time when someone was there for you or, more simply, an occasion when someone stretched out an arm or showed you encouragement.

2. **Allow yourself to re-experience the occasion.** Work through each of your senses as prompts. What can you see and hear; are certain smells or physical sensations associated with the memory?

3. **Experience a sense of connection between yourself and the other person.** Feel their sensitivity to your distress and their motivation to alleviate it.

   Stay with this for a while.

4. **Notice where you feel their compassion in your body and the emotions it evokes.** Maybe you feel a pull towards the other person as you experience a strong sense of connection with them. Maybe you feel a relaxation and softening in your body or a reconnection with a sense of sadness.

5. **Focus once more on the experience of compassion from the other person and allow this experience to sink in.**

Although an experience is in our past, we can choose to evoke the memory by bringing to mind the scene and re-experiencing it. The experience can be enhanced by recalling other sensory experiences such as smells and sounds. Because our mind and body reacts to recalled events in exactly the same way as it does to those in the present moment, we can use past experiences to re-experience compassion and develop our compassionate self.

Experiencing compassion from others in the moment

Experiencing compassion from others in the moment can have an extremely powerful impact on our wellbeing. It can also bring a sense of connectedness and usually enhances the other person's wellbeing too! However, hectic lives, concerns about judgement from others and judgements of ourselves can be just some of the reasons why we fail to experience compassion in the moment. (Chapters 6 and 7 review common blocks to compassion and provide some ideas of how to overcome them.)

The next exercise focuses your attention on experiencing compassion in the moment.

The next time you experience compassion from others, open your mind to it. It may be compassion from a stranger as you fall to the floor, struggle with a heavy load or face an anxiety-provoking situation. Alternatively, it may be compassion from someone you're close to as they give you a reassuring hug, express frustration on your behalf or make contact at a time of difficulty. Experience this sense of connection with others and savour it.

TIP

Compassion from others is dependent upon a range of factors, such as the availability of others and the things that are going on in our lives. Although we can't control when the opportunity to experience compassion will happen, make sure that you're open to the experience when it next arises and notice it in the moment.

Bringing your attention to key relationships

This exercise focuses on key relationships. Bringing to mind the image of someone you care about, and who cares for you, can have a powerful effect on your mind and body. It enhances your sense of connection with the person and develops your compassionate self.

If you're lucky to have people around you who are (in general) sensitive to your distress and motivated to prevent and alleviate it, slowly bring each of them to mind, one by one.

Allow yourself to experience a sense of connection with each person. Experience their compassion for you. Allow time for each experience to really sink in before turning your attention to someone else.

TIP

You may consider a religious or spiritual figure as one of your key relationships and may therefore decide to focus on them.

It's all too easy to take compassion from the key people in our lives for granted. For example, we're likely to really appreciate it when a stranger offers to carry our bags, but when someone familiar to us does the same thing we often fail to experience their compassion. Bringing our attention to key relationships, and maybe to some of the things these people do for us, can be a really good way to remind us of their compassion and experience it.

Visiting your compassionate place

In the next exercise you explore what a compassionate place may look like. Of course, places can't act with compassion; however, this is fantasy so you can allow your mind to create an image of somewhere that feels compassionate to you. The place you choose knows how you're feeling and can adapt itself to whatever you need in the moment.

Allow your mind to explore and 'try on for size' a place that you can connect with and experience a sense of compassion from. It may be somewhere indoors or out, somewhere magical or real, somewhere from the past or the future. Allow your mind to explore many different possibilities.

Gently visualise where your mind takes you, using your senses:

>> **What can you see?** Maybe objects, vegetation or animals, an expanse of water or a beach. What colours can you see?

>> **What sounds are around you?** Maybe the rustling of leaves in the breeze, water, the faint sound of music, muffled noises, children laughing or birds singing.

>> **How does the air feel?** Is it warm or cold? Do you feel the sun on your skin?

>> **Do you notice particular smells?** Maybe the scent of grass, the saltiness of the ocean, the smell of bread or an open fire?

>> **What's supporting your body?** Maybe the ground is contoured perfectly against it or you're sitting on a cool rock, a cosy bed or warm sand?

Now, with a clear (or fleeting!) sense of this place, imagine that it welcomes you. Its sole purpose is to adapt to your needs. It's sensitive to your distress and aims to alleviate it, creating a sanctuary you can return to whenever you require it.

TIP

A fleeting impression can be enriched by attention to your sensory experiences. Your compassionate place may be vivid or impressionistic, a real place or fantastical. Be playful and try different places on for size.

Although places are unable to practice compassion, we can award the images in our mind any quality we wish. The image of a compassionate place can provide us with the experience of receiving compassion, and so it provides us with a helpful way to develop our experience of compassion.

REMEMBER

We all need different things at different times, so your compassionate place may alter and change depending on your needs.

Finding your compassionate colour or light

While some find it helpful to develop clear images of people, mystical animals and places to experience incoming compassion, others find focusing on colours and senses of light to be equally helpful.

FINDING A SAFE HAVEN: SAFE PLACE IMAGERY

Safe place imagery, often recommended as a relaxation or meditation practice, can be used to create a very similar sensory experience to your compassionate place (refer to the nearby section, 'Visiting your compassionate place'). However, the use of the term 'safe', for a small number of people, triggers a sense of them being safe *from* something. Subsequently, they experience threatening or menacing images on the periphery of the 'safe place' image. As such, I suggest you begin by focusing on a compassionate place rather than a 'safe one' in the hope that this will reduce the likelihood of this happening.

That said, for some, the creation of an image that has defences against threat may be helpful in the early days, and you may wish to call this your safe place. Imagining that your place is surrounded by thick impenetrable walls, the ocean or a supernatural force-field may allow you to experience something that's helpful to you. As always, the key to any of these exercises is to experience compassion, and so the things that make up your image (and experience) are personal to your needs.

Imagine a colour or a sense of light that, for you, is associated with compassion. Imagine it surrounding you. Award it a sense of gentleness, warmth, strength, courage or wisdom. Experience the compassionate colour holding you, maybe like a blanket. It may be helpful to imagine breathing the compassionate colour in or watching the compassionate colour enter your chest.

TIP

Your compassionate colour or compassionate light is likely to change depending on your needs (just as with your compassionate place). It may be a warm and gentle pastel when you're feeling low and upset or a strong and bold colour when you need to conjure up strength and courage.

Although a colour or light is clearly not a person, it can be compassionate and is therefore sensitive to your needs and motivated to help. As such, colour- and light-based compassionate images can allow us to experience compassion in exactly the same way as we would do if it were visualising a person.

Some individuals report that their compassionate colour or compassionate light speaks to them and has a particular gender.

Cultivating a compassionate ideal

Revisiting memories, opening ourselves to acts of compassion as they happen and focusing on key relationships are all 'real world' experiences of compassion from others (refer to the earlier exercises on these real-world experiences). Compassionate places, colours or light are imaginary or 'synthetic' ways that we can experience compassion flowing into us (refer to the preceding two exercises). They stimulate exactly the same systems in our mind and body that 'real' experiences do and are therefore very helpful practices. This exercise on compassionate ideals, and the exercise in the next section about an older and wiser version of ourselves, provides additional imaginary ways for us to experience this inward flow of compassion.

Explore an image in front of you, in your mind's eye, that embodies compassion – an ideal compassionate image. It may help to consider it as your 'perfect nurturer', compassionate teacher, friend, guide or coach. It may take a human, animal or mystical form.

Allow your mind to wander and to try different images on for size, exploring the experience that different images, and the terms used to describe them, evoke.

Consider your ideal image's empathy and sympathy, sensitivity and distress tolerance, non-judgement and care for your wellbeing. Focus on its sense of wisdom, strength, courage and commitment.

Consider its tone of voice and facial expression. This may be pretty hard if the image that comes to mind is a great oak tree – but maybe then the sounds you hear would be the gentle rustle of leaves or a whisper conveying that everything will be okay. What emotions does it direct your way? What other sensory experiences come with this imagery?

Imagine being in the presence of this ideal, and in receipt of its compassion.

TIP

Terms such as ideal compassionate image, perfect nurturer, compassionate coach, guide or friend can all evoke different experiences and different images. While some people find it helpful to develop one image that's used universally across a range of situations, others find it helpful to have a range, or 'family', of images.

Cultivating a compassionate ideal, or set of ideals, allows you to be as creative as you want to be. With experience, you can use this exercise, and other exercises in this chapter, to calm you when times are hard, advise you when you need to consider a way forward, and provide the strength to face a difficult situation.

Checking in with an older, wiser version of you

Time, age and experience can give us greater insight. Thinking back to your teenage years, you may now see arguments and disappointments that seemed catastrophic at the time as petty. You may wish to reassure your younger self that everything will be okay and to give them a hug.

Waiting to be older and wiser is an option, but you can also imagine being in the presence of that version of you. With an older, wiser version of you in mind you may gain greater insight and develop the strength to put certain things into perspective.

Imagine being in the presence of an older, wiser version of you: a version of you that has complete knowledge of the difficulties you've experienced in your life and those that you continue to face.

Experience its compassion for you and the strength and courage it's sending your way.

Imagining an older and wiser version of ourselves can be a powerful way to experience compassion 'flowing in'. An older version of ourselves can channel its wisdom, strength and courage through to us. It can remind us that change is possible and support us in our efforts. As with other compassionate imagery exercises, we can use the image of an older and wiser version of ourselves to assist us when we're distressed.

Experiencing compassion from fellow readers

Books such as this wouldn't be published unless there were enough people interested in the approach. As such, although you may be reading this book for the first time, hundreds if not thousands of other people will have read it before you and practised the exercises.

In this exercise, you reach out to other readers and feel their compassion for you.

Allow yourself to experience the compassion being sent to you by all the other readers of this and other books about compassion. Experience a sense of commonality with them, their sensitivity to your distress, and their heart-felt wish for your distress to be alleviated.

REMEMBER

Common humanity is a cornerstone of CFT. If you're able to embrace that you're not on your own but that you're connected to and similar to other people in many different ways, it can transport you from a sense of 'aloneness' to a sense of 'togetherness'.

Receiving compassion from me

I write this book with the knowledge that life can be incredibly hard. Throughout this book, we look at how our tricky brains (refer to Chapter 3 for more on why our brains are so tricky!), threat-focused environments, experiences and the ways in which we relate to ourselves can have a devastating effect on our wellbeing.

My heartfelt belief is that everyone deserves and needs compassion. So open up to it and experience the compassion I'm sending your way.

Enhancing Your Experience of Compassion from Others

You may have found a number of the compassionate imagery exercises in this chapter difficult. Perhaps they illuminated obstacles for you. If this is the case, consider taking a closer look to see if you can overcome these barriers.

Of course, other exercises may simply not 'hit the mark', but hopefully you discovered some that allowed you to experience a sense of compassion from others or to appreciate the sensation of compassion flowing in towards you. Continue to practise these exercises in order to grow your compassionate practice and ultimately to further develop this aspect of your compassionate mind and compassionate self.

REMEMBER

Compassionate flow involves allowing compassion in, practicing compassion for others and experiencing self-compassion. Clear overlap exists between these different elements: for example, compassion from an older and wiser version of yourself may be viewed as a form of self-compassion, and there are also occasions when you're both giving and receiving compassion simultaneously. All elements are central to your wellbeing, and that of others. The key is to create balance between these aspects.

Chapter 12

Delving Deeper into Self-Compassion

When we wake up to the impact our evolved brain, experiences and social environment have on us, we realise that our shame and self-criticism is misplaced. We realise it's incorrect to blame and bully ourselves for things that are not of our making. Importantly, we also awaken to the fact that self-criticism and shame is unhelpful to us and to others.

Instead of relating to ourselves with hostility, we begin to view ourselves, and the difficulties we have, with kindness. We become sensitive to our distress and motivated to alleviate it. Warmly holding ourselves in mind, we relate to ourselves in the same way we'd relate to someone we care for. This is self-compassion.

But self-compassion isn't something that simply develops overnight. It's something we need to explore, practice and strengthen. By doing so, we become aware of some of the things that block us – usually the things we don't like about ourselves and would rather not think about. It's easy to practice self-compassion for those parts of us that we like, but the true test of our self-compassion is whether we can practice it for those parts of us we don't like so much.

REMEMBER

Compassion, be it compassion for others, from others or self-compassion, isn't about saying 'there there, never mind' when something needs to change. Compassion involves the strength, courage and conviction to act in a way that alleviates our own and other peoples' distress.

In this chapter, we look at how you can further evolve your compassionate mind and compassionate self by developing self-compassion. We look at a number of exercises from a range of different perspectives that can help you to better understand self-compassion, and we turn to your life story (from Chapter 5) so that you can treat the experiences that have shaped you with self-compassion.

Making Sense of Self-Compassion

Self-compassion involves sensitivity to our own distress and a motivation to prevent or alleviate it. It's supportive and forward-looking. A self-compassionate mind is very different from a *self-critical* mind, which is undermining and intolerant of the difficulties you experience, and backward-looking.

FEEDING THE WOLVES WITHIN

As nightfall approached, a Native American Cherokee elder sat quietly with his grandchildren. He gazed into the campfire.

'A struggle occurs within my mind and body. It's because of the two wolves that live within me.'

The children looked puzzled. 'Wolves, grandfather?'

He said, 'One wolf carries with it fear, anger, envy, sorrow, regret, greed, arrogance, self-pity, resentment, inferiority, lies, false pride, superiority and ego. The other is filled with joy, peace, love, hope, serenity, humility, kindness, benevolence, friendship, empathy, generosity, truth and compassion. They struggle for territory and influence. This fight goes on inside you too, and inside every other person.'

After a period of silence, a child asked, 'So, grandfather – which wolf wins?'

The old Cherokee paused for a moment and warmly replied, 'The one I feed.'

Of course, the experiences we have, the things we attend to and the relationship we have with ourselves can feed and strengthen our threat-focused mind. However, we can consciously choose to feed our compassionate mind, nurturing our compassionate self. In so doing we can quieten our tendency for anger, fear and resentment while opening ourselves up to joy, connection and compassion.

Imagine you're disappointed with how your contribution to a meeting went. A backward-looking and critical mind may go over and over the mistakes you made and is likely to be associated with anger, sadness or anxiety. It's likely to give an unrealistic appraisal of your performance and catastrophise. In contrast, a supportive and forward-looking mind would be realistic about the mistakes you may have made but will look to the future, with a warm emotional tone, and consider ideas for how things may be improved in the future.

Compassion involves six core attributes and skills (outlined in Chapter 2). Sympathy, distress tolerance, empathy, non-judgement, care for wellbeing and sensitivity are practiced/enacted by way of compassionate attention, imagery, reasoning, behaviour, feeling and sensory focusing. Self-compassion directs these attributes and skills inwards in order to develop a supportive relationship with ourselves, one that is encouraging and forward-looking.

Exploring and Developing Self-Compassion

In the following sections, I introduce you to some exercises that help you explore and develop self-compassion. They may make you aware of personal blocks you have to self-compassion (refer to Chapters 6 and 7 for ways to address these); because they aim to create an emotional connect with your own distress, these blocks can lead to a strong emotional response. As such, allow the time and headspace you need to fully engage with them.

Prepare for each of the following exercises by finding a place that is, as far as possible, free from distractions. Feel a sense of strength and alertness to your spine and relaxation in your body. If helpful, you can close your eyes, but you may prefer to settle your gaze on a low fixed point.

Use soothing rhythm breathing or mindfulness to create a sense of calm awareness in your mind and body (refer to Chapter 9 for specific information on these exercises). Evoke your compassionate self (turn to Chapter 10 for tips on developing your compassionate self), reminding yourself of the compassionate attributes and qualities I introduce in Chapter 2. Bring a warm expression to your face to enhance the experience before beginning each exercise.

REMEMBER

Throughout the exercises outlined in this book, your mind is highly likely to wander. When you notice that this has happened, gently bring your attention back to the focus of the exercise.

After completing each exercise, sit for a while and gently allow the experience to 'sink in'. Spend a few moments tuning into the feelings that arise in you, noticing in particular how and where you feel them in your body. Paying attention to the body, as well as the mind, can enhance your experience of self-compassion. You may also find it helpful to move around, have a stretch or to jot down some thoughts and reflections after each exercise. This can help to signify the end of the exercise, help you reflect on the experience, and allow you to hold onto any realisations or experiences that the exercise evoked.

We have many different versions of ourselves. At times we may be highly competitive and focused; at others, we may be calm and reflective. Much of who we are is not of our own making, but we do have the capacity to stop and consider which version of ourselves it's helpful for us to be and which it's helpful for us to cultivate. Compassion Focused Therapy (CFT) makes a case for and helps us to cultivate our compassionate self.

Compassion for your ordinary self

In this exercise, we focus compassion on your 'ordinary self'. In other words, the part of you that goes about your day-to-day activities and has day-to-day concerns. You may find this a good point to start from as you're less likely to hold strong views or emotions about yourself in such circumstances.

TIP

If your day-to-day life contains times of great stress, start by focusing on the more mundane parts of your day – the times when things are relatively easy or you're simply on autopilot.

Through the eyes of your compassionate self, see yourself as you go about your day – as if you're viewing a video of yourself. Watch as you wake up, brush your teeth, have a wash, get dressed and go about your other daily activities.

Notice how your ordinary self is troubled by all manner of things. Maybe it's worried about your appearance, how you're viewed by others, deadlines, money and your emotional state.

From the perspective of your compassionate self, extend compassionate feelings to your ordinary self, and a heart-felt desire for your ordinary self to be happy, well and free of suffering.

Consider what your compassionate self may say to your ordinary self. You can use or adapt the following phrases and add your name after each phrase as well as this helps to enhance the personal experience.

> May you be well . . .
>
> May you be happy . . .
>
> May you be free of suffering . . .

Tone of voice is incredibly important. For example, you can say one word to another person, such as 'smile', in a manner that conveys warmth, anger or even a sinister motive – and all these interpretations depend on your tone of voice. As such, consider how your compassionate self sounds. It's likely that a soft, warm and slow tone of voice will help to convey your compassionate mind. Saying phrases on the out-breath can also help slow your voice down, and this helps to create a stabilising rhythm.

Study your reflection in a mirror, through the eyes of your compassionate self. Experience a warm connection with yourself, understanding the difficulties that everyday life brings for you. Consider yourself as a whole, rather than considering a specific aspect of your life in this moment.

Once again, it may help to say the same compassionate phrases that you used in the preceding exercise. Say each phrase on your out-breath, using your name.

If you find using a mirror difficult, use a different reflective surface. Alternatively, you may find it easier to start with a photo or mental image of yourself.

Compassionate phrases can be said out loud or in your head. Each phrase can be adapted to suit your needs and situation; for example, you may choose to say 'Things are difficult for you right now, I will help you stay strong' or 'I want you to be happy'. Compassionate statements are as much about what you say as how you say it. Find something that works for you.

If you become self-critical, appreciate that you've just become aware of your own undermining. Return your attention to 'your ordinary self' and continue with the exercise. (In the exercise in the next section I focus on compassion for your self-critic, and this can help you relate to your self-critic.)

Compassion for your self-critic

It may be tempting to argue with your self-critic as it calls you names and angrily tells you about all the things you could or should have done. But it will just turn into a row, and your threat system will be further activated as you meet fire with fire (refer to Chapter 4 to discover more about your threat system).

From the perspective of our compassionate mind we realise that often, behind the self-critic's anger and negativity, lies fear and concern. We may, for example, fear messing up, being rejected and feeling isolated. As such, a compassionate response is called for.

In this exercise, we focus your compassionate self on your self-critic.

1. **Bring to mind a time when you were mildly self-critical.** Maybe you were late, lost your keys, made a mistake or forgot an important event.

2. **See the situation in your mind's eye.** If you could see your self-critic, what would it look like? Maybe it would have a wagging finger, an angry face or a disappointed expression (refer to Chapter 1 to familiarise yourself with your self-critic). Watch for a minute or so as you're undermined or bullied by your self-critic.

3. **Connecting with your compassionate self, consider what lies behind your self-critic's negativity and harsh comments. Extend compassionate feelings towards your self-critic.** Consider what your compassionate self may say to it and in what tone of voice it may say it.

Compassionate exercises such as those described in this chapter can reveal personal blocks (refer to Chapters 6 and 7 for more information on these blocks). When you become aware of one, gently consider why this may be difficult for you and explore ways to overcome it.

Directing your compassionate self to your self-critic means that you step out of your negative way of relating to yourself (sometimes called a negative self-to-self relationship or self-interaction). Your compassionate self helps you see that your critic is worried about something and is just responding in the only way it knows – through aggression. Your compassionate self helps you see the situation for what it is, softens your emotional experience and helps you think creatively and courageously about what may be helpful for you.

Compassion for your self-critic is also a form of compassion for others (refer to Chapter 10).

Compassion for your perceived flaws

You may not like your anxious, angry or sad self (see Chapter 17 for more information about your different emotions). Equally, you may not like something about the way you look or an aspect of your personality.

Viewing perceived flaws with compassion, as opposed to criticism, is what people tend to recommend to others. We can see the damage that shame and self-criticism can cause. But it's often a totally different matter when the focus is on ourselves. As such, we need to practice treating ourselves, and our perceived flaws, with the same kindness we would show others.

I use the term 'perceived flaws' because everything is a matter of perception. 'Flaws' mean that we're human: none of us are perfect, and I for one say thank goodness that's the case.

In this exercise, you use your compassionate self to connect with an aspect of yourself that you struggle with. Start by focusing on something that is relatively easy – something that doesn't bring with it strong emotions. As you develop your confidence with exercising self-compassion, you can work on the aspects of yourself that you have more difficulty with.

1. **Bring to mind something you struggle with.** Maybe your anxious, angry or upset self, an aspect of your appearance, or another personal characteristic.

2. **Through the eyes of your compassionate self, allow that part of you to appear in your mind's eye.** If an image doesn't appear, simply focus on your compassionate self's feelings towards the part of you that you chose in Step 1.

3. **Through your compassionate self, experience a sense of connection with the part of you that you struggle with.** Experience a sensitivity to your own distress and the strength and courage required to face, accept and overcome your difficulties.

4. **Imagine what your compassionate self would say if it were to speak about or to this other aspect of you. What would your compassionate self's tone of voice sound like?**

   Use or adapt the following phrases, perhaps adding your name after each phrase if this feels comfortable to you:

   May you be well . . .

   May you be happy . . .

   May you be free of suffering . . .

Some additional phrases may help you to deal with particular difficulties. If you're focusing on your anxious self, it may help to add phrases such as 'May you be free of agitation' and 'May you find a sense of calm'; for your angry self, you may say 'May you be free of tension and frustration' and 'May your voice and concerns be heard'; and for your sad or upset self you may say 'May you find comfort and contentment' and 'May you feel the warm connection of others'.

By developing compassion for our perceived flaws, our mind becomes a much calmer and more supportive place to inhabit. For some aspects of ourselves, we may develop a sense of compassionate acceptance; for others, we may develop the strength and courage to make helpful changes.

Compassion for yourself when you experience a sense of shame

Shame is a powerful feeling. It can lead to low mood, anxiety, anger and isolation. The first step in overcoming shame is often to develop self-compassion for the thing that we feel shame about. We can then begin to connect or reconnect with others.

Try this exercise:

1. **Bring your mind to something you feel a degree of shame about, something that it is relatively easy for you to think about.** It may be something that has happened, an aspect of your appearance or an aspect of how your body or mind works.

2. **From the perspective of your compassionate self, create a mental image of what you feel shame about. If this is something that has happened to you, recall the memory. Alternatively, imagine the aspect of yourself that you experience shame about.** Allow compassionate feelings to emerge and flow towards the part of you that you're focusing on.

3. **Consider what your compassionate self would say to this younger or other aspect of you, and how it would say it.** Maybe it would begin by acknowledging that this part of you is in pain and offer some reassurance. You can then use the specific phrases described in the preceding exercise to focus your compassion.

   In relation to those things we feel shame about, additional helpful phrases, said with warmth and kindness, may include 'You're not the only person to have ever felt like this', 'You're not the only person to have ever experienced this' and 'May you develop the strength and courage to reconnect with others'.

TIP

As you develop your compassionate self (refer to Chapter 10 for more on this) and understand yourself more, it's likely that your experiences of shame and self-criticism will decrease. As this happens, you may choose to move on to more difficult memories and experiences.

TIP

Shame-based memories can trigger the threat system (refer to Chapter 4 for more on your threat system). This trigger can result in intense anger, anxiety and fear. Shame-based memories can also trigger a 'shut-down' response where you experience an absence of feeling, as though a switch has been flipped.

If this is the case, or you feel stuck, it may help to speak to your GP or to seek a professional therapist who may be able to offer advice or work with you to overcome such difficulties.

Compassion for a younger you

It's much easier to be compassionate towards babies, toddlers and young children than adults. While we often perceive the former as free from blame, placing responsibility for their behaviour at the door of their parents or society, or on their developing brain, the same isn't true for how we perceive adults.

In exactly the same way, it can be easier to have and develop compassion for a younger version of ourselves.

This exercise therefore gently builds your self-compassion by focusing your compassionate self firstly on the younger you. It can illuminate points in our lives when self-criticism took hold, as well as the events associated with this. Such insights and potential blocks may benefit from further exploration.

1. **Bring to mind an image of yourself as a new-born.** Experience compassion flowing from your compassionate self to you as a baby.

2. **Move ahead in time by a year or so. Extend your compassion to the slightly older version of you.**

3. **Move yourself through each year of your life – right up to the present day. At each age, extend your compassion to yourself.**

4. **As you move through each year, consider using the phrases provided in the exercise in the earlier section, 'Compassion for your perceived flaws', to imagine what your compassionate self may say to the younger you. Alternatively, you may have other thoughts about what your compassionate self may say to the younger you that may have been beneficial at that age.** Consider the tone of voice that your compassionate self would use.

In Chapter 14, you use writing to further develop your compassionate mind. However, it may be beneficial for you to put pen to paper (or finger to touch-screen!) at points during or after this exercise and make note of what your compassionate self may say to the younger versions of you.

TIP

It may help to focus on specific events or experiences. Photos may also help you connect with the younger you.

Most people have no problem being compassionate towards themselves as a baby but find it trickier as they move towards specific points in their lives and particular ages. If you find this to be the case, gently consider the reasons for this. Is there something you're blaming yourself for or telling yourself off about?

In contrast, others find that focusing compassion on a younger version of themselves can be emotional due to the difficulties on the road ahead for them as a child. This can trigger a sense of grief and strong emotions. If you find this to be the case, gently proceed at a pace comfortable for you and use your soothing rhythm breathing, mindfulness and other practices to assist you.

REMEMBER Focusing our compassionate self on different points in our lives can broaden and enrich our experience of self-compassion. It can gently make us aware of our personal blocks to self-compassion and provide an opportunity to address and overcome these.

SELF-COMPASSION VERSUS SELF-ESTEEM

Self-esteem is generally defined as an evaluation of our worth. If we evaluate ourselves positively, we feel positive. If we evaluate ourselves negatively, we feel negative. Such evaluations are often based on comparing ourselves favourably or less favourably to others.

In recent decades, improving self-esteem has become a popular focus. Thousands of initiatives, self-help guides and magazine articles focus on how to improve self-esteem for greater wellbeing and happiness.

But what happens when other people *are* more attractive, fitter, stronger, brighter or more socially skilled than us? What if our physical or mental health, our environment, or our age mean that we can't do things? What happens when we mess up, things don't go to plan or we experience set-backs? You guessed it – our self-esteem takes a nose-dive, negative thoughts multiply and our mood drops.

One solution is to criticise and push ourselves to get things right, make improvements and achieve our goals. But, once again, what happens when we can't achieve our goals? This is where self-compassion can help. It allows us to step out of such a competitive and stressful way of living our lives. It doesn't mean that we're apathetic; instead, it motivates us to work towards helpful goals and helps us to stop constantly drawing comparisons between ourselves and other people – judging some to be 'worse than us' and others to be 'better'. By relating to ourselves in a supportive and encouraging manner, whether things are going well or not, we're actually more likely to achieve our goals and be happier in the process.

Research suggests that self-compassion results in a calmer mind, better relationships, less anxiety and low mood, and a steadier feeling of self-worth than self-esteem.

Reviewing Your Life Story with Self-Compassion

In Chapter 5 you develop your *life story* – a diagram that places you in the context of your life. This diagram brings together the factors that shaped and continue to shape you, your fears and concerns, and your ways of coping and their drawbacks. In this section, we return to this diagram (if you haven't already produced your life story diagram, you may want to turn back to Chapter 5 first).

Evoke your compassionate mind and reflect on your life story through the eyes of your compassionate self. Slowly review each section, allowing compassion for the things that have shaped you, the concerns you have and so on.

From this perspective, what may it be helpful to say? Are there additional conclusions that you can draw to further develop your life story? It may help to jot some of these down and expand on the work you did in Chapter 5.

From the perspective of your compassionate self, experience a sensitivity to your own distress and the difficulties outlined in the diagram. Experience your compassionate self's motivation to alleviate such difficulties and also prevent difficulties in the future.

Stay with this experience for a while in order to enhance your emotional connection with your life story and allow any realisations you have to 'sink in'.

REMEMBER

Developing your compassionate mind and compassionate self doesn't mean that you'll transform into someone who never gets angry, anxious or upset. However, it will help you develop a more supportive way of relating to the parts of you that you struggle with and you want to change.

As you begin to view your fears and concerns, coping strategies, and their unintended consequences in the context of your experiences and biology, you gradually replace shame and self-criticism with warmth and compassion. With an inner sense of support, you're better able to make helpful choices and commit yourself to the changes you need to make.

4

Compassionate Practices

IN THIS PART . . .

Focus on the cultivation of compassionate thoughts.

Investigate the power of writing to help you develop your compassionate mind and compassionate self.

Take compassionate action.

Discover compassionate ways to express yourself.

Grapple with the different parts of yourself using chair work.

Consider how to continue your compassionate journey.

Chapter 13

Cultivating Compassionate Thoughts

O ur minds are the playground for an array of thoughts and images that bombard us on a day-to-day, hour-by-hour basis. We think about one thing, and then another, and get interrupted by yet another. Even when we're asleep we can be running through a never-ending stream of past events and future possibilities. It's as though the brain is running a continuous programme or 24-hour commentary.

We can also think in more complex ways: we can intentionally think about the past and look ahead to the future. We can think about ourselves, what others are thinking and even think about thoughts. These amazing capabilities have been hugely important for our survival because, among other things, they allow us to reflect on events, plan for the future and avoid danger.

Both the content of our thoughts and their emotional tone have a big impact on how we feel. Our thoughts may be critical and harsh or wise and supportive.

In this chapter we look at compassionate thinking – what it is, how it sounds in your head and how you can use it to develop your compassionate mind and ultimately your compassionate self. We also consider the challenge of changing our thinking – which is easier said than done! Finally, I take you through six steps that help to guide you towards thinking more compassionately in your everyday life.

Introducing Compassionate Thinking

Our brains are threat-focused (refer to Chapter 4 for more on this), which means that our thoughts are more likely to focus on negative or threatening things (be they in the past, present or future). This tendency to focus on the negative can be strengthened by negative experiences. As our brains attempt to work out what has happened and how to respond, we can easily get caught in seemingly never-ending loops of worry and rumination. This can cause anxiety and lower our mood.

THE INFLUENCE OF THE CULTURE WE'RE BORN INTO

Your thoughts can be influenced in many subtle ways. This relates to the culture you're born into and the views that others hold within it. For example, while growing up in the UK I was exposed to, experienced and therefore inherited a way of thinking about others and myself. As a child, I developed views about democracies versus dictatorships, women and men, religion, cultures, sexuality, and many other topics. This is understandable given my experiences and the impact my environment had on me. Pausing for a moment, imagine if I'd been born 200 years earlier, in the very same town. I may have held very different views than I do now. I may have condoned or been party to certain behaviours that I would now view as unacceptable and abhorrent. I may have felt anger, anxiety or disgust towards certain groups and gone along with the idea that women shouldn't vote.

Our views and thoughts are developed by exposure to the dominant belief systems of the time or culture into which we're born. The consistency between our views, and those around us, gives us a sense of connectedness and belonging. The flip side of this is that it can also give rise to the negative thoughts and views of those who have differing views to us.

An awareness of the lottery of our birth is central to Compassion Focused Therapy (CFT). It suggests that it's helpful for us to question why we hold the views we have, be they about ourselves or others, and to consider who such thoughts serve and whether alternatives may be more helpful to ourselves, others and society.

The good news is that we can choose to use our brain's mindful and compassionate capacities to break these difficult cycles. By observing, reflecting, reasoning and re-evaluating the thoughts we have, we can then decide what may be helpful to us. *Compassionate thinking* allows us to stand back and use our brains' amazing mindful and compassionate capacities, instead of simply utilising only our more reactive and primitive ones – capacities that can get us into trouble or make us less likely to achieve our goals, such as doing something out of spite or anger or avoiding situations we feel anxious about. Your *compassionate thoughts* have a warm emotional tone (see the next section, 'Voicing Our Emotions') and come from a perspective of true care for the wellbeing of ourselves and others.

REMEMBER

Using our compassionate mind, we can broaden our attention and warmly consider the factors that have influenced us in the past and things that influence us on a moment-to-moment basis. Compassionate thinking can significantly change how we feel and, in turn, this can influence what we do.

Voicing Our Emotions

Paul Gilbert, the founder of CFT, observed that many people suffering with low mood were able to generate supportive statements and 'alternative thoughts' but that this had no positive impact on them. Wanting to understand this, he realised that the *way* someone spoke to themselves could turn a supporting and validating statement or thought into something that's experienced as undermining. The tone of our internal voice comes hand-in-hand with a matching set of emotions, physical sensations and a motivation to behave in a certain way.

CFT emphasises the need to explore not only what we're thinking, but also the emotional tone in which we're thinking it. The following exercise helps to illustrate this.

Consider this statement:

'Everyone deserves to be happy.'

Take a few calming breaths and say this statement to yourself, in your head, in a warm and supportive way. You don't need to say this aloud – just think it. Allow this experience to sink in.

Now, move around your room for a minute or so, or maybe have a stretch. Having had a little break, say exactly the same statement to yourself – but this time change your internal tone of voice to one of sadness or despair. Repeat the statement to yourself. Experience how this feels.

Once again, move around or enjoy a stretch. Having had a little break, say the same statement to yourself again – but this time change your internal tone of voice to one of anger or frustration. Repeat the statement once more. Experience how this feels.

What did you notice? Did you experience the thought in different ways? Did you notice any other changes? Maybe a warm expression on your face on one occasion and a furrowed brow and a tense expression on another? You may have also felt differences in your body.

Interesting, isn't it? You say the same statement but have a very different experience.

The way we speak to ourselves, not just the words that we say, is incredibly important.

REMEMBER

Changing How We Think

Ever had a 'the penny's dropped!' moment, or an epiphany? Such experiences can be very powerful and can rapidly change the way we think about things. Usually when this happens we sit for a while in stunned silence – allowing the revelation to sink in. It's as if a wave of change occurs across a whole range of areas. Wouldn't it be great if everything was this simple? Unfortunately, changing the way we think is usually a much slower process.

Three related factors affect the speed at which we can change our thinking:

>> **Rules:** Our brains create rules that can't be easily broken.

>> **Habits:** Our brains create strong loops, or *habits*, that we can't simply rewrite in an instant.

>> **Time:** Our brains take time to learn something new.

If we understand these three things, it can prevent us from giving ourselves a hard time when change is slow – as is normal. In the following sections, we look at each of these factors in turn.

REMEMBER

Change can be achieved, but it takes time. However, once your changes become habit, and your brain gets used to working in new ways, it will begin to create new rules – rules for happier, more compassionate living!

Creating rules for living

To help us navigate the complex world we live in, our brain has developed a way of drawing snap conclusions and making instantaneous predictions – creating a set of rules or beliefs that applies to a whole range of domains, including our physical surroundings, other people and ourselves. We call this our *automatic pilot* mode and it allows us to focus our energy on other things.

REMEMBER

These automatic rules for living influence how we think, feel and behave. They often develop as a consequence of information being 'programmed' into us.

Check out the following exercise for an example of how your brain may become programmed with information that can develop into a potential automatic rule for living.

Imagine that you grew up with only positive experiences of dogs and were never given any messages to the contrary. Physically, how might you feel when a dog runs towards you? What are you likely to do? What kind of thoughts are you likely to have about dogs? What rules or beliefs in relation to dogs may you have?

Now imagine that you observed one of your parents behaving anxiously around dogs. You were warned that they could be dangerous. Maybe you were knocked over by one or snapped at as a child. Physically, how might you feel when a dog runs towards you? What kind of thoughts are you likely to have about dogs? What rules or beliefs in relation to dogs may you have?

Finally, how may your experience of dogs affect your attention when you're out walking in an open space? If you're aware of a dog who is off the lead, how much would it grab your attention, how would it affect you physically and what kinds of thoughts would occupy your mind? You may find that the thoughts you have match the rules or beliefs that you hold.

The following example introduces Stacey, a young girl who likes to sing.

EXAMPLE

When Stacey was younger she liked singing, but was constantly told to be quiet by her parents. 'Sounds like a cats' chorus' her dad would say. As a consequence, Stacey developed the rule or belief that she simply couldn't sing.

One day, while at school, Stacey's class was asked to sing as a group while the music teacher wandered around and tuned in to each pupil in turn. She recalled the teacher stopping in front of her for a considerable amount of time and then beckoning her colleague over. They stood for what seemed like ages, listening to her intently. When they walked away, Stacey saw them exchanging smiles.

Consider the following questions in relation to Stacey's story:

>> What is Stacey likely to take away from this experience?

>> How might this affect her singing?

>> How might this influence her rule or belief about her singing?

Stacey may have decided that the behaviour of her teacher and the colleague provides further evidence that she can't sing. Her singing voice may be affected by anxiety; however, her teacher may have stopped because she realised that Stacey had a good voice, and beckoned her colleague over to hear her sing.

Both of these exercises demonstrate that the beliefs we form can affect our subsequent experiences and fix us in a seemingly never-ending pattern of reinforcement. This reinforcement can be both positive and negative and lead to both positive and negative beliefs and assumptions.

Key to wellbeing is the ability to question the assumptions and rules we have in order to gain a clear and balanced perspective. So, it isn't necessarily advantageous for us to think that everyone should love our singing voice, or that all dogs are friendly, but it certainly is problematic if we think that we have a horrible singing voice that shouldn't be heard, or that all dogs are dangerous!

REMEMBER

Information is filtered by the rules we establish for ourselves, others and our environment. Our thoughts reflect this. Changing these patterns takes time and effort.

Strengthening learning, for good or ill

They say that practice makes perfect – but, of course, we can't all be perfect at everything. However, practice and reinforcement can strengthen our learning. But what if we have learnt something that is unhelpful? In this case, practice creates habits that are difficult to break.

In the preceding section, we saw that we create automatic rules for living by rein-forcement of certain information or behaviour. In this section, we consider the effect our subsequent behaviour has on us. In other words, even when our experi-ences have changed (maybe we meet nice dogs, or have a partner who likes dogs or even our singing), our habitual responses and feelings remain difficult to change. The nearby sidebar 'Old habits die hard' provides an illustration of this.

REMEMBER

If you've been thinking in a negative way for a long time, you become very good at it! You may have an amazing capacity to think in this way again and again. But when we become aware of the things we're saying to ourselves, and the negative impact that this can have, we begin to have a choice. Do we continue to listen to the critical thoughts, or do we consider their usefulness and develop thoughts that will be more helpful to us?

OLD HABITS DIE HARD

For four years, in order to gain access to my office, I had to go to the secretary's room and pick up a key from a little box that was located above the filing cabinets. I did this for five days a week, 46 weeks of each year.

When the box was moved to a different location, intellectually I 'knew' it had moved. If someone asked me how much I believed it was in its new location, I would've said 100 per cent. But, on almost a daily basis, where did I go when I went to get my key? Yes, you guessed it – I walked straight up to the filing cabinets, time and time again. Eventually, I got the hang of it – just before I left the department!

Although this example relates to my behaviour, the same thing can happen with our thinking. When I consciously began to address my own shame and self-criticism, I was 34. Years later, I was a little frustrated with myself because I still had quite a long way to go (I was self-critical of still being self-critical!).

I therefore sat and worked out how long I'd been thinking in a self-critical way versus the time I'd spent working on a more compassionate version of me.

I discovered I'd trained my brain, on and off, for about 23 years. I'd been working to enhance my compassionate self for almost half this time. Was it any wonder that I still fell into the trap of self-criticism?

So habits, be they my walk to the old key cabinet or the way I relate to myself, are hard to change. Awareness brings choice. Is it helpful for me to keep walking to the location of the old key cabinet? The answer is clear: absolutely not. But equally, is it helpful to me to continue relating to myself with negativity? A resounding and compassionate no! And yes, like so many other people, I'm still a 'work in progress'!

Timing is everything

If we go to the gym once, we're unlikely to gain much long-term benefit; however, if we make a commitment to regular exercise, we experience the benefit of increased fitness.

Thankfully, with time, we can train ourselves in all sorts of new skills, new routines and new ways of thinking. CFT therapists often refer to the exercises associated with CFT as compassionate mind training. This is also referred to as 'physiotherapy for the brain' or 'brain training', because we strengthen the links and circuits in our brain with repeated practice.

REMEMBER

Changing what goes on in our minds can be like turning around a huge cruise liner! It takes time. It also takes sustained effort – but this investment of time and energy is worthwhile. Negative thoughts increase our risk of experiencing mental health issues. They also maintain difficulties, such as anxiety and depression. In contrast, compassionate thinking is associated with, among other things, improved personal wellbeing and relationships. The choice is within your grasp.

Taking Six Steps towards Compassionate Thinking

It's helpful to break things down into manageable chunks, so here I share six steps you can take towards compassionate thinking. Once you're well practiced with each step, you may choose to employ one or two right up to all of them as part of your everyday life – they begin to become second nature!

REMEMBER

Our compassionate mind and compassionate self is something we need to enhance and maintain on a regular basis. As such, it's helpful to engage in the exercises in each step regularly. With time, you may begin to work through the steps in your head, but it can help to regularly return to the questions, make notes and re-read these.

TIP

We start by looking at everyday situations, and the thoughts that occupy your mind in relation to them. As you develop your confidence with these six steps, you can use them to review experiences from much earlier in your life that were difficult, or to help consider rules and beliefs that you hold about yourself, other people, the future and life in general. As you develop your compassionate mind, you'll find that these steps can help while you're *in* situations, not just afterwards.

I use a number of examples to help illustrate how the different steps work.

Step one: Becoming aware of your thoughts

Some people are acutely aware of the thoughts that occupy their minds. Others aren't. We start by considering a recent experience and exploring it in more detail.

1. **Bring to mind a recent occasion on which you felt anxious, disappointed, sad or angry.**

2. **Close your eyes and re-familiarise yourself with the situation for a few moments.**

3. **Consider the following questions.** Write your responses on a sheet of paper (or on a mobile device or computer screen where you can save them) so that you can re-read them later.

   - What were the thoughts that occupied your mind at the time?

   - What are the thoughts that occupy your mind now that you're recalling the experience?

   - Did you draw any conclusions about:

     – Yourself?

     – Other people?

     – The situation?

     – The past?

     – The future?

4. **When you feel you've explored the situation in enough detail, move your attention away from the difficult situation by evoking your compassionate mind.** It may help to adjust your posture as you inhabit your compassionate self. Refer to Chapters 10–12 for ways to do this.

5. **Remind yourself of your wisdom, strength and courage, focusing for a short time on how compassion feels in your mind and body.**

Elaine's story illustrates how a difficult event can trigger a range of thoughts about ourselves, other people, the situation, the past and the future. Becoming aware of how these thoughts can be triggered is the first step towards doing something about them.

EXAMPLE

Elaine had been bullied at school and felt like the 'outsider', even within her friendship group. Keen to leave school as soon as she could, she got an apprenticeship and threw herself into that. Elaine made little, if any, contact with her old school friends over the following 12 months.

While shopping one day, Elaine bumped into one of her old friends and, having heard she had changed jobs, immediately asked how it was going. 'Interested now, are we? Don't tell me you care about anyone but yourself,' her old friend responded, and walked away. Later that evening, Elaine completed the step one exercise to cultivate compassionate thoughts:

What were the thoughts that occupied your mind at the time?

> I don't know what to say.
>
> I look like an idiot.

What are the thoughts that occupy your mind now that you're recalling the experience?

> I'm so selfish and get caught up with so many other things.
>
> I'm a rubbish friend.
>
> Who else may she have told?

Did you draw any conclusions about:

Yourself?

> I'm not a good friend.

Other people?

> Nobody really likes me.

The situation?

> I must have looked shocked and pathetic.

The past?

> My bullies were right, I am pathetic.

The future?

> I'm not going to have any friends.
>
> She'll get other people to side with her.
>
> I won't be able to go back into town or anywhere I could bump into her.

REMEMBER

Of course, during this step you may find that all your thoughts are centred on a particular theme or a particular emotion. However, you may have had competing thoughts and competing emotions. If you have found this to be the case, the following exercise will help you explore this in greater detail.

1. **Bring to mind a recent occasion on which you experienced a mixture of emotions about something.**

2. **Close your eyes and re-familiarise yourself with the situation.**

3. **Consider the following questions.** Write your responses on a sheet of paper (or on a mobile device or computer screen where you can save them) so that you can re-read them later.

   - Was there an anxious part of you and, if so, what was it thinking?

   - Was there a sad or disappointed part of you and, if so, what was it thinking?

   - Was there an angry part of you and, if so, what was it thinking?

   - Were all the thoughts directed towards yourself, or were you also thinking about other people (that you haven't noted elsewhere)? If you had additional thoughts about other people, what were they?

   - Did you have any thoughts about the world in general?

   - Are there any rules that you're applying to yourself, to other people or to the world in general (refer to the earlier section 'Creating rules for living' for more on such rules)? These rules may begin with wording such as 'I am . . .', 'Other people are . . .' or 'Emotions are . . .'.

4. **When you feel you've explored the situation in enough detail, move your attention away from the difficult situation by evoking your compassionate mind.** It may help to adjust your posture as you inhabit your compassionate self. Refer to Chapters 10–12 for ways to do this.

5. **Remind yourself of your wisdom, strength and courage, focusing for a short time on how compassion feels in your mind and body.**

One situation can lead to a range of different thoughts and emotions. These can be associated with different physical sensations and motivate us to do a range of different things. It's helpful for us to realise this because sometimes the most dominant emotion, and our related thoughts, can grab all of our attention while others remain unchecked. We look at this in more detail in the following example, which explores Graham's story. (Chapter 17 explores further how situations can lead us to have many different thoughts, feelings and physiological reactions and considers additional ways it may be helpful to work through these.)

EXAMPLE

Graham worked in a busy office. Decisions were made quickly and much of the office-based communication occurred by email. Having circulated something that he had actioned that morning, he received an email in which his colleague Jack had criticised this action. A whole number of people were copied into it too, which meant the issue was really public.

Graham was aware that he had mixed emotions about the situation, so he decided to consider the thoughts that came with each emotion:

Was there was an anxious part of you and, if so, what was it thinking?

> Other people will think I'm no good at my job.
>
> I won't be able to face people at the next meeting because they'll see I'm wound up.

Was there a sad or disappointed part of you and, if so, what was it thinking?

> I'm crap and I have crap ideas.
>
> I just can't keep on doing this.

Was there an angry part of you and, if so, what was it thinking?

> He just doesn't recognise the input of people and is full of himself.
>
> He wouldn't know a good idea if it slapped him in the face.
>
> I can't believe I did it to myself again – I'm so stupid.

Were all the thoughts directed towards yourself, or were you also thinking about other people (that you haven't noted elsewhere)? If you had additional thoughts about other people, what were they?

> None over and above what I've already written down.

Did you have any thoughts about the world in general?

> What's the point of all of this?
>
> People are cruel and insensitive.

Are there any rules that you're applying to yourself, to other people or to the world in general?

> People should be aware of the feelings of others at all times.
>
> I should have ideas that everyone sees as good all of the time.

Simply becoming aware of our thoughts (whether they're the product of just one emotion or many) and our rules or beliefs can have a positive impact on us. For example, in Graham's case, realising that he'd applied the rule 'I should have ideas that everyone sees as good all of the time' brought a smile to his face and dissolved some of the difficult emotions he was feeling.

TIP

If you found it difficult, in the exercises in this section, to recall a time when you experienced strong emotions, think about a time when you felt a change in your bodily sensations (such as stomach churning or tension in your face). Maybe there are times when you feel a strong craving to eat, smoke or drink. Maybe you can recall a time when you felt the urge to hide or lash out? Use such changes in your bodily sensations or urges as a cue to gently consider what was going on at the time and explore the questions starting from this point.

Step two: Gaining the perspective of your compassionate mind

Your compassionate mind helps you to stand back from situations and consider different perspectives. You can then consider what thoughts are likely to be more beneficial.

REMEMBER

A compassionate viewpoint doesn't involve simply saying 'there there, never mind', 'you're amazing' or 'it's someone else's fault'. Your compassionate mind and its embodiment in your compassionate self provides the strength and courage to see a situation from different perspectives: it supports you to take appropriate levels of responsibility, helps you bear pain and disappointment and provides you with the commitment to address the difficulties you experience.

Try this exercise to explore this concept further.

1. **Bring to mind the difficult situation you explored in step one (refer to the preceding section – maybe it's a time when you felt strong or mixed emotions).**

2. **Evoke your compassionate mind and inhabit your compassionate self, using a strategy that you have previously found helpful.** This may involve adjusting your posture and using an imagery exercise such as those you find in Chapters 10–12.

3. **As your compassionate self, slowly consider the following questions.** Write your responses on a sheet of paper (or on a mobile device or computer screen where you can save them) so that you can re-read them later.

- As I stand back from the situation, is there another way of viewing it?

- Is there any information that runs contrary to the thoughts I was having or the conclusions I drew?

- If I wasn't experiencing strong emotions, would I think any differently about the situation, about myself or about other people?

- If I were looking back a year from now, would I view things in the same way?

- If someone I cared for was thinking in this way, what would I say to them?

- What would someone who cares about me say? (It can be helpful to bring different people to mind and consider what each may say. Alternatively, recall the exercise in Chapter 1 involving the two teachers. Ask yourself: 'What would the compassionate teacher say?')

- Have there been occasions in the past when I've thought this way, but the conclusions I drew proved to be incorrect?

- Am I expecting unrealistic things of the situation, other people or myself?

- What may have been going on for the other people involved? (If there was more than one person in the situation, consider each in turn.)

- If my conclusions are indeed correct (for example, maybe your anxiety did result in you doing a bad presentation and thus receiving negative judgement from others), what would my compassionate self say that would be helpful?

It's important to pay some attention to our anxious, angry and sad selves, but a balanced and considered perspective is often more helpful. This is where your compassionate self can help. Your compassionate self will listen to the different parts of you. It will reassure (where reassurance is needed) and assertively prevent you from acting impulsively. Your compassionate self takes a balanced perspective and can guide you towards thoughts, feelings and behaviours that will be helpful to you and others.

In the preceding step (refer to the section 'Step one: Becoming aware of your thoughts') you met Graham, who was having some difficulties at work. We return to his story as he explores his situation from the perspective of his compassionate self.

EXAMPLE

Having evoked his compassionate mind and moved around, embodying his compassionate self, Graham calmly sat down and engaged in the second step of the process. He asked himself the following questions:

As I stand back from the situation, is there another way of viewing it?

Maybe Jack wasn't being critical of me personally.

Is there any information that runs contrary to the thoughts I was having or the conclusions I drew?

I know that other people think that I'm good at my job; more importantly, they like and support me.

I'll be able to get through the next meeting – I'm just feeling a bit raw. Things will improve.

I keep on trying to improve things, which is a good thing – not everything will take off.

Maybe, as I reflect on things, Jack has a point.

If I wasn't experiencing strong emotions, would I think any differently about the situation, about myself or about other people?

Having re-read his email in the cold light of day it wasn't as bad as I thought.

If I were looking back a year from now, would I view things in the same way?

No – I would just see it as a blip. If it ends up being a turning point for me maybe that will be a good thing.

If someone I cared for was thinking in this way, what would I say to them?

I would say 'I can understand why you're upset – I would be upset. I would be anxious and furious too.'

'It's awful to feel criticised – especially in front of other people.'

What would someone who cares about me say?

Clare would give me a hug and say, 'Sod them!'

James would have a rant and tell me about similar situations.

A compassionate teacher or coach would support me in facing Jack and give me the strength to have a conversation with him.

Have there been occasions in the past when I have thought this way, but the conclusions I drew proved to be incorrect?

I have got people wrong before – read things in a negative way – and things have blown over.

Am I expecting unrealistic things of the situation, other people or myself?

> Maybe I'm being unrealistic. In my work life I will disagree with people at times; I'm going to have ideas that other people don't agree with and people, being people, will at times not be aware of others' feelings.

What may have been going on for the other people involved?

> I think Jack was potentially busy and responded quickly.

> In actual fact I know that some of the others have been in my situation before so they may be aware of how I might be feeling.

> I know Jack feels a lot of pressure at the moment – it must be difficult for him.

If my conclusions are indeed correct, what would my compassionate self say that would be helpful?

> I can get through this but it's understandable that I'm upset at the moment.

> The fact that I have ideas and share them is a good thing – I'm trying to improve things.

> It's helpful for me to see this as a knock and something I can learn from.

From the perspective of his compassionate self, Graham was able to stand back and consider a more helpful way of viewing things. This didn't mean that he undermined his initial responses, harshly told himself he was overacting or made excuses for Jack (who could be difficult at times). Instead, Graham's efforts during the exercise helped him to calmly return to his work, recognise his qualities and interact with Jack in a more productive manner.

REMEMBER

You don't have to kid yourself into new ways of thinking; rather, you take time to draw conclusions that are considered and compassionate.

Step three: Getting deeper into your compassionate mind

Steps one and two help us to review situations and consider alternative ways of viewing them. It's also helpful to bring our attention to the aspects of ourselves and our environment that can cause us problems (refer to Chapters 3–5 for more information on the challenges you face, the three circles and the experiences that have shaped you, respectively). Bringing our attention to such things allows us to be more compassionate to ourselves and others. Step three takes you through this process.

Returning to the situation you wrote about in steps one and two, consider the following questions. Write your responses on a sheet of paper (or on a mobile device or computer screen where you can save them) so that you can re-read them later.

TIP

» Are there additional things I can bring my attention to that may help?

Consider your 'tricky' brain, your biology and how previous experiences have shaped you (refer to Chapter 3 for more on why your brain is so tricky!). Connect with a sense of common humanity as you recognise that others struggle too. Recognise that life can be hard and sometimes people do things that hurt us. Sometimes we don't act in the way we'd hope.

TIP

» If the situation involved other people, are there additional ways I can sensitively take into account other people's perspectives?

Consider other people's tricky brains, their biology and how previous experiences have potentially shaped them. Connect with a sense of common humanity and the fact that they struggle too. Recognise that life can be hard and sometimes people do things that hurt us. Sometimes other people don't act in the way we'd hope.

The influence of your biology and experiences can enhance your compassionate mind and compassionate self as you come to connect with a deep sense of common humanity.

REMEMBER

Being compassionate towards others doesn't involve 'letting them off the hook' or explaining away their behaviour. It involves seeing people as human beings, shaped by their biology and experiences, who are simply trying to get by. Head to Chapter 6 for more on the myths associated with compassion.

We now return to Graham, who engaged with step three in order to connect further with his compassionate mind and compassionate self.

EXAMPLE

As he engaged with the questions in step three (refer to the preceding exercise), Graham wrote:

Are there additional things I can bring my attention to that may help?

I have a tricky brain and this has been affected by many of the experiences I had when younger. This is a difficult situation. My tricky brain is looking to the negative and jumping to conclusions – because that's what it's designed to do. In addition to this, my reactions are related to some of the experiences I've had. Because I was bullied at school and on the receiving end of some very unkind words, it makes sense that I'm often quick to assume that people are getting at me and don't like me.

Many other people will have had similar experiences and will also struggle. It's helpful for me to stand back and not just look at this situation but also look at it in the context of my life and biology.

If the situation involved other people, are there additional ways I can sensitively take into account other people's perspectives?

Jack has a tricky brain too, as we all do. I'm sure he doesn't intentionally want to undermine or upset me. Biology and life experiences impact on how he behaves. At the moment I'm unsure what's going on in his head, but I'm hurt by it. It would be helpful for me not to just ignore it, undermine myself or label him but to find a helpful way through this – for everyone's benefit.

Turn to Chapter 3 for more on the nature of your tricky brain.

REMEMBER

Writing your thoughts down can help to focus the mind. A compassionate perspective can also prevent emotions such as anxiety, anger and hopelessness running the show.

TIP

Writing compassionate thoughts and statements on postcards or sticky notes and carrying them with you or placing them strategically around your house can be helpful. Other people may have statements printed on poster-boards or framed.

Step four: Creating extra sticking power

In this book, I emphasise the importance of truly 'connecting' with your compassionate mind and compassionate self and the experiences it creates. This can turn an intellectual exercise into a helpful, longer-lasting emotional experience.

This step towards compassionate thinking gives your new thoughts and views more sticking power or Velcro! In other words, the exercise allows you to be more reassured by your thoughts and to connect with them further.

The exercise for this step asks you to compassionately review the answers to the questions that you wrote down in steps one, two and three. This will help you move from an intellectual to a more lasting emotional understanding.

Evoke your compassionate mind, and embody your compassionate self. Slowly read through the things you wrote down in in the preceding sections: in the exercises for steps one, two and three. 'Stay with' the experiences this evokes, maybe for 10 seconds or longer. These may include emotions, images and physical sensations.

This exercise helps create longer-lasting and more powerful realisations that not only change how you think but, more importantly, how you feel.

This exercise is helpful to return to. You can make it the focus of your regular practice to develop your compassionate mind and compassionate self – holding compassionate thoughts in your mind and experiencing them.

Thoughts are experiences that our mind brings into our awareness. Thoughts are not who we are, they're just part of us. At times it's helpful just to let them be; at other times, it's helpful to look at them in more detail and consider if they're helpful or even true.

Step five: Capitalising on your motivation

Although this chapter focuses on generating and enhancing your compassionate thinking, you may find that as you do so, you feel motivated in a slightly different way and towards certain different behaviours. You may feel more motivated to face a difficult situation or talk things through with someone.

The following exercise explores this motivation in more detail.

Having completed steps one through four, evoke your compassionate mind, embodying your compassionate self once more. In light of the compassionate thoughts you generated during the preceding steps, now consider what you feel motivated to do. Commit these thoughts to paper (or write them on a mobile device or computer screen where you can save them) so that you can re-read them later. Write in a way that conveys emotion, rather than simply writing a list of things to do.

It may help to consider Graham's example below for a few ideas.

Engaging in step five, Graham wrote:

> It's helpful to be compassionate to myself regarding this situation. When I'm in a stronger and calmer frame of mind, I'll attempt to speak with Jack. The conversation won't be driven by anger or hurt. I'll conduct it in a way that acknowledges his situation and his feelings, as well as my own. I'll calmly ask to discuss the situation in an open and curious way. I can prepare by using the material covered here as a basis for a letter to myself.

Graham may also have found some useful advice on how best to speak to Jack in Chapter 16 – as may you!

To enhance the believability of and sense of connectedness with your compassionate thoughts, it can be helpful to make them the focus of a compassionate writing exercise. Committing your thoughts to writing can also be an extremely helpful way to review and re-evaluate your thoughts. By using your compassionate mind and embodying your compassionate self, you can generate helpful balanced thoughts, feelings and behaviours that you can make note of. Chapter 14 focuses on the use of writing within CFT. It may give you some helpful tips and ideas.

Step six: Reviewing your progress

After you've worked through the exercises in steps one to five, it can be helpful to review your progress, looking for any blocks that may interfere with the changes you hope to make.

The next exercise will take you through this process.

Evoke your compassionate mind, embodying your compassionate self and, in relation to the answers you've written down for the exercises in each of the preceding steps, slowly consider the following questions:

>> When I read the things I've written (whether silently or out loud), is my tone of voice warm, soothing and ultimately helpful?

>> When I read through the things I've written, can I evoke a sense of emotional warmth?

>> When I read through the things I've written, do I discover any personal blocks, such as thoughts that I'm kidding myself, anxiety that thinking in this way may cause me problems, or residual feelings of anger that get in the way?

TIP

If you're aware of blocks, warmly hold them in mind and consider their discovery as a further opportunity to explore things in more detail. You may use them as the focus of an imagery exercise (refer to Chapter 11), chair work (see Chapter 17) or a compassionate letter (see Chapter 14). It may also help to speak to someone you trust or to consider the blocks within the context of your 'life story' (refer to Chapter 5).

Asking yourself the questions provided in this step is helpful and highlights blocks and obstacles to the development of your compassionate mind and compassionate self. Changes aren't immediate; they occur gradually over time. Reviewing your progress at regular intervals is key to negotiating obstacles and creating long-lasting change.

TIP

You may find that certain themes come up time and time again, and despite your best efforts they don't seem to change. If this is the case, it can be helpful to speak with someone who has your best interests at heart or a professional who may further support you in this process.

Chapter 14

The Power of the Pen: Writing to Strengthen Your Compassionate Mind

We developed writing as a means to communicate with each other. Since then we've also discovered how to use it to communicate with ourselves. While writing can help us remember what we need to get from the shops or the chores we need to do, writing can also help us to:

>> Slow down our thinking, especially when we're bombarded with information, thoughts and images

>> Stand back, reflect and evaluate

>> Consider different choices and which may be most helpful

>> Get things 'out of our head' and on to paper

>> Generate new insights and ideas

>> Work through strong emotions

>> Understand ourselves and other people better

>> Generate inner support

In this chapter, I explain how you can practise compassion through writing, using a variety of different exercises. Writing with care for your wellbeing, sensitivity, sympathy, empathy, tolerance for any distress and non-judgement strengthens your compassionate mind and compassionate self.

Writing can take many forms. You can write in a physical diary or journal, or in a word-processing document on a computer, tablet or phone, or an email. You can write letters, record short statements, summaries and prompts on sticky notes, text messages to yourself or, my personal favourite, the back of your hand.

TIP

Different materials can enhance the emotional connection you have with your writing and can also help when you re-read it. You can use pen or pencil, colours, highlighters, upper or lower case, lined or blank paper, pictures or emoticons. Be creative, try things out and find what benefits you most.

REMEMBER

Some people benefit from writing on a daily basis. Others report that writing with such regularity can reduce the benefits of the work. You may choose to write every few days and supplement this with re-reading what you've already written. The important thing is to find what works for you, and this may be different at different points in your life.

Writing from the perspective of your compassionate mind and compassionate self is often referred to as compassionate letter writing. This is because many compassionate writings are written to the part of you that is distressed and take the form of a letter. However, compassionate writing can take a whole number of different forms.

Preparing for Compassionate Writing

Before you begin the compassionate writing exercises in the next section, bear in mind these ideas and suggestions.

Time is of the essence!

Most of us, when we see a beautiful view, stop for a while, bring our complete attention to the experience and allow it to sink in. We just find ourselves doing it – nobody tells us to. Pausing in this way is associated with stronger and longer-lasting memories. They have a richness to them and combine visual memory, feelings, and maybe sounds and smells too.

Because we want this work (on practising compassion through writing) to have a lasting emotional impact, try to slow things down to allow the experience to sink in. In doing so, you connect with the work in a stronger and more meaningful way and increase the likelihood of lasting change.

Here are some ideas for taking things slowly:

>> Initially try to set aside 30–40 minutes to write that's as free from distractions as possible. Later, you may find that you prefer to set aside a longer or shorter time, depending on the focus of your writing and the time you have available. Choose a time of day or point in the week that's likely to be advantageous. Factors such as your level of alertness, temperature and hunger can all play a part in how much you can engage with compassionate writing.

>> If you find remaining focused on your writing difficult, build in breaks. Get up and move around; engage in your soothing rhythm breathing (refer to Chapter 9) or an imagery exercise (refer to Chapters 10–12). Return to the writing exercise when you feel ready.

>> If you feel you simply don't have the time to put pen to paper for half an hour, try this three-minute compassionate writing exercise. If you find it helpful you can then expand it.

- **Minute 1:** Engage in your soothing rhythm breathing or an imagery exercise (explained in Chapters 9–12).

- **Minute 2:** Write a single statement to yourself from a place of inner support. It may help to use your name. For example, you may write: 'Things are difficult for you at the moment Mary and it's helpful to simply recognise this.'

- **Minute 3:** Evoke a compassionate voice in your mind and imagine hearing the statement being spoken to you warmly. Alternatively, you may choose to say the statement out loud using a warm tone of voice.

>> Build pauses into your writing by using multiple full stops (ellipses). Doing so helps to slow things down. Here's an example of a short but very powerful piece of writing:

'Life can be REALLY difficult . . . stand tall . . . breathe . . . know that you are not on your own with this . . . feel a sense of connection with others . . . feel an alertness in your spine yet relaxation in your body . . . breathe.'

By taking the time to slow down and engage fully in the exercises, we actually speed up the development of our compassionate mind and compassionate self. So by slowing things down, we speed things up!

For your eyes only

Our self-critic, that negative voice in our minds that can undermine our efforts (explored more fully in Chapter 1), can make us think that grammar, spelling and handwriting matter here. They don't! Write using single words, sentences, bullet points or paragraphs. Whatever works for you.

The aim of the exercises in this chapter is to call upon your compassionate mind and utilise its capacity for inner support, wisdom, courage and strength, not to win any literary prizes! No one else is going to read what you've written, so you don't need to worry about what people may think of you.

I or you?

Most people naturally write from a first person singular perspective ('I'). However, it can be interesting to experiment by using 'you' instead and reflecting on the impact that has. For example, if you write, 'I have been struggling today because . . .', consider experimenting and writing, 'You have been struggling today because . . .'.

Similarly, you may naturally write in the present tense or in the past. Work out what's helpful and, at intervals, experiment.

Allow space for emotions

Sorrow, anger and anxiety are just some of the emotions that we all experience. Emotions can indicate that we need to do important work in relation to the situation they're attached to.

When emotions arise while writing, staying with them and exploring them can be helpful. This may involve pausing and simply allowing the emotion to be present for a time.

At other times you can use your compassionate mind to assist you. For example, pausing and engaging in an imagery or soothing rhythm breathing exercise can help you to stay with, work through and come to terms with the emotions you feel during writing. (Refer to Chapters 9–12 for more on these exercises.)

REMEMBER

Developing a balance between creating space for our emotions and using our compassionate mind to reflect on them is a *dynamic process*. In other words, at times it may help to simply experience emotions such as sadness or anger, while at others it may be helpful to try to make sense of their causes and consider alternative ways of viewing the situation. Most importantly, be guided by what you feel you need at the time.

The accumulator effect

The Compassion Focused Therapy (CFT) exercises I describe in this book often enhance and build upon each other. For example, before, during and after compassionate writing you can use soothing rhythm breathing and/or imagery. You can enhance your compassionate thinking and compassionate action plans (Chapters 13 and 15) with a writing exercise, and in the later section 'Making sense of things' you use your 'life story' as a focus (Chapter 5 helps you explore your life story). Hopefully, as Aristotle suggested, 'the whole is greater than the sum of the parts'.

Putting Pen to Paper

In this section, you put pen to paper, with different exercises to help develop your compassionate mind and compassionate self.

Before each exercise, prepare in the following way:

» Find a place, free from distractions, where you can be for 30–40 minutes. If this timescale seems too daunting, start by aiming to work on this exercise for a shorter time (refer to the earlier section 'Time is of the essence!').

» Sit holding a posture that brings with it a sense of strength and alertness in your spine yet relaxation and openness in your body.

» Engage with your soothing rhythm breathing or an imagery exercise to evoke your compassionate mind (refer to Chapters 9–12).

» Soften your facial expression to create a sense of emotional warmth and inhabit your compassionate self.

» If helpful, use a particular compassionate smell, sound or piece of music to assist you in connecting to your compassionate mind (head to Chapter 11 for more on this).

ENHANCING THE POWER OF YOUR WRITTEN WORDS

You can enhance your compassionate writing in the following ways:

- Speak out loud. Using a warm voice, read one of your written exercises into a voice-recording device, perhaps on your phone. Play it back when you're in need of compassion, or at the start or end of the day.

- Read a compassionate statement while looking at yourself warmly in a mirror.

- Read your writing aloud to a photo of yourself, perhaps taken at a key point in your life.

- Write on the back of postcards you can carry with you.

- Scent your paper with a soothing smell that evokes a sense of inner warmth.

REMEMBER

Your compassionate mind and its embodiment in your compassionate self helps you intellectually *and* emotionally connect with the focus of the exercise by helping you to generate new insights and ideas and develop a lasting sense of inner support.

TIP

Begin by focusing on situations in which you find it relatively easy to have a degree of compassion for yourself. Gently build up to writing about more difficult and complex situations associated with stronger or mixed emotions.

In some cases, you may only need a few words to access inner support and compassion, while in others more detail may be required to get to a similar place. Don't worry about how much you write; focus on how it makes you feel.

Dealing with day-to-day difficulties

Ever feel like your head is in a washing machine on a never-ending cycle? To make it worse, the contents aren't getting any cleaner! In such cases it can be helpful to stop the cycle and sort things out. Writing can help with this. It can create a space where you can see things more clearly.

We develop CFT skills by initially focusing our efforts on relatively simple aspects of our lives that aren't associated with strong emotions. As your confidence, compassionate mind and compassionate self builds, you can then consider and write about more complex situations and times of strong emotion.

The following exercise asks you to focus on a time when things have been difficult but not overwhelming for you – a time that has been associated with some difficult emotions, but not particularly strong ones.

1. **Bring to mind a disappointment, mistake or difficulty you've recently experienced.** Allow yourself to become familiar with the emotions, thoughts and physical sensations associated with it.

2. **When ready, use the following prompts to guide you through the writing exercise:**

   ● It is understandable that I found . . . difficult/disappointing/unsettling. This is because . . .

   ● A number of thoughts and images ran through my head such as . . .

   REMEMBER

   Thoughts fall into different categories. They may involve what you think about yourself (for example, 'I'm an idiot' or 'I'm stupid'); what you think about others ('They're stupid', 'They're insensitive' and so on); what you think other people think about you (for example, 'They think I'm stupid' or 'They think I'm pathetic'); and predictions such as 'They don't care about me' or 'They're out to get me'.

   Images may be of other people, the future or yourself. For example, they may involve everyone staring at or looking down on you, a flash-forward into the future that you fear, or an image in which you focus on an aspect of your body, or where you look flushed or panicky.

   ● These thoughts and images came into my mind because I felt . . . (emotion). This is because . . .

   ● Other emotions I felt included. . . . This is because . . .

   ● I was motivated to . . . (behaviour) because . . .

   ● Other things I did/was motivated to do included . . .

   Engage with your compassionate mind again for a few moments, embodying your compassionate self. Head to Part 3 for more on developing your compassionate mind and compassionate self, particularly Chapters 10–12 (for specific exercises). Use the following prompt to develop your letter further:

   With a warm and supportive tone of voice, my compassionate mind would remind me . . .

3. **After you feel you've written enough, evoke your compassionate mind, inhabiting your compassionate self again.** Now slowly read through your letter with warmth and a sense of inner strength. Allow what you've written to sink in.

EXAMPLE

John had recently been promoted to head up a new team at work. He felt a bit out of his depth and undermined by his colleague Paul, who seemed to resent his promotion. Paul's comments and manner chipped away at John's confidence. Here's an example of John's first compassionate writing task:

> It's understandable that I found the recent meeting difficult because on a number of occasions Paul interrupted me and spoke over the top of me.
>
> A number of thoughts and images about myself ran through my head such as 'I'm an idiot; I'm useless'. I also had thoughts about other people such as 'Nobody cares about me or values my contributions'. They just want to make a fool out of me. An image of people laughing at me pops into my mind.
>
> These thoughts and images come into my mind because I have a tendency to give myself a hard time and criticise myself. Sometimes I think people really don't like me. Other times I think my anxiety gets the better of me and kicks me when I'm down. This has been a familiar pattern throughout my life.
>
> I feel anxious because I want to do well at work. I feel angry when I think that Paul undermines me. After the event I feel down on myself because these things keep on happening.
>
> I wanted to tell them to stick their job so they can't make a fool out of me anymore. I also felt trapped because I need the job and the money so I have to stay. That evening I had a lot to drink because I just wanted to forget about it.
>
> With a warm and supportive tone of voice my compassionate self would remind me that change takes time. I'm not going to feel better overnight. It will also take time for others to change how they are towards me. It would be helpful not to give myself such a hard time. Instead, it's helpful to access some inner support for myself. It's helpful for me to develop my compassionate mind and compassionate self to help me see things more clearly, to gain courage, strength and wisdom.

By writing down a range of difficult thoughts, John was able to make sense of the strong emotions he felt. Writing from the perspective of his compassionate self, John was then able to take a kinder and more realistic perspective of himself, other people and the situation.

Making sense of things

Chapter 5 helps you make sense of the things that have shaped you, such as your experiences, biology and culture. It also helps you to take account of the fears and concerns you hold, including how you cope and the problems that sometimes arise. In this exercise, you use writing to emotionally deepen this understanding.

1. **Familiarise yourself with your 'life story' that you developed in Chapter 5 for a few minutes (if you haven't developed your life story yet, you may want to turn to Chapter 5 first).**

2. **When you're ready to start writing, use the following prompts to guide you:**

- All humans have difficulties to contend with. This is because . . .

- A whole range of experiences and influences have impacted on me. These include . . .

  Include both past experiences, current circumstances and the impact your wider community and society have on you. It may help to write about your tricky brain (refer to Chapter 3 for more on this) and how your tricky brain relates to the difficulties you have.

- It's understandable that I've developed concerns and fears about . . .

  Include things you worry other people are thinking about you and also things you may be thinking about yourself.

- I have coped by . . .

- But there have been unintended consequences and drawbacks, such as . . .

- This is not my fault. I can make some changes and I can use my compassionate mind to guide me. With a warm tone of voice, my compassionate self would remind me that . . .

TIP

Avoid using words such as *should* and *must*. Keep your words encouraging and nurturing.

3. **When you feel you've written enough, re-engage with one of the exercises you find helpful. This may be a mindfulness exercise, your soothing rhythm breathing or an imagery exercise (refer to Chapters 9–12). When you're ready, slowly read through your letter while feeling warm and strong, and allow the words to sink in.**

EXAMPLE

Stephanie often felt an outsider and this meant that she struggled with her mood. She was highly self–critical and worried that life would always be this way. To help her make sense of things, Stephanie wrote:

All human beings have difficulties to contend with. This is because we have tricky brains. Our old brain's motivations and new brain's reflective and thinking capacities get us caught in loops. I, like most people, have a fundamental need to be with others, to feel a sense of connection and affection, and it's understandable that I struggle when these needs are not met.

A whole range of experiences and influences have impacted on me. These include growing up with a much older sister, and feeling on my own for much of the time. My parents worked hard so they weren't around much. We lived a distance from my friends, which meant seeing them outside of school was difficult.

Growing up on a farm was tricky as my friends did not understand my way of life. Even now I realise that my life and my experiences are very different to other people's.

It's understandable that I've developed concerns and fears about fitting in. I often felt an outsider and worried that if people really knew me they would judge me to be weird and wouldn't want to know me. Now I have concerns that people don't like me. In actual fact I really don't like aspects of myself. I judge myself to be boring and an outsider.

I've coped by only opening up in certain ways to people – image manipulation. I wear a social mask. Sometimes I have a drink to help me in social situations; most of the time, I just withdraw to the sidelines or don't go out at all.

I give myself a hard time in the vain hope that this will make things better. I am often very critical of myself.

But there have been unintended consequences and drawbacks to my way of coping, such as loneliness, never truly getting to know people, low mood, anxiety, regret and more self-criticism.

This isn't my fault. I can make some changes and I can use my compassionate mind to guide me. With a warm tone of voice my compassionate self reminds me that I am a human being with a tricky brain who is living a tricky life and just trying to get by. It's understandable that I struggle at times. In this moment I am doing the best that I can. My compassionate mind and compassionate self encourages me to develop and enhance my inner strength and courage to make changes that will be helpful to me.

Writing from the perspective of her compassionate mind, Stephanie was able to place her difficulties in the context of her early experiences and 'life story'. As she wrote to herself slowly, in carefully considered sentences, Stephanie's compassionate understanding became more meaningful and a sense of inner warmth and inner support replaced a sense of shame and self-criticism (head to Chapter 1 or more on shame and self-criticism).

Helping with strong emotions

When we experience strong emotions we can worry about being overwhelmed. As such we may 'keep a lid on them' or not allow ourselves to 'go there'. We may distract ourselves by work, focus on other worries, use drugs, alcohol or food, or replace one emotion with another.

Unchecked and unresolved, this avoidance and distraction can lead to emotions bubbling away and creeping up when we least expect them. We may, for example, have a big reaction to a seemingly small situation.

Talking about our emotions with someone we trust can help. Writing, using our compassionate mind and compassionate self, can also be of benefit.

Write a letter from the perspective of your compassionate mind, inhabiting your compassionate self. Experience a sense of emotional warmth as you write your letter.

1. **Bring to mind something you have strong emotions about, something that you feel relatively comfortable to explore.**

2. **Write about the situation from the perspective of your compassionate mind or compassionate self.** Consider what your compassionate mind or compassionate self wants you to know. For example:

    'It's understandable for me to feel strong emotions because . . .'

3. **Alternatively, write as if your compassionate self were speaking to you.** For example:

    'I'm sorry that this is painful/difficult for you and evokes difficult emotions . . . I can understand why this would be . . . It is part of the human condition that we can feel such strong emotions . . . You are courageous to embark on this work . . .'

4. **Engage in soothing rhythm breathing and imagery to assist you during the writing and at the end.** These are explained in Chapters 9–12.

5. **Slowly, re-read what you've written.** If you feel that re-reading your letter would be too difficult at this point in time, it's okay not to do so. Commend yourself for the fact that you've written it and take a break. You can return to the letter at a later date. Be guided by what you think would be helpful.

EXAMPLE

Ravindra often felt overwhelmed by strong emotions. In the past he'd considered suicide as the only solution to his difficulties. More recently, Ravindra had decided to seek help and, having developed the courage to speak with his GP, he had started to see a therapist and engage with CFT. Ravindra decided to write a letter to himself from the perspective of his compassionate mind. He wrote:

> I'm so sorry that things have been really difficult for you and you've been struggling to cope. I know at times you've felt that you've been drowning. I know you've felt on your own with all of this. This has filled you with terror and at times you've felt as though things will never change. You've wanted to give in because fighting your difficulties all the time is exhausting.

> Remember I am here for you. Reach out to me and I will give you the strength and courage to face this. I can help you face the things that are so upsetting, so frustrating and so anxiety-provoking. I am sending you warmth. Move closer to me and we can face this together.

Having completed his letter, Ravindra no longer felt as isolated as he had been. He was able to look forward with hope that things could change for him in the future.

AND IF YOU NEED A LITTLE MORE PERSUASION: THE POSITIVE IMPACT OF WRITING

James Pennebaker, author of *Opening Up by Writing It Down* (The Guilford Press), has spent much of his career studying the positive impact of writing. One of his research projects involved setting people a simple assignment to write down their deepest feelings about an emotional upheaval in their life for 15 or 20 minutes a day for four consecutive days. The simple exercise resulted in many people experiencing an increase in the functioning of their immune system. Students found that their grades improved; the writing task improved memory and sleep.

Pennebaker's research also suggests that the ability to move from a personal perspective to the perspective of others during the course of writing can have positive benefits for the individual. This involves viewing a situation from multiple angles. For example, you may initially write about a situation from your anxious or angry perspective but then widen your writing to include other people's viewpoints, including that of your compassionate mind.

In addition, those individuals whose narrative evolved during the course of a writing assignment improved their immune system to the greatest extent. In other words, if we go round and round in circles we're likely to feel stuck and less likely to experience a change. In contrast, those who gradually develop a more coherent story are more likely to feel better (as long as the conclusions they draw aren't critical of themselves!).

Considering dilemmas and conflicting emotions

Wouldn't it be great if everything was simple? We liked something or didn't; we wanted to move house or change our job – or we didn't. More often than not we get caught in dilemmas and experience mixed emotions. This can be exhausting and we can feel as if we're going round in circles.

The following exercise helps you explore your dilemmas and mixed emotions through writing – compassionately!

1. **Bring to mind a dilemma, or someone or something you feel conflicting emotions about.**

2. **Connect with each option or emotion in turn and let your pen do the talking.** The exercise is for your own purposes and no one else's, so don't hold back or keep yourself in check.

TIP

You may like to divide your paper or screen into sections and use the following headings: Angry Self, Anxious Self and Sad Self (or whichever emotions you're feeling). Once you've familiarised yourself with each emotional state, write from that particular viewpoint. In doing this, you're less likely to overlook key emotions.

Alternatively, allow yourself to become in touch with difficult feelings by sitting in different 'chairs'. (For more on using chairs within CFT, head to Chapter 17.)

3. **As you finish what you want to say in relation to each aspect of the dilemma or emotional state, stand up and warmly say goodbye to that part of you, and then begin to explore another feeling.** Do this until you've explored the different views or different emotions you're experiencing.

4. **Use your soothing rhythm breathing or an imagery exercise to evoke your compassionate mind, inhabit your compassionate self and write from this perspective (refer to Chapters 9–12).** It may help to sit in a chair that you nominate as the 'compassionate chair' and, from this perspective, take into account the other emotional states you experience in respect to the situation and viewpoint.

REMEMBER

Understanding and exploring the different aspects of ourselves is important, because internal conflicts are often at the heart of emotional difficulties.

EXAMPLE

After a difficult month and heated arguments, Charlie was experiencing the conflicting emotions of love and anger towards his partner, Helen. Charlie wrote:

It's understandable that I feel these different emotions about Helen at the moment. Human beings are complex and we often have conflicting feelings. Right now I feel really angry towards her and want to get away from her but at the same time I love her deeply. When I get like this I often criticise myself for being too harsh or too soft.

It's helpful to remind myself that experiencing conflicting emotions is hard and it's understandable that I feel these difficult things. If I can support myself, and not fall into self-criticism, maybe I can work through these strong emotions and later consider some helpful actions.

TIP

When writing from the perspective of your compassionate mind or compassionate self, avoid *shoulds* and *musts*. Consider language such as, 'It may be helpful for me to consider . . .'.

Developing compassion for others

The *flow* of compassion is a key part of CFT. The three components involve *self-compassion*, the experience of compassion *from* others and the experience of compassion *for* others. The next exercise focuses on developing your compassion for others.

1. Remind yourself of a recent situation in which someone upset you, or made you angry or anxious (one that you feel comfortable to explore from a perspective other than your own).

2. Write down what you thought and felt about the situation.

3. After a few soothing breaths, consider the situation from the other person's perspective. Gently, consider and write down their potential motivations, thoughts, emotions, behaviours and how they may have felt physically.

4. Consider what your compassionate mind and compassionate self would say about the situation and, if it helps, write this down too.

TIP

If multiple people are involved, it can help to literally draw out different perspectives by using simple stick figures with boxes and arrows to convey the thoughts, feelings, physical sensations and behaviours you think they may experience.

Writing to guide your behaviour

We can use our compassionate mind to focus on a range of past, present and future situations. Writing can lead to changes in the way we feel, think and behave. In the following exercise, you use your compassionate mind to consider what it may be helpful for your compassionate self to *do* and commit these actions to writing.

Evoke your compassionate mind, embodying your compassionate self, and consider small steps or changes that it may be helpful to make. Maybe you've been avoiding certain things or falling into seemingly unhelpful patterns of behaviour. From the perspective of your compassionate self, write down ideas that can encourage and support you to face difficulties and make helpful changes.

REMEMBER

Changes may involve getting in contact with someone you've been avoiding, working towards a healthier diet, engaging in more exercise or putting yourself forward for something. However, they may involve more subtle changes, such as allowing yourself to feel sadness or anger about something, expressing how you're feeling or not pushing yourself so much.

COMING UNSTUCK: DEVELOPING YOUR COMPASSIONATE MIND AND COMPASSIONATE SELF

EXAMPLE

If you become aware of potential difficulties and/or sticking points as you write, warmly and curiously consider the following questions:

- Is any of your writing associated with coldness, indifference or even hostility?
- Does your self-critic step in at any point and undermine your efforts?
- Is this the type of letter you'd write to someone you cared about? If not, in what ways is it different?
- Does your drive or threat system kick in (refer to Chapter 4), leading you to write statements such as 'You should do X' and 'You shouldn't do Y'?

All observations direct us towards further exploratory writing that may be of value. It can be helpful to explore the obstacle itself, or write about the sense of 'stuckness' you feel when writing. It may also be helpful to imagine what your compassionate mind, compassionate self or perfect nurturer (refer to Chapters 10–12) may say or to ask for the input of someone you trust.

Damien was dyslexic, and because of this, and a number of his physical attributes, he was bullied at school. Deciding to put pen to paper, he felt a pang of anxiety and the same sense of frustration he felt at school when asked to do a writing task. Preferring to try and address rather than avoid this, Damien wrote:

> At times when I write, I begin to feel anxious and frustrated. I then start to tell myself I need to 'pull myself together'. I quickly revert to thinking I'm pathetic. This doesn't put me in the best frame of mind to write and I can be tempted to rush it. I know that this relates to my dyslexia and how I was treated in the past by others – especially when I was at school. I know it wasn't helpful for people to bully me and I can make a decision not to do it to myself. Reminding myself that I deserve to prioritise me is helpful. Being patient with myself and writing for 30 minutes every few days can make a huge difference. So, when I get frustrated, it's helpful to notice it and rather than bully myself, be supportive of my efforts.

Reviewing Your Compassionate Writing

Reviewing your compassionate writing by asking the following questions about it can be useful. They may point you in a new and fruitful direction.

Ask yourself:

>> Have I been sensitive to, and accepting of, the emotions I experience?

>> Have I spent time conveying understanding, acceptance and caring?

>> Have I explored the reasons why I may be struggling with certain things?

>> Have I taken time to reflect that humans are a complex species and that this means that we often struggle?

>> Have I written in a way that demonstrates my sense of connectedness with, rather than difference from, others?

>> Have I written about our natural tendency for self-criticism and the fact that, although the self-critic may have my best intentions at heart, it often goes about things in an unhelpful way?

>> Have I conveyed openness, curiosity and non-judgement?

>> Have I spent time reflecting on the blocks and barriers that I experience in relation to the development and maintenance of my compassionate mind?

>> Have I allowed myself to be moved by my experiences?

>> Have I spent time reflecting on others and their actions through my compassionate mind?

>> If I think compassionate writing is helpful to my general wellbeing, how can I ensure that I prioritise it in my life?

REMEMBER

Practising compassion through writing can be an important cornerstone for the development and maintenance of your compassionate mind and compassionate self. With practice, you become aware of your own idiosyncrasies. These may involve a tendency to suppress particular emotions, be judgemental of yourself and others or prioritise other things over the development of compassion into your life. As such, it may be helpful to develop a list of questions that are more tailored to you, or to ask for the regular input of someone who has your best interests at heart, such as a friend or therapist.

ADDITIONAL WAYS IN WHICH WRITING CAN HELP DEVELOP YOUR COMPASSIONATE MIND AND COMPASSIONATE SELF

Here are some additional tips for using writing to enhance your compassionate mind and compassionate self:

- Sit facing an empty chair and evoke your compassionate self or you at your best (refer to Chapter 10). While inhabiting this part of you, read out one of your letters. Once finished, move to the second chair and experience what you read.

- Make a note of positive events, interactions and thoughts as they occur during the day. Explore and expand on these positive experiences during a writing exercise in the evening.

- Write a letter to your self-critic. Compassionately explain to it what your needs are.

- Consider how you're likely to think and feel about a current situation a week, month or year from now. Write to yourself from this perspective.

- Write a letter to people who have hurt you – tell them how you felt and how you feel now. This can be an emotional exercise so remember to evoke inner strength, support, wisdom and courage from imagery or breathing exercises. The intention isn't to send the letter (although you may choose to do so) but to enable you to work through strong emotions.

- Write to your younger self. What messages and emotions does your compassionate mind or compassionate self want you to hear and feel?

- Write to yourself from an older, wiser, compassionate you. What would you say and what emotions would you be directing your way?

Chapter 15

Taking Action!

We can spend much of our lives simply moving from one thing to another without considering what we *really* want for others and for ourselves. Left unchecked, our threat and drive systems can be easily activated and run the show (Chapter 4 explains what your threat and drive systems do). Life can seemingly pass us by – as though we've stepped onto an escalator with a predetermined destination.

Compassion Focused Therapy (CFT) advocates that we regularly turn to our compassionate mind to consider the difficulties we face and ways forward. Our compassionate mind may consider it helpful to change our course or *consciously* continue on our current path. Whatever we decide to do, we refer to behaviour that is motivated by our compassionate mind as *compassionate action* – and it's our compassionate self that takes such action. Compassionate action involves doing things to prevent and respond to difficulties. It helps us to develop, flourish and improve, whether in relation to ourselves or other people. This may be in contrast to living a life on automatic pilot or a life motivated by fear and pressures that often result in unhelpful outcomes.

In this chapter, I provide you with the information you need to help you take compassionate action in your life. I guide you through the process step by step, first helping you to get started and to identify your goals before considering how you can take compassionate action to work your way through challenging situations. I also remind you to regularly review your progress as you take action and continue to develop your compassionate mind and compassionate self.

Exploring the Broad Range of Compassionate Actions

Compassion involves sensitivity to distress *plus* a motivation to prevent or alleviate it. As such, there are two components to compassion. It may help to think of these as 'sensitivity' plus 'action'.

CFT helps us to develop our compassionate mind, and its embodiment, the compassionate self, by the development of compassionate attributes. These attributes allow us to be sensitive to the difficulties we and others experience.

CFT considers distress to be a consequence of a complex interplay between our biology, experiences and environment (head to Chapter 2 for more on the attributes of compassion, Chapter 3 for more on the challenges we face, and Chapters 10–12 for specific exercises to develop your compassionate mind and compassionate self).

Based on this compassionate sensitivity and understanding, we then become motivated to take action. We develop ideas of what action it may be best to take. Such actions are defined as *compassionate actions*.

Importantly, compassionate actions can vary greatly. While some compassionate actions are big and bold, others are small or may involve doing nothing. The following example helps to illustrate the range of compassionate actions it may be useful to take given a single situation.

Imagine that you're experiencing pressure at work. As a result, you experience troubled sleep, strained relationships, worry and low mood. The following compassionate actions may help you:

» Engaging in a range of compassion exercises such as compassionate imagery (refer to Chapters 11 and 12), soothing rhythm breathing (refer to Chapter 9) or compassionate writing (refer to Chapter 14)

» Speaking to your boss

» Talking it through with a friend

» Looking for another job

» Taking a few days off work to do something that helps to reduce your stress levels

» Working a few evenings to get through the backlog and get back on top of things

» All of the above!

Any of these actions, if done excessively, exclusively or without much consideration of potential drawbacks, can cause problems. For example, if your strategy was always to look for another job, speak to your friend or work in the evenings when stressed, this may result in problems. In contrast, considered and flexible actions are less likely to result in problems.

You're unlikely to find a right or wrong action to take straight away. But if you regularly use compassion to motivate yourself, you present yourself with the opportunity to take *potentially* helpful action. You can then engage in an ongoing cycle of adjustments and changes, and review your progress.

If you use your compassionate mind to guide your actions, you're more likely to follow a steady and consistent course in life. This is because your compassionate mind is consistently motivated by care for your own and other people's wellbeing. This is in contrast to leaving yourself open to constantly changing social pressures, expectations and the agendas of other people.

Because compassionate action requires us to make changes, we emphasise the role of our compassionate self. Our compassionate self is the embodiment of our compassionate mind, or our compassionate mind in action.

Both your self-critic and your compassionate self have your best interests at heart. However, while your self-critic employs hostility, blame and anger to motivate you, your compassionate self creates a sense of inner support and encouragement. In a compassionate frame of mind, you're more likely to work to resolve the obstacles you face, even when things seem difficult. This is in contrast to the avoidance and denial that self-criticism often evokes.

In the following example, we see that Andy struggles in a range of social situations and, determined to overcome his difficulties, he begins using CFT to help. His example helps illustrate the different actions we may take dependent upon whether we listen to our self-critic or compassionate self.

Andy loved playing the guitar. For years he'd considered joining a folk group who practised at the local pub. However, his self-critic told him that under the scrutiny of others he'd make a fool of himself. Images of him sitting with the others and making continuous mistakes, or even freezing mid-song, kept popping into his mind. He imagined others looking on bemused, critically or even in a pitying way. As a result, Andy didn't join the group.

After working to develop his compassionate mind and compassionate self, Andy considered that making some changes would be helpful, as he was simply not leading the life he wished to lead. He was able to reassure himself that, when relaxed, he could play the guitar to a good standard. He acknowledged that most people would experience anxiety when first joining a group and that, although this may affect his performance, his confidence was likely to grow as he became more comfortable with the people and his surroundings. Andy recognised that his self-critic was just worried and that maybe it would be helpful to reassure his self-critic that, though anxiety-provoking, this was a step he should take.

Although our self-critic is often acting out of a protective instinct, listening to it and acting on its warnings can hold us back. In contrast, our compassionate self recognises that things are difficult, supports us in our efforts and continues to provide the strength and courage to continue our efforts, regardless of whether things go well or not.

REMEMBER

There may be a number of reasons why you are reading this book. You may be reading it because someone has told you that you have to. As such, you may be feeling slightly resentful or anxious while reading! You may want to learn more about different forms of therapy. As a result, you may feel curious or even buzzy as you acquire new knowledge. Alternatively, you may be reading these words because you wish to develop your compassionate mind and compassionate self out of care for your own wellbeing.

In real terms, it's likely that you're reading for a combination of reasons, but these reasons demonstrate that although our behaviour is important, the *why* or the motivation behind us doing something has a big effect on our experience and potentially the outcome.

TAKING INSPIRATION FROM OTHERS

Compassionate writing (refer to Chapter 14) in the form of letters, statements or single words can be extremely helpful to us. Famous quotes can also provide us with the additional strength and courage to face difficult situations. Here are some of my favourite quotes that I often turn to when I need to summon the strength to take action:

'You gain strength, courage and confidence by every experience in which you really stop to look fear in the face . . . you must do the thing you think you cannot do.' Eleanor Roosevelt

'Courage is not the absence of fear, but rather the judgment that something else is more important than fear.' Ambrose Redmoon

'Courage does not always roar. Sometimes courage is the quiet voice at the end of the day, saying, "I will try again tomorrow".' Mary Anne Radmacher

'Action expresses priorities.' Mahatma Gandhi

Preparing Yourself for Action

Good preparation can make it more likely that you achieve the things you aim for. You can prepare yourself for compassionate action by using your compassionate self to help you break the process into stages. The following sections take you through each stage, from identifying your goals and considering which action to start with, to recognising the steps you need to take and making a detailed plan.

In some ways, the term 'goals' can detract from the process of working towards something. After all, in football very few goals are scored by a single strike after a won ball – most are the result of a combination of actions. Practice at playing the whole game improves the players' confidence, leading to a more successful run of play – even if it doesn't result in a goal being scored.

REMEMBER

All parts of the process contribute to a helpful learning experience.

Discovering your goals

The goals that you decide to focus your efforts on can be big or small. They may involve developing your compassionate self, becoming more confident, feeling a greater sense of connection with others or making new friends.

REMEMBER

Engaging with your compassionate mind and compassionate self can help you to consider your own wellbeing as well as that of other people. It may be helpful, therefore, to consider other people as you work to identify your goals. After all, the wellbeing of others isn't just important to them but can also have a positive impact on you!

The following exercise will help you begin this process. Goals generated from your compassionate mind and compassionate self can be very different to those your pragmatic or intellectual self may generate. Engaging with your compassionate self can also deepen the experience, making it more emotional and ultimately more motivating.

1. **Find a place that is, as much as you can predict, free from major distractions.**

2. **Engage with a posture that brings with it a sense of strength and alertness in your spine, yet relaxation and openness in your body.** You may find it easier to sit for this exercise.

3. **Engage with your soothing rhythm breathing or an imagery exercise to evoke your compassionate mind.** Refer to Chapter 9 for guidance if you need some help to get started.

4. **Generate a warm facial expression to help enhance a sense of emotional warmth and inhabit your compassionate self (head to Chapter 10 for more guidance on developing your compassionate self).** If helpful, use a particular compassionate smell, sound or piece of music to assist you in connecting to your compassionate self.

5. **When you've engaged your compassionate mind, inhabiting your compassionate self, ask yourself what goals it would be helpful for you to work towards.** Make a note of things as they come to mind.

TIP

If you find it difficult to generate goals, consider a time when you've been self-critical or experienced strong emotions. Now consider what may have helped you at that time.

It may also help to re-familiarise yourself with your 'life story' (refer to Chapter 5 for more on developing your life story). Reflect on your experiences and influences, your fears and concerns, your coping strategies and their drawbacks. Consider the difficulties you, at times, experience and whether it may be helpful to develop goals around these difficulties.

If your self-critic steps in, stating 'You need to be less anxious', 'You need to get a grip on yourself' or 'You need to get a life', thank your self-critic for its input and recognise that it has your best interests at heart, and then return to the exercise. Evoke your compassionate mind and inhabit your compassionate self once more and ask for its input. Maybe it suggests in a warm tone, 'It would be helpful for me to develop my confidence' or 'It would be helpful for me to develop some hobbies that I can feel good about'. Your compassionate self is warm, supportive and forward-looking. From this perspective, you're sensitive to the difficulties you face and you're motivated to prevent and alleviate them.

REMEMBER

It's perfectly normal to feel overwhelmed, daunted or even to avoid putting down certain goals because they're associated with strong emotions or you think they're too difficult to achieve. If this is the case, you can break your goals down into smaller steps that move you towards something that you hope for. You can then proceed at your own pace.

If you're still struggling to generate goals that feel right for you, consider some of the diverse goals that other people have used:

>> Be able to apologise when you know you're at fault

>> Be able to ask for help

>> Be able to assert yourself

>> Be able to put your point of view across to others – be they people you know well or those you don't

- » Be able to speak fluently to a group

- » Be able to tell people how you feel

- » Be comfortable handing in a piece of work that isn't perfect

- » Develop friendships

- » Do things just for pleasure

- » Give yourself less of a hard time

- » Look after your health

- » Put yourself forward for career opportunities

- » Say no to people

- » Say yes more

- » Spend less time worrying

- » Stop apologising for everything

- » Stop putting yourself down endlessly

TIP

If you're still finding it difficult to generate some goals, it may help to speak with a close friend or family member, someone who has your best interests at heart. Motivated by compassion for you, they may be able to help you generate some ideas.

In the following example we meet Mira, who turned to her compassionate self in order to generate some goals.

EXAMPLE

Mira's life seemed to be going relatively 'okay' but sometimes she had periods of low mood that were associated with feelings of boredom and thoughts that life was monotonous or simply passing her by.

Using the preceding exercise, Mira reconnected with her compassionate self and generated the following goals:

- » To feel a greater sense of fulfilment

- » To improve my relationship with others

- » To be less critical of Paul (her partner)

- » To be more self-confident

- » To reduce my experiences of low mood

Mira reflected that while her goals were extremely meaningful, and changes in these areas were highly likely to result in improvements to her life, none had a clear means by which she could measure her progress. She therefore recognised that it would be helpful to her to break them down into clear steps that she could focus on. (We tackle this in the later section, 'Moving Yourself Forward: Taking Compassionate Action'.)

Considering where to start

When you have your list of goals (refer to the preceding section), you need to consider a starting point on which to focus your efforts. You may select your most pressing goal, the one that you think is the easiest to achieve or the one that will have the greatest impact on your life.

To help you get started, try out the following exercise.

Evoke your compassionate mind and inhabit your compassionate self (refer to the exercise in the preceding section for some guidance if you need it) and review the personal goals that you generated. Number or rewrite your list to reflect the order that you think you'd like to follow. Alternatively, circle or highlight an initial goal – you can always return to your list once you have made progress on your first goal.

Moving Yourself Forward: Taking Compassionate Action

Compassionate action can be difficult. It often involves doing things we have been avoiding due to concerns, worries and fears. As such, recognise and validate the efforts that you're making and the difficult emotions you're likely to feel during the process.

REMEMBER

CFT involves evoking your compassionate mind and embodying your compassionate self in order to create a sense of inner support, especially when you're facing difficult things. From this secure base, you face rather than avoid difficulties as a means to prevent or alleviate them.

Research by American social psychologist Amy Cuddy and colleagues suggests that 'faking it until we feel it' or even 'faking it until we become it' can have a positive impact on what we do and how we feel. If you're feeling anxious but you adopt a posture and facial expression of confidence, this can help to reduce your anxiety.

TIP

Many actors begin to get into character by adjusting their facial expression, posture, tone of voice and walk in order to create in themselves the thoughts and feelings of the characters they want to portray. So do as actors do!

The following sections explore how you can break your compassionate actions into steps and make a plan for taking these steps to generate compassionate actions.

Taking compassionate action, step by step

Breaking things down into manageable steps can help us think things through logically and make things feel less overwhelming.

Try the following exercise to see if you can break your goal into steps.

Write down the goal that you want to start with (the goal that you identified in the preceding section). Evoke your compassionate mind and inhabit your compassionate self (refer to the exercise in the earlier section, 'Discovering your goals', if you need guidance to help you get started) and consider the steps it will be helpful for you to take to achieve your goal through compassionate action (remember that each step is in itself a compassionate action). Write down as many steps as you see fit.

TIP

For some goals, the steps will be clearly sequential; for others, it may be helpful to try a range of different things simultaneously or in a less linear way.

If you find the preceding exercise challenging, consider the following examples to inspire you.

EXAMPLE

Mira, having generated a range of goals, decided that she wished to prioritise her efforts on the development of her self-confidence. She broke her goal down into the following manageable steps:

1. Spend 20–30 minutes a day, for one week, writing to further understand the difficulties I have with my self-confidence by:

   - Focusing on my newly developed compassionate understanding of the fears and concerns I have

   - Exploring how I currently cope with my fears and concerns and how this can be problematic for me

2. Consider alternative coping strategies and employ them one by one. These strategies include:

   - Evoking my compassionate self and asking for support and guidance rather than listening to my self-critic

   - Not putting myself down when I'm with other people

   - Not having a drink to calm my nerves before going out

   - Contributing my own thoughts and views to discussions (maybe starting with situations in which I feel more comfortable)

- Putting myself forward for things that I want to do but are currently outside my comfort zone

- Asking for input and feedback from others at work rather than telling myself I should do everything under my own steam

3. Review how things are progressing on a weekly basis, using my compassionate self to think things through.

EXAMPLE

Tom had a busy career, which often meant that he worked at the weekend. This had been okay before he had a family, but increasingly Tom became frustrated and self-critical because he spent too much of his weekend at his desk and not enough time with his children. His relationship with his wife Alice was also suffering, and they often became critical of each other.

One of Tom's goals was to develop a better relationship with his children. He broke his goal down into the following manageable steps:

1. Write compassionately (refer to Chapter 14) to myself to consider why it's important to spend quality time with my children and to consider why this may be difficult at times.

2. Decide on a time in the week when I can spend good quality time with both children.

3. Decide on a time in the week when I can spend good quality one-to-one time with each of my children.

4. Switch off my phone when I'm with my children to remove myself from distractions that may interrupt this time.

5. Make a list of activities that I can do with the children.

6. Speak to Alice while in a compassionate frame of mind about how we can support each other (rather than be critical of each other's parenting).

7. Review things with Alice fortnightly to iron out any difficulties.

EXAMPLE

One of Stephen's goal was to conquer the art of public speaking. He broke his goal down into manageable steps that he can follow over eight weeks:

1. Decide on a topic for a five-minute talk.

2. Prepare the talk.

3. Using soothing rhythm breathing, evoke my compassionate self (refer to Chapters 9 and 10) and then:

- Present my talk in front of a mirror

- Present my talk in front of a video-recording device

- Practise, practise, practise until I feel more comfortable
- Present my talk in front of a small group of supportive people
- Briefly speak at a team meeting
- Put myself forward for a small talk at work
- Ask for feedback and input from others after my talk

4. Review my progress at regular intervals and adjust the steps if required.

EXAMPLE

Jana presented a version of herself to the outside world that was in control, organised and unflappable. She suppressed emotions such as anxiety and frustration, but this took its toll. She felt a fake and questioned whether people would still like her if they truly knew her.

Jana's goal was to express her feelings more and not to let them get the better of her. She broke her goal down into the following manageable steps:

1. Continue to develop my compassionate self.

2. Write a compassionate letter to myself whenever I feel strong emotions (refer to Chapter 14). In each letter, explore why I feel the way I do, validate the feelings that I currently have and look at things from different perspectives.

3. Using the support of my compassionate image (refer to Chapter 11):

- Speak to Claire (close friend) about how I sometimes feel and get her input
- Begin to voice my anxiety, anger or frustration to close friends

4. Ask for feedback from friends when appropriate.

EXAMPLE

Tracey had never learnt to drive and, after moving to a rural location, she relied on her partner for lifts. Aware of the impact this had on her partner, Tracey felt she was becoming a burden and this affected her confidence.

Tracey's goal was to gain more independence. She broke her goal down into the following manageable steps that she can take over 12 months:

1. Find out more about public transport routes.

2. Try out public transport.

3. Research the price of a car and driving lessons.

4. Set a date to start driving lessons.

5. Save money and create a budget.

6. Ask friends and family for instructor recommendations.

7. Look for a regular slot in my diary for lessons.

8. Make an appointment for my first driving lesson.

9. Take each lesson one at a time.

TIP

You can break your steps down further if you find it helpful. For example, one of Tracey's steps involves saving money and budgeting, and so this may be broken down further into setting up a savings account, reviewing her current incomings and outgoings, looking for ways to save on her household bills, and so on.

If you're struggling to identify the steps you need to take, or you're finding it difficult to visualise the outcomes, it may be helpful to consider some problem-solving and imagery techniques. The following sections look at tips for working around problematic areas and consider how you can use compassionate imagery to gain a fresh perspective on your goals.

Coming unstuck

TIP

If you're finding it hard to break your goal down into manageable steps, ask someone whose opinion you value for their input into how you can proceed – someone you feel has your best interests at heart and will be open and honest with you. Remember to take notes, because sometimes it's easy to forget things – or our threat system (refer to Chapter 4) can skew what people have said to us over time. Alternatively, ask them to write a few things down for you – they may have the key to helping you move forward.

Compassionate action is motivated by care for your own wellbeing and the wellbeing of others. You don't take compassionate action because you feel you've got to do something or take action on automatic pilot.

REMEMBER

Using your compassionate mind to guide your behaviour can result in broaching a difficult subject with someone or working up to presenting to a large audience. Equally, it can involve you allowing yourself to explore or sit with strong emotions.

So, although taking compassionate action can transform our lives, and the lives of others, the steps we need to take are often difficult and require strength, courage and commitment.

Using imagery and imagination

You may be aware of some imagery-based strategies designed to make you feel less intimidated, such as imagining interviewers, audience members or assessors in their underwear or sitting on the toilet. Such images can be helpful as they make us laugh, remind us that we're all human or give us a sense of superiority, but within CFT we use compassionate imagery. (I cover compassionate imagery in more detail in Chapters 11 and 12.)

In this section, we look at how compassionate imagery and imagination can help prepare you to take compassionate action. Slowly stay with the feelings from each exercise, allowing these feelings to have optimal impact.

The first exercise looks at imagining when you achieve your goal.

Evoke your *compassionate self* and slowly imagine yourself successfully engaging in your next goal or step (refer to Chapter 10 for more on evoking your compassionate self). In your mind's eye, explore the scene as you successfully achieve your goal and work through each of your senses in turn: what you see, smell, hear, feel and maybe taste.

It can help to both observe yourself achieving your goal, as a compassionate onlooker, and also to imagine yourself achieving your goal, seeing the scene through your own eyes as you take the action yourself.

If the step you plan to take involves other people, turn your attention to them, individual by individual. Consider what they're likely to be experiencing. What are they thinking? Attempt to take a comprehensive and compassionate view of each person.

Imagining ourselves achieving our goals can help us develop our confidence to face difficult situations and consider how we may go about things, negotiate obstacles and practice what we may do and say in certain situations.

This exercise can also help us gain a greater perspective on a situation. Considering the minds of other people can make us less prone to negative predictions. For example, an interviewer is likely to want us to do well at interview, a cashier is unlikely to be consumed by judgments of us if we attempt to take something back to their store, and a friend is more likely to experience a sense of connection with us if we show vulnerability than judge us to be weak.

The next exercise encourages you to imagine the positive outcomes that may result from compassionate action.

Imagine the positive feeling you're likely to experience after you've taken the steps you hope to take. Stay with this feeling for a while.

Imagining how you may feel after successfully achieving a step towards your goal can enhance your motivation to take action. After all, if you've given yourself a taste of how you may feel it may help you to counteract fear, avoidance or apathy.

Taking another perspective can also help you to explore your compassionate activities.

Imagine that you're a compassionate observer looking at the situation you plan to engage in. Consider what the compassionate observer may think and feel and what emotions they may be directing your way as you engage in a difficult activity.

This particular imagery can provide us with a sense of support when we actually do what we plan, and are maybe fearful of doing.

Compassionate imagery can help to prepare us to take compassionate action.

TIP

If, at any point during these exercises, you notice that your threat system has been activated and you feel strong emotions such as anxiety or anger, re-engage with an exercise to evoke your compassionate self (refer to the earlier section, 'Discovering your goals' for a starting point). Resume the exercise when you feel ready.

Making a detailed plan

It can be helpful to make a detailed plan to prepare you for a specific compassionate action you're hoping to take. Your plan may include things that help get you in the best frame of mind (such as wearing clothes you feel more confident or comfortable in or arranging to see a close friend afterwards). Plans can also help you to think through obstacles, recognise your means of overcoming them, and set out the things you need to do and the things you may need to remind yourself at certain stages.

The nearby sidebar 'Exercises to generate inner support' provides examples of ways you can generate additional inner support before, during or after taking compassionate action.

It is often helpful for us to consider obstacles that may stand in the way of achieving our goals or making steps towards them. The following exercise helps you to explore obstacles that you may be well aware of, as well as those that you haven't yet considered. The exercise also helps you to develop some ideas to decrease or overcome such barriers. As they say, 'forewarned is forearmed'.

1. **At the top of a blank sheet of paper, write down a step that you plan to take, one that is likely to create challenges for you.**

2. **Evoke your compassionate mind and adjust your posture and facial expression in order to inhabit your compassionate self.** Refer to Chapters 10–12.

EXERCISES TO GENERATE INNER SUPPORT

Here are some familiar as well as some additional ways to generate inner support while taking compassionate action:

- Before, during and/or after taking compassionate action, use mindfulness or soothing rhythm breathing to create a sense of calm awareness and wellbeing. (Refer to Chapter 9 for more on this.)

- Evoke your compassionate image (be it your perfect nurturer, compassionate coach, compassionate friend or ideal compassionate image) to enhance a sense of strength, courage and commitment for your actions. (Refer to Chapter 11.)

  Imagine your compassionate image alongside you or at your shoulder to create a sense of support in whatever you plan to do.

- Use a compassionate posture that has strength and alertness and a warm facial expression to assist you.

- Generate compassionate thoughts (refer to Chapter 13) before, during or after taking action. This can be particularly helpful if negative thoughts or images interfere with you taking the compassionate actions you planned. Such exercises can help you develop a supportive and more balanced way of looking at things.

- Write compassionately to yourself before or after taking compassionate action in order to help plan or review the exercise. Acknowledge the strength and courage it takes to do something difficult. Remind yourself that any situation is an opportunity to learn more about yourself and others. Refer to Chapter 14 for more on compassionate writing.

- Consider using music, a smell, a photo or written prompts to help you prepare, take or reflect on your compassionate actions. Such practices can help you step out of your threat system (refer to Chapter 4).

3. **Write down the ways in which you can prepare to take this step.** Include ideas that will put you in the best frame of mind to take compassionate action.

4. **Consider the potential obstacles you may come across. Take time to problem-solve and write down what you can do to help negotiate your way past these obstacles.**

5. **Ask yourself, 'What would it be helpful for me to remind myself before, during and after taking this step towards my goal?'**

Of course it is impossible to predict or plan for every eventuality. Even when we know a situation inside out, something may happen that can throw us off course. However, allowing time to calmly consider obstacles, minimise their likelihood and plan how to overcome them can reduce your anxiety and provide you with a greater sense of confidence.

In the following example, we return to Andy's story (which we originally looked at in the earlier section, 'Exploring the Broad Range of Compassionate Actions'). Andy has made a detailed plan, which includes an exploration of potential obstacles and ways of overcoming them. His story may give you a few ideas as you plan to take action.

In preparation for attending his first folk group session, Andy wrote:

EXAMPLE **The step I am now going to take is:**

Attend my first folk group evening.

The things I can do to help me prepare for this are:

Double-check the venue and the time the folk group meets.

Visit the venue the evening before just to familiarise myself with it.

Wear something I feel comfortable in – something I'm not self-conscious wearing.

Set off in good time so that I'm not in a rush and flustered when I arrive.

Play some relaxing music on the way there, something I enjoy and that will get me in the right mood.

Use breathing and then an imagery exercise before I go in to calm my mind and get in contact with my strength and courage.

Imagine my compassionate coach is at my shoulder.

Remind myself that we're all going to be there because we love listening to and playing music.

The potential obstacles I can see are:

I may freeze due to my anxiety and think that everyone is judging me negatively.

I may freeze because I'm giving myself a hard time.

I can do the following things to help me negotiate the obstacles:

I can assume a relaxed, open posture and a warm facial expression, even if I don't feel that way.

I can use my soothing rhythm breathing and then compassionate imagery to access inner support.

I can simply say I feel a bit awkward and maybe say I was just aiming to meet people rather than play at the first meeting.

I can smile, clap and sing with the group, which will be enjoyable in itself – after all, while songs are being played it's quite relaxing, with no pressure to talk.

The things it would be helpful for me to remind myself before, during and after the situation are:

This will help me learn about myself – whichever way it goes.

Afterwards I can give myself a pat on the back for facing the things I'm fearful of.

I can always revert to my soothing rhythm breathing/take a break/use some compassionate imagery if it's difficult.

I can play my guitar to a good standard when I feel relaxed.

Other people struggle as I do, it's not just me – in fact, many musicians say they feel socially awkward without their instrument.

My confidence is likely to build with time.

If I focus on other people, such as what music they like and how they play, it may take my attention away from myself.

If there are awkward silences or I am put on the spot, I can ask some general questions about the group.

It is helpful to reassure my self-critic that, although this is anxiety-provoking, it's a helpful step for me to take and a step I'm ready for.

Working out a detailed plan in this way can motivate us and help us to overcome our anxieties and fears. It can also help us to prevent or deal with worrying thoughts that go round and round in our heads.

Reviewing Your Progress

Life is a series of experiences from which you learn. Reviewing our progress in a step-by-step, supportive and forward-looking way can help us negotiate setbacks and ultimately achieve our goals.

Unfortunately, even when something has gone well, minutes, hours, days or weeks later your self-critic can turn something that went relatively well into something so terrible that it's never to be repeated.

It can therefore be helpful to compassionately review your progress in written form soon after each step taken. Review events in a balanced and considered manner, neither saying everything went terribly nor amazingly: your compassionate self supports your efforts, and its forward-looking approach helps you consider the next steps. Later, you can look back on what you've written and reassure your self-critic that things aren't as bad as it seems to think.

After completing each step taken, consider the following exercise:

1. **At the top of a blank sheet of paper, write down the compassionate action that you took.**

2. **Evoke your compassionate mind. Adjust your posture and facial expression to embody your compassionate self.** Refer to Chapter 10.

3. **Consider the things that you've learned about yourself from the step you took and write these down.** If relevant, consider the things that you learned about other people as well.

4. **Make a note of potential adjustments you can make in the future.** For example, it may help to try this step at a different time of day, in another location or with another person.

5. **Taking all this into account, what may your next step involve?** It may help to briefly make some notes, and this can become the focus of a 'taking action' exercise in the future.

6. **Summarise the progress you've made, making it as long or short as is helpful.** This may be a statement on a sticky note or take the form of a compassionate letter.

7. **Allow yourself a little time for the experience of reviewing your progress to 'sink in'.** It may help to engage with your soothing rhythm breathing, compassionate imagery or another practice as you recognise the strength, courage and commitment it took to take action.

We now return to Mira, who we met in the earlier section, 'Discovering your goals'.

EXAMPLE

At work, someone proposed moving a regular meeting to the end of the working day. As it often over-ran, Mira felt concerned that this change may risk her being late to pick up her children. She realised that voicing her concerns may be a good way to help develop her confidence. Having planned to take action, she courageously voiced her point of view. Later, Mira reviewed the step she had taken and wrote the following:

The step I took involved:

Contributing my own thoughts and views to a discussion.

The things I learnt about myself through the exercise were:

It was anxiety-provoking and it took a considerable amount of personal strength to put my concerns across, but I can contribute to discussions if I put my mind to it.

I was hesitant at first and my voice may have been a bit wobbly, but my point of view is valid. I can do more than I thought.

It's worth experimenting with situations.

Being anxious is uncomfortable, but it's helpful to consider whether to avoid things or face them. If I face them I'm more likely to grow in confidence.

If I'm asked for my opinion it's appropriate to give it – in an ideal world I'd be able to do it without strong emotion, but I will learn, with time, to be able to do that.

The things I learnt about other people were:

Other people took on board what I had to say, and although they may have picked up that I was anxious, this didn't seem to detract from the point I made. In fact, by their response, it seemed to emphasise to others how important I felt my point was.

One person seemed to be a bit dismissive and seemed to want to hurry me along, but maybe she is just like that – maybe over time she will listen to my opinion more if I become more confident.

Some people will ignore me, disagree, hurry me along or speak over me at times – this is what happens when a group of people come together.

When I looked around me, I could see that maybe I voiced something that other people agreed with – there were nods of agreement and other people said they agreed.

Things hardly ever go perfectly, and even confident people sometimes struggle to get their point across for all sorts of reasons.

People were no different towards me after the meeting so I don't think they thought negatively of me for contributing my opinion.

The potential adjustments that I could make to myself or other aspects of the situation in the future are:

I could practise my soothing rhythm breathing for a short while before meetings. (Refer to Chapter 9 for more on this.)

I could calm myself during the meeting, as the agenda item approaches, by breathing in my compassionate smell.

I could speak more in support of other people if I think they made a good point just to get used to speaking more in that forum.

Taking all of this into account, my next step may involve:

Taking other opportunities to express my thoughts and opinions with colleagues, friends or family. I experience so many occasions on which I don't say something because I'm worried about whether it will come out right and what people will think. Using my compassionate mind, I can harness my strength, courage and commitment to speak up at such times also.

In summary:

I am aiming to develop my confidence and it will take time. With my best interests at heart, it's helpful to encourage myself to face difficult things.

A PERSONAL NOTE FROM MY COMPASSIONATE SELF

I'm a great believer in the power of putting pen to paper to help me focus my mind. I find this helpful both at the time of writing and also later when I look back, as I'd look through a photo album.

I wrote the following summary after I experienced a knock to my confidence. Sat in front of an amazing view, I cried for a while. I then took some mindful breaths, evoked my compassionate self and wrote:

Smile an inner smile when you realise you've got something wrong or realise you've been utterly naive. It's yet another opportunity to learn about yourself and other people. See mistakes or disappointments as an opportunity to change things and grow.

Don't worry that other people know more than you, are better than you or have more experience – see them as a source of support and input for your learning. Think about what you can offer them in return and don't undermine what you have.

May you never stop realising the edges of your knowledge and experience and therefore may you continue to grow. I hope you continue to fall off your bike but also continue to get back on it!

In all honesty, when I wrote that diary entry a part of me didn't believe my compassionate mind's advice. But I suppose that's the point. Developing our compassionate mind is helpful *because* life is hard, and because doubts and worries occupy our minds. But developing some support in the face of these challenges is a good thing.

Chapter 16

Expressing Yourself

H ave you ever kept your mouth firmly shut for fear of saying something wrong? Or maybe you summon the courage to say something but it comes out all wrong and it seems that you've made things a whole lot worse? Situations such as these often lead to frustration and upset. We can find that we're not taken seriously, thrown into an argument or racked with self-criticism.

So, how do we become more authentic? How do we express our feelings, needs and views in a way that's neither too passive nor too aggressive? Where do we start?

In this chapter, we take a look at how you can address these questions using compassionate assertiveness. We also consider how you can manage resistance to the changes you make from those around you, and how you can use compassionate constructive feedback as a further way to express yourself to the people in your life.

Asserting Yourself with Compassion

We can use our compassionate mind to consider situations from our own and other people's perspectives. Through this process we can then discover what we want to do. Our compassionate mind may lead us to decide to courageously do nothing. More often, though, we feel motivated to address an issue with someone in a way that has both our own and the other person's wellbeing in mind. When we engage in discussions from this perspective, we're practicing compassionate assertiveness.

Compassionate assertiveness has two components:

>> It requires you to consider a situation from the perspective of your compassionate mind. In so doing, it may be helpful to consider both our own and other peoples' perspectives and wellbeing.

>> It involves embodying your compassionate self and courageously instigating a conversation or dialogue, the aim of which is to alleviate or prevent difficulties we may experience. In so doing, it is hoped this is also beneficial for others.

The compassionate assertiveness strategies in this chapter can provide a framework for addressing difficulties with others. They help us to express ourselves in a non-apologetic or aggressive way, while also being respectful of other people. Using such strategies makes it more likely that we can achieve the outcomes we're hoping for.

In the following sections I help you to find the words to express yourself, and then ask you to use your compassionate mind to consider alternative viewpoints. I suggest ways in which you can prepare and practice for the conversations you hope to have, and then help you review your progress after you've given compassionate assertiveness a try.

Finding the words to express yourself

In this exercise, you develop a way to express your thoughts, feelings or needs. You can do this exercise anywhere; however, it can help to find a place that is, as far as possible, free from distractions – somewhere you can be for 15 minutes or so.

You may like to use soothing rhythm breathing, a mindfulness practice (both outlined in Chapter 9) or another form of exercise to create a sense of calm awareness in your mind and body before engaging in this (or, indeed, any) exercise.

To prepare for this exercise, sit in a relaxed, open posture with strength and alertness to your spine. Soften your facial expression, slightly relaxing your jaw. When you feel ready, take the following steps:

1. **Bring to mind a relationship that you find difficult.** Maybe you often feel resentful around this person, tend to have arguments with them or the relationship feels generally strained.

   Choose a relationship that you want to improve and that you feel motivated to change. It makes sense to choose a relationship that you find relatively easy to begin with (you can tackle more challenging relationships as you develop your confidence with this exercise).

2. **Evoke your compassionate mind and spend a little time re-familiarising yourself with the attributes and skills associated with your compassionate mind.** Refer to Chapter 2 to re-familiarise yourself with your compassionate mind's attributes and skills. Embody your compassionate mind as your compassionate self. Refer to Chapter 10 for more on embodying your compassionate self.

3. **Experience a sense of compassionate connection with the person you're focusing your attention on.** Consider that, like you, they wish to live a life that is free of distress, difficulties and disagreements.

4. **From the perspective of your compassionate mind and compassionate self, use one of the following formats to help outline what it may be helpful to say to this person.** This may relate to a specific situation or the relationship as a whole:

   > I think/feel/need . . .
   >
   > This is based on . . .
   >
   > I think it would be helpful if . . .
   >
   > Can we discuss this?

   Alternatively:

   > When you do/say . . .
   >
   > I feel . . .
   >
   > and I would prefer . . .
   >
   > Can we discuss this?

5. **Jot down your ideas so that you can play around with the wording and refer back to them later.** (The exercises in the following sections ask you to consider these thoughts further.)

One approach addresses your own needs, feelings or thoughts first, while the other turns this around and puts the other person's actions or words first. You can approach compassionate assertiveness exercises either way – there's no right or wrong here. Find something that works for you and seems to match up with how you speak naturally.

TIP

Finishing with the question, 'Can we discuss this?' acknowledges that the other person may have important thoughts and feelings about this that you may not be aware of, and that it may help to discuss these thoughts and feelings too.

If you're finding it difficult to imagine how this conversation may go in practice, the following examples provide an idea:

> *I think* I am not being taken seriously at work *because* none of the ideas I come up with in meetings are ever acted upon. *I think it would be helpful if* you could give me feedback so that I can understand why my ideas may not be viable. *Can we discuss this?*

> *When you don't* put things away after yourself *I feel* as though you don't care about me and just expect me to tidy up after you. *I would prefer it* if you cleaned up after yourself or if you could tell me why this is difficult for you so that I can understand it better. *Can we discuss this?*

> *I need* to have some time to myself every so often. *This is because* it helps me to get a bit of perspective, especially when things are so busy and stressful. *I would like* to think that you would support me in this. I am not sure what you think. *Can we discuss it?*

You can use this strategy in a range of ways. You can also amend the wording to suit your needs. For example, it may be that you replace 'based on' with 'because', or 'I would prefer' with 'I would like', as different terms may feel more natural to you.

When you say 'I feel' it leaves less opportunity for people to disagree with you, whereas statements such as 'You make me feel . . .' are more likely to trigger disagreement. As such, 'I' statements are often more helpful than 'You' statements.

Considering alternative views

When we focus on our need to compassionately assert ourselves, it may seem odd to spend time considering the other person's viewpoint – but doing so can be extremely important. It provides us with more insight into a given situation, which can help us to adjust our own perspective. It can also help us to see them as another human being just trying to get by, because it helps us to feel less intimidated when we come to express our own views – after all, we're muddling through this life together!

Feeling compassion for others and considering their viewpoint doesn't mean that we 'let them off the hook' – it actually helps us to develop the strength and courage to face (and hopefully resolve) difficulties, for everyone's benefit. Head to Chapter 6 for more on the common myths associated with compassion.

The exercise in the preceding section helps you to develop a way of articulating difficulties in relation to someone you want to have a better relationship with. In the following exercise, you use your compassionate mind and compassionate self to consider the other person's viewpoint.

To prepare for this exercise, sit in a relaxed, open posture with strength and alertness to your spine. Soften your facial expression, slightly relaxing your jaw. When you feel ready, take the following steps:

1. **Evoke your compassionate mind and embody this as your compassionate self.** Refer to Chapter 10 for some tips to help you get started if required.

2. **In relation to the issue you looked at in the preceding section, consider the other person's perspective.**

3. **Consider what you know about the person – their experiences and what has led them to be as they are.** Maybe they're stressed, anxious, frustrated or simply unaware of the impact they have on you.

4. **Consider that they too may benefit from truly healthy relationships.** Just like you, they may see the benefit of having open and honest relationships.

5. **Make notes as you consider the other person's perspective on the situation.** You may begin 'Zayn is human too. He doesn't want conflict either. He may himself benefit from a conversation to iron out the difficulties between us,' or 'Irene has had a lot on her plate at the moment. Although it doesn't excuse her being snappy with me, it helps to consider the stress she is experiencing.'

6. **Having considered the other person's point of view, review the statements you developed in the exercise in the preceding section.** You may consider changing the wording or tone of voice you imagine using when you take the next step of compassionately asserting yourself (which we cover in the next section).

In some circumstances it can be very difficult to see a situation from the other person's perspective (for example, if someone is verbally abusive towards you and appears to enjoy seeing you squirm, it can be hard to consider their viewpoint).

You may therefore find it helpful to initially focus your efforts on relationships that are relatively easy – ones that you want to improve and feel motivated to change. As you develop your compassionate mind and compassionate self, and your confidence builds, you can then begin to focus your attention on more difficult relationships.

Practising compassionately asserting yourself

The more we rehearse what we want to say, the more naturally this way of expressing ourselves becomes, even when we're feeling high levels of anxiety, sadness or anger. Because practicing compassionate assertiveness is difficult, it's good to prepare as best we can.

The following exercise provides you with some different ideas to help you practise the statements you considered in the preceding two sections. With practice, you may feel more confident as you contemplate expressing your views with compassionate assertiveness.

Begin by evoking your compassionate mind and inhabiting your compassionate self in a way you find helpful (refer to Chapter 10 for advice on getting started). After you've engaged your compassionate mind and embodied your compassionate self, try some of the following approaches:

>> Read out loud the statements you noted down in the earlier section, 'Finding the words to express yourself'. Do they sound okay? Are there any adjustments you can make that help the statements to flow or make your point better? (You may also want to consider your further reflections on these statements, as you explored in the preceding section, 'Considering alternative views'.)

>> Practise saying the statements in front of a mirror.

>> Talk into a recording device and then play it back.

>> Ask for the input of someone you trust and role-play the situation with them. Maybe ask them to say very little at the start and later ask them to be a little more difficult. Another person's support and feedback may be incredibly helpful.

REMEMBER

As we compassionately assert ourselves, tone of voice can make all the difference. Use your voice to express openness, non-judgement, curiosity and warmth (head to Chapters 1, 9 and 13 for more on the importance of voice tone).

By trying out these different approaches to practising your compassionately assertive statements, you can develop your confidence or adjust what you intend to say based on your own (and maybe other people's) reflections.

Preparing to express yourself

After you generate your statements to address to the person at the centre of the difficult relationship in your life, consider other viewpoints and rehearse the conversation you hope to have (as you explore in the preceding three sections), it's time to take action. But before you do, here's an additional step to help you prepare.

In the minutes leading up to your interaction, engage in an exercise to evoke your compassionate mind. Remind yourself of the key compassionate attributes (refer to Chapter 2 for a reminder of these). Feel a sense of warmth and calmness, together with strength and courage. Adjust your posture, feeling strength in your spine and openness and warmth in your facial expression. In so doing, you embody your compassionate self. Remind yourself that the person with whom you aim to compassionately assert yourself is another human being, with a tricky brain (head to Chapter 3 for more on our tricky brains) and a unique set of experiences that influence them. Feel a sense of common humanity.

When ready, approach the person and express yourself using the statements you developed in the preceding three sections.

TIP

With compassion for both yourself and the other person, consider the best time to attempt to have the conversation you've planned. Pick a time when neither of you are likely to be stressed or busy. Maybe aim for a time when you're both feeling calm and relaxed (as much as you can predict).

Reviewing your progress

It's helpful to review your progress – we're all on a learning curve and none of us are the finished article. Things don't always go to plan, but you'll understand more about yourself and the other person after you speak with them.

The following exercise will help you to review your experience as you develop the confidence to assert yourself with compassion.

To prepare for this exercise, have a pen and paper to hand (or a computer/mobile device). Sit in a relaxed, open posture with strength and alertness to your spine. When you feel ready, take the following steps:

1. **Evoke your compassionate mind and embody your compassionate self as you soften your facial expression and slightly relax your jaw.** Refer to Chapter 10 for guidance if you're unsure on how to get started.

2. **On a sheet of paper (or a computer screen/mobile device), write down the step you took to compassionately assert yourself.** Think through the preceding four exercises (in the preceding four sections), and what led you to the point where you had the conversation with the person you identified at the start of this process.

3. **Consider and write down what you discovered about yourself through compassionately asserting yourself.** Perhaps you found that you have more courage than you thought? (Head to Chapter 14 for ideas about how to express yourself through writing and the benefits of doing this.)

4. **Consider and make note of what you discovered about the other person.** Maybe their reaction surprised you, which may have been good or bad.

5. **Consider what it may be helpful to do or say in the future based on this experience.**

TIP

It can help to write compassionately about the things you've discovered about yourself and other people (head to Chapter 14 for more on compassionate writing). If things didn't go quite as you'd hoped, compassionate imagery (refer to Chapters 11 and 12) may help you to generate some inner support and maybe some new insights.

TIP

You can't plan for or be *proactive* about every situation. Some situations require you to be *reactive*; you may be put on the spot and need to say something quickly. In such situations, it's helpful to pause and take a soothing breath, feel strength in your spine and bring to mind the statements you developed in the earlier section 'Finding the words to express yourself'. The more you do this, the more naturally these words will come to you.

Managing Resistance to the Changes You're Making

Unfortunately, other people may resist the changes you're making. People get used to you behaving in a particular way and may interact with you accordingly. This resistance to change can be very frustrating! If you find that the people in your life are resisting your efforts to make changes to your life and relationships, you may want to address the issue directly.

EXAMPLE

Mira, a 34-year-old legal secretary, struggled with her confidence. Having decided to make changes and developed some ways to express herself, she practised making particular statements, both in the mirror and with the help of a trusted friend.

When Mira used the statements she'd developed at work to express her point of view, things went well. However, when she tried a similar approach with Paul, her partner, he simply responded: 'Have you been reading that self-help stuff again?' Even more frustratingly, when Mira raised an issue with her sister, again using the same formula, she shrugged her shoulders and said she didn't have the time to discuss things.

Mira thought long and hard about what Paul had said. Concerned that she would get the same response again, she took the time to follow the steps outlined in this chapter (in the earlier section, 'Asserting Yourself with Compassion') and write the following note to him:

> When you asked if I had been reading self-help books again it hurt, because I feel as though you don't want me to be more self-confident and that you're undermining my efforts. I am trying my best. It would be great if you could help me with this because I think it would be good for me and for our relationship. Can we discuss this?

With her sister, Mira decided to leave it for a while before bringing up the issue again. She then rang her sister and, using notes she had made to assist her, in a warm, confident and open manner, said:

> I know you said you didn't have time to discuss things, but this just makes me feel that you don't care. It would be good if you could spare some time to talk. Maybe we can go out for a walk and properly catch up about all sorts of things – it might be that there are things that you would benefit from talking through with me too, it's been so long since we properly caught up. If you can't that is okay as well – maybe we can do it some other time when you have more time.

These strategies resulted in good but different outcomes. With Mira's partner, Paul, the very first conversation after he had read her note brought them closer together. He started to take an interest in the changes she was trying to make and, in addition, changed his own behaviour towards her. Although Mira still had to bring things up from time to time, she noticed that Paul started to use this way of expressing himself as well – which was good all round.

With respect to her sister, they agreed to meet but her sister cancelled at the last minute. She did it again on two further occasions. Although it hurt, Mira felt proud that she had expressed her feelings and stopped beating herself up about being submissive around her. Mira wrote in her journal:

> This is about her, not me. I have tried to be more open and closer to her but she is unwilling or unable at this point in time to take this further. Maybe there is something going on for her that I don't know about. I will focus on the things I can change for the time being and I will be open when she feels ready to talk.

REMEMBER

Despite your best efforts, people may resist the changes you make (head to Chapter 7 for more on barriers to the changes we attempt to compassionately make). In such cases it may be helpful to simply maintain our commitment and try again. As Mira found in the preceding example, her initial efforts failed to produce the discussion she wanted with her partner Paul, but a different approach (whereby she wrote him a note) led to a more positive outcome.

It's also helpful to remember that although we can't change others, we can change ourselves. Despite Mira's second failed attempt with her sister, she felt a sense of pride, and ultimately an increase in confidence, due to her ability to compassionately assert herself.

TIP

If things don't go the way you hope, writing a compassionate letter to yourself (refer to Chapter 14), using compassionate imagery (refer to Chapter 11) and trying out chair work (see Chapter 17) are just some of the practices in this book that may help you.

Giving Constructive Feedback – Compassionately!

Many of us avoid giving honest feedback for fear of upsetting people. We may then become frustrated with others (and ourselves!) as unhelpful patterns of behaviour go on repeating themselves.

While compassionate assertiveness can help in such cases, so too can compassionate constructive feedback. Where the former tends to focus on asserting our own views, feelings and needs, the latter is more focused on our desire for the other person to be at their best and acknowledges our role with respect to this.

TIP

In the workplace, you may be expected to manage or supervise others, and so the focus should be on the other person's needs rather than your own. Try not to bring your own anxieties about being liked (or not) into your workplace interactions.

If you have difficulty giving constructive feedback, in any area of your life, try working through the following exercise.

1. **Think about a person to whom you wish to give some compassionate constructive feedback, and bring to mind the specific issue you want to deal with.** It may be their timekeeping, an aspect of their work or the manner in which they communicate with yourself or others.

2. **Take a few breaths and evoke your compassionate mind and compassionate self. Connect with the key compassionate attributes, especially strength and courage, empathy and non-judgement.** Refer to Chapter 10 for guidance on evoking your compassionate mind, and Chapter 2 for a reminder of the compassionate attributes.

3. **Remind yourself of your wish for the other person to be the best that they can be. Remind yourself of the important role you can play in their development.**

4. **Think about what the person in question needs to know, employing the following formula:**

    I want you to know that . . .

    It is important that I tell you this because . . .

    Can we discuss this?

TIP

Refer to the earlier section 'Finding the words to express yourself' for some other example scripts.

5. **Practise – be it on your own, with someone you trust or in front of the mirror.** Refer to the earlier section, 'Practising compassionately asserting yourself' for additional ideas.

6. **Plan how and when you're going to give your feedback.** Meeting one-to-one may be best, ideally at a time when you won't feel rushed or stressed, and you have enough time to discuss things fully.

7. **Make use of exercises you have previously found useful.** Perhaps making a detailed plan (refer to Chapter 15), writing a compassionate letter (refer to Chapter 14), cultivating compassionate thoughts (refer to Chapter 13) or using imagery to help you prepare further (refer to Chapters 10–12) have been helpful for you.

8. **Just before you meet with the person you're going to give feedback to, evoke your compassionate mind and inhabit your compassionate self.** You're then ready to provide constructive feedback to this person.

9. **Review your progress!** Again, it may help to write a compassionate letter, cultivate compassionate thoughts or consider using compassionate imagery to help you – especially if things don't go quite as you'd hoped. Refer to the earlier section, 'Reviewing your progress' for more on this.

EXAMPLE

Tony struggled to give constructive feedback to staff within his team at work. He found he either avoided giving it, fearful of potential confrontation, or ended up saying something when he was wound up and angry. He wasn't progressing as he'd hoped within his organisation and, in his recent appraisal, people management was identified to be a key factor.

He found that one of the new members of his team, Andrew, regularly completed work after the deadline he'd been given. At first he ignored it, thinking Andrew was just starting to familiarise himself with his new job and new roles. He reassured himself that eventually things would sort themselves out. Unfortunately, as time went on the problem continued.

Tony started commenting on Andrew's missed deadlines, to which Andrew would quickly respond, 'I'll get it to you tomorrow.' Invariably he did get the work to him on the following day, but it didn't stop his tasks being handed in after the deadline that Tony had originally set. Tony began to give Andrew false deadlines, a few days before work had to be in, but he resented having to do so. 'You're taking the mick out of me,' Tony thought. This was quickly followed by a tidal wave of self-criticism. 'Stand up for yourself', 'You're pathetic' and 'Loser' were just a few of the self-critical statements he bullied himself with.

He found that he was often short with Andrew, tended to look at his work with a more critical eye, and even began to leave the room when Andrew came in as he felt that his blood was boiling.

This was clearly not a good situation for Tony, Andrew or the rest of the team. Others saw Andrew getting away with missed deadlines, felt resentful and were aware of tension in the workplace.

In this situation, it seemed inappropriate for Tony to be talking about his own needs, feelings and thoughts because it was clear that Andrew was breaching clear deadlines and not meeting the targets set out in his job description. Tony felt that talking about his own needs, feelings and thoughts would only confuse and cloud the matter. Instead, he decided it would be helpful to give Andrew some compassionate constructive feedback from the perspective of his compassionate self. That evening he used compassionate imagery to remind himself of the key compassionate qualities, especially courage, empathy and non-judgement, and thought about the situation with Andrew from this perspective. Tony embodied his compassionate self and wrote in his journal:

> I want him to be the best that he can be, and I am potentially doing him a disservice by not addressing this issue with him.

Tony imagined himself saying to Andrew:

> I want you to know that deadlines are important for the smooth running of the department, and yet I've noticed that you regularly hand in your work late. It's important that we address this, because it has an impact on you, the work you do and the rest of the team. Can we discuss it?

Tony decided that it would be best to have the discussion away from the main part of the office and any potential interruptions, to allow plenty of space and time for this conversation. He ran through what he was going to say a few times, and used compassionate imagery and soothing rhythm breathing (refer to Chapter 9) to recruit a helpful frame of mind, one that would be non-judgemental, warm, empathic and strong.

The next day Tony engaged in his soothing rhythm breathing, reminded himself of the key compassionate attributes, embodied his compassionate self and, with warmth on his face and in his voice, asked to speak to Andrew. After he'd said what he had to say, Tony calmly waited for a response. Andrew paused and sat quietly for a few moments. He then responded, 'Yes, I know I'm terrible at working to deadlines. All I can say is that I'm sorry and I will make a concerted effort from here on in.' They discussed ways that Tony could help Andrew develop the skills he needed to work to deadlines. At the end of the meeting, Andrew shook Tony's hand and said, 'Thanks for being so good about it; I will do better.'

From a compassionate perspective, we hold in mind the other person's needs when we offer feedback, and we have their true interests at heart. This perspective is different from being self-focused and worrying how we're coming across and what the other person thinks about us.

Worrying too much about upsetting people can do that person a disservice and can make matters worse. We may fail to give them the feedback they need to be the best that they can be.

Turning your focus from your own worries to the other person's needs can give you the strength and courage to act. In Chapter 1, I introduced the story of the compassionate teacher. Their role was to nurture those around them to be the best they could be. This involves curiosity and the provision of feedback without judgement. Such a compassionate stance is beneficial for others, but ultimately it's also beneficial for ourselves because it improves our confidence, relationships and wellbeing.

Chapter 17

Understanding the Different Aspects of Yourself

The human brain has evolved over time to give you the capacity for fighting, hunting, seeking sexual partners and defending territory. You also have the capacity for caring for others and being cared for, relationship-building, playing, and creating social hierarchies. Your brain has developed the capacity to think into the future and the past, experience a sense of self and self-identity, and put yourself in other people's shoes and consider what they're thinking.

These different aspects are within all of us. They come with different motivations and emotions, physical sensations and thinking styles. Although such a tricky brain brings with it amazing capacities, it also predisposes us to conflict between these different aspects of who we are. We can become critical about what we're capable of, and confused by mixed emotions and motivations (refer to Chapter 3 for more on our tricky brains and the challenges we face).

In this chapter, I introduce the concept of using chair work to help you understand your various mindsets and their potential for conflict. I also explore how your compassionate self can help you to further the relationship between your self-critic and your criticised self. Finally, we take a look at how different emotions can be attached to the same situation and consider chair work as a means to work through these emotions.

Taking a Different Chair: Introducing Chair Work

A range of different therapies use physical movement between chairs (*chair work*) to explore the different aspects of ourselves and to create a dialogue between them. Within Compassion Focused Therapy (CFT), the key focus is the presence of a compassionate chair to nurture an awareness and understanding of the different parts of ourselves. From this perspective we warmly generate helpful feelings, behaviours and thoughts to our 'other selves'.

Chair work can help us tease out different aspects of ourselves, such as jealousy and disgust, boredom, anger, anxiety, a sense of feeling 'stuck', or hopelessness. It can help us see the relationship between our self-critic and criticised self.

Isolating the different aspects of ourselves can help us compassionately realise how complicated we are and therefore how difficult life can be. By recognising our competing feelings, thoughts and urges, we can begin to feel less shame and self-criticism and make more informed and helpful choices. Chair work, and personal understanding, can also help us understand others and their actions so that we move beyond the simple yet tempting idea that some people are good and others are bad or evil (see the nearby sidebar, 'Beyond good and evil: Different versions of you' for more on this).

REMEMBER

Chair work is thought to enhance our ability to understand our feelings, motivations and behaviours. This ability is often referred to as *mentalisation*. Improvements in mentalisation are associated with a greater ability to manage emotions and relate to others.

TIP

Although we often use different chairs to signify and separate the different aspects of ourselves, you may prefer to use cushions on the floor or specific spaces within a room.

Engagement with the chair-based exercises in this chapter will help to develop and strengthen your compassionate mind and compassionate self. The exercises may also highlight blocks and barriers that may benefit from further exploration.

For example, you may realise that while the anxious part of you is easy to connect with, anger or sadness isn't. Alternatively, you may find it difficult to be compassionate to a particular part of you. In realising any of these things, explore these discoveries with warm curiosity. It may be helpful to return to your life story (refer to Chapter 5) to explore why this may be; to check out Chapters 6 and 7 to explore common blocks and barriers to compassion; to use the compassionate practices outlined in Chapters 10–12; or to write a compassionate letter to yourself or an aspect of you (refer to Chapter 14).

BEYOND GOOD AND EVIL: DIFFERENT VERSIONS OF YOU

It can be protective to think that bad things are carried out by 'bad' or 'evil' people. This being the case, all we'd need to do would be to avoid certain people! But the reality is that we all have an incredible capacity for great compassion, kindness and care – *and* great cruelty. The circumstances of our lives dictate the *version* of us that inhabits the world.

If I was brought up by a different family, in the very same town I grew up in, I may have become a very different version of Mary Welford. Had I been brought up in a war-torn environment, perhaps the contrast between these two different versions of me would be even greater. I may have caused other people significant suffering and I may have killed people. Had I been born in eighteenth-century England I may have viewed hangings and executions as entertainment; had I been born into the early twentieth century I may have believed same-sex relationships were 'unnatural'; and had I been born in the nineteenth century I may have seen the slave trade as acceptable. I may have even been involved in such a barbaric act!

Even in this moment, my present-day actions (or inactions) may be viewed as cruel. I live in a house and within it I have more than I need to eat and clothe myself. I have much more 'stuff' than I need and yet I will still go out and 'acquire' more. Yet here I sit with the knowledge that others are in need of food, shelter and clothes. We can easily dissociate ourselves from these tough realities.

It can be sobering to realise these modern-day challenges. Only when we understand that we all have such startling capacities for compassion through to dissociation, denial and cruelty do we truly begin to address the issues that surround us and move, inch by inch, day by day, towards a compassionate approach for ourselves and others.

Practising Compassion for Your Self-Critic and Your Criticised Self

CFT recognises that self-criticism is at the heart of many psychological difficulties, and the CFT approach uses a range of ways to address and overcome this. Central to addressing self-criticism is the realisation that we have evolved brains and bodies that create many challenges that are not of our making (head to Chapter 3 to become familiar with the challenges we face). We're also the product of many experiences and influences that we wrongly blame ourselves for (refer to Chapter 5 for more on life stories).

In this section, we take a closer look at your *self-critic* (the part of you that's critical of yourself) and your *criticised self* (the part of you that's on the receiving end). With the help of different chairs, you first take on the role of a self-critic and experience this part of you and then, moving to another chair, explore what it feels like to be on the receiving end of your self critic (your criticised self).

In becoming aware of these different aspects of ourselves, we can begin to step back and make helpful choices. Do we let our self-critic rule the show, or is it helpful to develop compassion for both the self-critic and our criticised self and work to help them both? (For further information on self-criticism, head to Chapter 1.)

TIP

Throughout the exercises in this chapter, you'll be asked to assume the role of different aspects of yourself through chair work. Although it can be difficult, imagine that you are playing a character and stay in each role as much as you can. Explore and enact how that part of you may speak and how they may sit. Speak directly as this part of you. For example, instead of saying 'This part of me thinks . . .', say 'I think . . .'.

In the next exercise, you use chairs to enact both your self-critic and criticised self. You then use a third chair, evoking your compassionate mind and compassionate self, to view the argument that goes on within you and consider a more compassionate way of relating to the different parts of you.

Find a suitable place, free from distractions, where you can be for 20–30 minutes. If this timescale seems too daunting, start by aiming to work on this exercise for a shorter time.

1. **Arrange two chairs, directly facing each other. Allocate one for your self-critic and the other for your criticised self. Place a third chair facing the space between the other two (as though the third is dividing the attention equally between them).** You can use this third chair for your compassionate self.

2. **Before sitting in any of the chairs, bring to mind a time when you have been critical of yourself.** Maybe a time you told yourself off for something you did or didn't do.

3. **Sit in the chair allocated to your self-critic. Close your eyes and embody that part of you.** Think about how your self-critic feels, its tone of voice and its posture.

4. **Open your eyes and, facing the chair that will become your criticised self, say what's on the self-critic's mind, as though you're talking directly to another person.**

5. **Having explored the dialogue, tone of voice, feelings and posture of your self-critic, stand up, step out of that role and thank it for its input.** It may help to have a brief walk around the room, to stretch for a while or to engage in a mindfulness or compassionate imagery exercise (refer to Chapter 9 for more on these).

6. **When you're ready to resume this exercise, sit in the opposite chair to before – the chair for your criticised self. Become your criticised self and experience how it feels to be on the receiving end of your self-critic's words.** Consider the impact that your self-critic's tone of voice, means of interacting and facial expression has on you.

7. **Respond to your self-critic.** Consider your tone of voice, posture and feelings as you speak as your criticised self. If you are unable to respond in words, simply notice how your self-critic makes you feel.

8. **After a short time, thank your criticised self for its input.** Step out of the role of the criticised self and engage in a practice that's helpful to you (as you did earlier in the exercise, in Step 5).

9. **When you're ready to resume this exercise, return to the self-critic's chair and respond to what your criticised self communicated.**

10. **Thank your self-critic and engage in an exercise to help you again switch roles (refer to Steps 5 and 8). Return to the criticised self chair to place yourself on the receiving end of your self-critic's response once more.** Imagine the words and emotions that have been directed your way and consider the impact these have on you as you inhabit your criticised self.

11. **Thank your criticised self for its input.**

12. **Stand up and let the experience of inhabiting those different parts of you fade.** Move around the room or engage in a practice that's helpful to you (refer to Step 5 for inspiration) to distance yourself from the interactions between your self-critic and your criticised self.

13. **Sit in the third chair. Evoke your compassionate mind and embody your compassionate self. Remind yourself of the qualities associated with your compassionate self.** Evoking a memory of a time when you were compassionate may help you. For more on evoking your compassionate mind and compassionate self, refer to Chapters 10–12.

14. **Connect with a sense of compassion for your self-critic and your criticised self in turn.** Spend time being sensitive to the distress each part of you feels, and motivated to help.

15. **Consider what your compassionate self may say to your self-critic and your critical self.** From the perspective of your compassionate self, try to understand these different aspects of you, the feelings that your compassionate self may experience and its tone of voice and posture.

16. **Staying in the compassionate self chair, move your attention away from the critical and criticised parts of you that have been enacted.** Close your eyes, or lower your gaze and engage once more with an exercise that you find helpful. Refer to Step 5 for some inspiration for suitable exercises.

REMEMBER

The compassionate stance is not to 'get rid' of your self-critic but to understand its motivations and the concerns that lay behind its actions, and to practise compassion for it. However, the response of your compassionate self isn't to say 'there, there, it doesn't matter'. Your compassionate self responds to and understands the motivations of the self-critic, and meets these motivations with compassion. Your compassionate self may also say, with warmth and authority, 'I hear what you're saying, but this is unacceptable'.

This exercise can bring into sharp focus both the fear that motivates your self-critic and the damage it can do when you're on the receiving end of it. A question that can be important to ask is, 'Even though I know what my critic is trying to achieve, is the way it's going about it helpful to me?' The answer is, probably, no. In contrast, your compassionate self gives you the strength, courage and commitment to face the difficulties you need to face and to work to alleviate your distress.

TIP

From the perspective of your compassionate self, it can be helpful to convey the thoughts, feelings and emotions you have towards your self-critic and criticised self in writing (refer to Chapter 14 for the benefits of committing pen to paper and some exercises that can help you do this). Remember to remain in the role of your compassionate self and try not to allow your self-critic to take over and become critical!

When finished, take a break and then, having evoked your compassionate self once more, re-read what you've written. It may help to do this out loud, using a tone of voice that expresses warmth and care for your wellbeing.

REMEMBER

Abuse can result in individuals internalising the voice and words of their abuser. If you identify that your self-critical voice comes from another person, rather than being a part of you, it may be helpful to address the voice of the abuser more assertively. Sometimes, simply recognising this to be an echo from the past can be a powerful tool to help you distance yourself from it. It may also help to use your compassionate self to address the other voice more assertively.

TIP

If working your way through this exercise leads you to identify the voice of an abuser or another negative influence that goes beyond your own self-critic, you may find it helpful to talk to someone who has your best interests at heart, or to ask your GP to refer you to a professional.

Understanding Our Mixed Emotions

We often experience strong but differing emotions about singular events (be they in the past, present or future) or different people. *Mixed emotions*, and the thoughts, feelings and behaviours associated with them, are very common but can result in us feeling overwhelmed and confused. It can feel as though a game of pinball is being played out in our minds, with one thing leading to another and forming a loop over and over. Head to Chapter 3 for more on life's challenges.

At other times, particularly strong emotions can dominate or rule the show while others get suppressed and squashed.

EXAMPLE

Here are a few examples of situations that can bring about mixed emotions. Maybe you have experienced something similar to them:

» Motivated and excited to go on a date, learn to drive, go for an interview or gain a qualification, you find that as the test, date, interview or exam approaches, you become increasingly anxious. You may notice a racing heart, a dry mouth, churning stomach or sense of light-headedness. You may then worry that you're going to have a heart attack, choke, be sick or faint. With your head filled with such worries, your anxiety level rises even more.

You may begin to tell yourself off for putting yourself in such a situation or for feeling anxious. At the same time, the criticised part of you may feel sapped of energy and defeated. You may become motivated to avoid the situation, which is contrary to the excitement you initially experienced and your true intent and wish!

>> A close friend or relative says something that's hurtful. You feel criticised and anxious, and want to escape the situation. Part of you feels angry and wants to confront them or 'get them back'. In addition, you try to work out why they said such a thing, tell yourself off for over-reacting or worry that you do indeed have 'issues' that need to be addressed. All of this can go through your head in the space of five minutes: your mind goes round and round (caught in a mental loop), bouncing from one thought, emotion and behaviour to another, then another, then another!

>> Having had an offer accepted on a house or been successful at an interview, you become excited and simultaneously scared to death. A flurry of thoughts occupies your mind. Have I done the right thing? My old job wasn't that bad. Do I really want to move? This is going to be brilliant! You may find that you double-check aspects of the new job or house move, doubting whether it's the right decision. You may even decide to stay put.

Interesting, isn't it! It's rare that we experience one pure emotion about an event or person, but we often expect this of ourselves and become confused if we feel different things, seemingly at the same time. Mixed emotions can pull us in different directions. We may want to do something but be scared stiff and experience an urge to avoid doing it at the same time. We may feel angry towards someone, but this may hide a great deal of upset and hurt.

Exploring your different emotions, allowing time to work through them and using your compassionate self to assist you can be extremely beneficial.

Using the same methods outlined in the preceding section, you now use chairs to explore and work through different emotions. You can then recruit the help of your compassionate self to relate to and advise the different parts of you.

Common to most difficulties are the emotions of sadness, anxiety and anger. During the following exercise, you'll be asked to begin by exploring and working through strong emotions. For some this is easy because such emotions are readily accessible, but others can feel overwhelmed by them.

As the exercise proceeds, you'll be asked to consider those emotions that are more hidden. As such, the exercise changes. Take your time to connect and experience the different parts of you. Take breaks if you need to by getting up and moving around or engaging in exercises that you have previously found helpful, such as those provided in Chapter 9.

1. **Arrange four chairs in a circle.**

2. **Bring to mind an argument, disagreement or rupture in a relationship.**

3. **Sit in the first chair. Consider what emotion the argument, disagreement or rupture evokes in you most strongly. It may be anxiety, sadness, anger or another emotion. Name the feeling and therefore the chair you're sitting in. Familiarise yourself with the emotion. Slowly and gently consider the thoughts that accompany this emotion and their tone.** Voice the thoughts, as if that part of you is speaking. Where do you feel it in your body and what are you motivated to do?

4. **When you've explored this part of you, stand up and thank that part of you for its input. Engage in an exercise to calm your mind and body. Now move to the second chair and explore another emotion that is related to the argument, disagreement or rupture. Again, this may be anxiety, anger, sadness or a different emotion. Slowly and gently bring your attention to the thoughts that accompany this emotion and their tone.** Voice the thoughts, as if this part of you is speaking. Notice where you feel it in your body and what you feel motivated to do.

5. **Repeat Step 4 with the third chair and explore a third emotion.**

6. **Having sat in the first three chairs, move between them once again, and as you move around, consider what each part of you thinks of the other two.** For example, what does your angry self feel about your anxious and your sad self? What does your sad self feel about your anxious and your angry self? What does your anxious self feel about your sad and your angry self? It can be helpful to voice these thoughts rather than just think them.

7. **Sit in the fourth chair. Evoke your compassionate self. Remind yourself of the qualities associated with it.** It may help you to evoke a memory of a time when you were compassionate towards somebody else. For more on evoking your compassionate self, refer to Chapter 10.

8. **Connect with a feeling of compassion for each of these parts of yourself in turn.** Spend time simply sending compassion to each part of yourself.

9. **Consider what your compassionate self may say to these different parts of you.** From this perspective, consider the feelings that your compassionate self may experience, and the tone of voice and posture that your compassionate self may have.

Most people find particular emotions difficult to experience or acknowledge, be it anxiety, anger or sadness. Such emotions can be left unresolved and cause us problems This is normal. Allow yourself time to explore and consider these three different emotions with a sense of curiosity.

Additional emotions you may experience include jealousy, disgust, contempt or humiliation. Alternatively, you may prefer to use terms such as scared or nervous instead of anxiety; furious or raging instead of anger; down or blue as opposed to sadness.

If you still find a particular emotion difficult, ask yourself, 'What might I think and feel if I did feel anxious, angry or sad? What might I feel motivated to do and what would I make of the other emotions?' Doing this may unlock an emotion that you were previously unable to acknowledge or experience.

Donna's example helps illustrate how chair work can be used to help you work through strong emotions while relating compassionately towards your anxious, sad and angry selves.

Donna was an only child and had very dominant and authoritarian parents. Growing up, she suffered with anxiety, constantly questioned herself and, from time to time, suffered bouts of low mood.

In her twenties, Donna met Mark and had a family. Their supportive and nurturing relationship meant that Donna was able to keep much of her anxiety and worry at bay and her mood was good.

One thing that predictably set her back, however, was spending extended periods of time with her parents. Donna wanted to do this as she loved them greatly and always hoped that things would be different. In reality, time spent with them resulted in her feeling like a child again, and all her worries would come flooding back. Later, Donna would criticise herself for letting them get under her skin.

Following a difficult visit to her parents, Donna decided to make this visit the focus of a chair work exercise. Because anxiety was the main emotion she felt, she started in this chair. Donna found she had no problem enacting her anxious self: 'I can't cope with life', 'I'm useless and pathetic' were just some of the things she found herself saying in a hesitant voice. Donna felt a knot in the pit of her stomach, a racing heart and an urge to curl up in a ball.

Saying thank you to this part of her, Donna stood up and engaged in her soothing rhythm breathing for a short while. She then sat in a second chair that she named as her sad chair: 'It's so sad I can't spend quality time with my parents,' she said. 'I wish they could see me as an adult and not a young child.' 'It's unlikely to ever change,' she added. Donna felt her energy drain away and a heaviness in her chair. She felt the urge to take herself to bed.

Saying thank you to this part of her, Donna once again stood up and engaged in her soothing rhythm breathing. She sat in the third chair, but found it difficult to connect with any sense of anger. She considered some of the things that Mark sometimes voiced and put them in her own words. Tentatively she said 'This isn't fair, they're treating me like a child' and 'They should back off and be less critical of me.' Feeling tension in her body, Donna became aware that her posture had changed and she was alert in her chair, her chin slightly raised. She felt motivated to continue, this time with more anger in her voice. 'They're responsible for many of my hang-ups and they take no responsibility for them. Instead they harass me about things I should and shouldn't be doing and impose their views on me.' Donna was surprised by how much she got into the role of her angry self, and she continued to do so for some time.

When she felt ready to leave her angry self, Donna got up and walked around, this time taking a bit longer to engage in her soothing rhythm breathing and say goodbye to that part of her. Finally, she settled into her compassionate chair and engaged in an imagery exercise to evoke her compassionate mind and inhabit her compassionate self. Softly, she began to speak to each part of her. 'This is an extremely hard situation and I can see why you feel anxious and sad about it. I can also see that anxiety and sadness often means that I avoid dealing with the situation. Anger gives me energy that's helpful, but I need to be mindful that, left to its own devices it could damage relationships further.' Feeling a relaxation in her body yet alertness in her spine, Donna brought a warm expression to her face and continued.

'It's helpful for me to acknowledge that my anxious, sad and angry selves are all there for a reason. As my compassionate self, I can bring the strength, wisdom, courage and commitment to address the difficulties I have with my parents or support myself through it if they're reluctant to make changes.'

Donna then sat in the compassionate chair and one by one held the different parts of her in mind, relating to them with compassion.

Having completed the exercise, she sat with a warm drink. Donna was better able to be fully present with her own family that evening, instead of ruminating or worrying about her relationship with her parents.

Focusing on the core emotions of anxiety, sadness and anger is a good starting point for chair work. During the exercises, if you become fleetingly or maybe powerfully aware of other emotions, simply add more chairs, attempting to inhabit and enact that part of you by giving it a voice.

Becoming more aware of our emotions, giving them space and relating to them with compassion allows us to understand our emotions and ourselves more. We can then make more helpful choices with respect to the parts of us we wish to nurture and develop – for me, my sad, anxious and angry self require airspace, but the strengthening of my compassionate self wins every time!

Chapter 18

Placing Compassion at the Centre of Your Life

When deciding to be fit and healthy, it's tempting to make short-term commitments, such as giving up chocolate or opting for the stairs instead of the lift for a month. It's also tempting to be hard on yourself as a means to motivate yourself. This may involve sternly telling yourself, 'I'm fat and I've got to lose weight', 'I've let myself go and I've got to be fitter', 'I'm a slob and I've got to keep the house tidier' or 'I'm lazy and I've got to be more productive'. Achieving your goals in this way may mean that you feel great, but the improvement in your mood, waistline, fitness or tidiness is often short-lived as you lurch to achieve another goal or experience a setback.

The combination of short-term goals and self-criticism (refer to Chapter 1 for more on your self-critic) can actually mean you're less likely to achieve your goals, and you may be more prone to low mood, anxiety and avoidance.

In contrast, instead of motivating yourself through short-term goals and self-criticism, how about developing life-long compassionate commitments to yourself and others and working to achieve these goals through developing your compassionate mind and compassionate self? After all, if you're worthy of fitness and health, a nice environment, and greater wellbeing now, surely you're also worthy of such things in years to come?

When we motivate ourselves out of true care for our wellbeing, we're more likely to be supportive of ourselves and our efforts, achieve our goals, and maintain them. From this perspective, we're also better able to acknowledge the likelihood of good days and setbacks too. A commitment to a compassionate way of life gives us a long term perspective of the person we wish to be, and the process by which we do it. Motivating ourselves through compassion enhances our mood, and makes us much less likely to throw the towel in!

Living your life with a long-term view and a compassionate relationship with yourself means that compassion becomes part of who you are, and not just something you're successful at.

In this chapter, we consider what you've found helpful and develop long-term commitments for your future. We think about how you can bring compassion into additional, and maybe overlooked, areas of your life, and focus your efforts to maximise its effect. Finally, we consider obstacles that may get in the way of your personal practice, and explore some of the ways you can overcome them.

Placing Compassion Centre-Stage in Your Life

In this section, we start by reminding ourselves why developing a supportive relationship with ourselves is more beneficial than a critical one. Maybe you'll also identify with the scenario and it can give you some ideas about small yet very significant changes you can make to additional areas of your life.

Imagine that you have a difficult phone call to make, one you've managed to avoid so far, and, in a harsh tone of voice, tell yourself, 'You've got to make that call tonight.' Consider the feelings and physical sensations that this evokes within you. Also, consider how motivated you feel by this internal conversation.

Now imagine that, instead of being hard on yourself, you calmly and warmly recognise that continuing to avoid making the call is likely to cause you more stress in the long run. Consider how, out of care for your wellbeing, it may be helpful to pick up the phone at your earliest convenience and make the difficult call.

Which strategy is the most helpful – being hard on yourself or being supportive?

Being motivated by care for your own wellbeing doesn't mean that you say, 'There, there, you don't need to make the call. You can do it another time.' Your compassionate self recognises that the call may be difficult, and understands why we all avoid such things. But it also acknowledges that continuing to avoid it is likely to bring further problems in the short and longer term. Your compassionate self warmly supports you to help you face that which you find difficult.

The Dalai Lama is associated with the practice of compassion. He's unlikely to get to the point of saying, 'That's it, I've done my bit, I'm up to the brim with compassion and I'm now going to do something completely different!' Instead, he's likely to continue living a compassionate life because he's lived with the experience of it helping himself and others – this is how he chooses to spend his life.

Compassion isn't something we do and then stop doing. It's a way of life. It's a way of viewing ourselves and a way of viewing others.

Head to Chapter 21 for further ideas on how to bring compassion into your life and the lives of others.

Developing Your Daily Practice and Identifying New Frontiers

This book is full to the brim with exercises, and it's easy to forget the specific ones that we found helpful and those we found more difficult.

We begin by identifying the exercises you've found helpful throughout this book, and we make note of these in order that they can become the bedrock of your regular compassionate practice. We also consider those exercises you found more difficult and reflect on whether these highlight barriers it may be useful for you to work on and overcome. It may be helpful to view these as the *next frontiers* upon which to focus your efforts.

Consider all the different exercises you've tried while reading this book. Which exercises have you found helpful? Some may have helped you address specific difficulties, while others may have resulted in improvement in your mood, relationships and general wellbeing. Maybe you benefitted particularly from specific mindfulness or imagery exercises, letter writing, compassionate thinking or compassionate assertiveness?

It may help to flick through this book or the Table of Contents pages to remind yourself of all the different things you've tried.

Make a list of the exercises that you find helpful. You can then use these exercises to form the foundation of your personal practice as you continue to develop your compassionate mind and compassionate self.

Now consider the exercises or practices that you find difficult. These may highlight blocks or barriers for you. For example, you may have found experiencing compassion from others, or self-compassion for aspects of your life story, difficult (refer to Chapter 5 for more about your life story, Chapter 11 for more on experiencing compassion from others, and Chapter 12 for more on self-compassion). Consider whether it may be worthwhile to focus more effort on these challenging exercises to help you overcome these barriers.

Make a list of the exercises that you find difficult. You can set aside time to take another look at such areas and then use these exercises to form the new frontier of your compassionate development.

You may choose to write your personalised list of exercises out as a checklist so that you can tick them off on a daily basis. The following points may also help you to successfully integrate and build your compassionate mind and compassionate self into your everyday life:

>> Place the list of exercises in your diary, on your calendar or maybe on the front of your fridge.

>> Use colours, fonts and images that enhance your motivation and compassionate self.

>> Tie your personal practice in with other daily activities. For example, mindfulness may be practised when you're walking or washing your hands. It may help to engage with 'you at your best' whenever you have a warm drink or when you first wake.

>> Buddy up with someone and engage in exercises together or talk through ideas. You can also discuss the blocks and obstacles that you come across and help keep each other focused, motivated and on track.

>> Experiment with one of the many apps that are available to act as a helpful reminder or to structure your practice.

Compassion Focused Therapy (CFT) emphasises an individualised approach to bringing compassion into our lives. After all, although we're incredibly similar, we're also amazingly unique in a whole range of different ways. What works for one person won't work for another and, just to confuse things more, what works for you now may not be what works for you in the future.

Developing a flexible plan that you compassionately support yourself to follow, and reviewing it at intervals, is key to making compassion centre stage in your life.

TIP

Reviewing your progress on a daily or weekly basis can help you maintain momentum and tailor your practice based on the things you learn about yourself and others. As you develop your practice, you may then find it helpful to review your progress less frequently.

Overcoming Obstacles to Progress

In the following sections, we look at some of the common obstacles you may encounter while you're trying to implement compassionate practices into your everyday life, and consider some ideas that may help you to overcome these difficulties.

I keep forgetting to practise

Busy lives mean that our attention is easily grabbed by all manner of different things. Before we know it, we can end up living on autopilot. Our lives and our living environment can end up dictating what we do with our time and can move us away from what we would prefer to be focusing on. Frequent distractions may mean that we simply forget to work on developing our compassionate self.

TIP

Similar to the practice of mindfulness, when you become aware that you've forgotten to engage with your self-practice exercises and strategies on a regular basis, warmly see this as an opportunity to refocus your mind and to return to your true intention. Evoke your compassionate mind, embodying your compassionate self, and consider how you can remind yourself to work on your exercises and to practise compassion in your daily life. (The earlier section 'Developing Your Daily Practice and Identifying New Frontiers' offers some helpful advice for making compassion a part of your everyday life.)

REMEMBER

When you notice that you've drifted away from your goals, instead of being self-critical, take a soothing breath, create a warm facial expression and thank your brain for bringing it to your attention – it's trying to help you out and point you in a helpful direction.

I don't have the time

If you feel that you can't make time for your compassionate practice, it may be helpful to remind yourself of the benefits associated with developing your compassionate mind and compassionate self. Enhanced creativity and mood combined with less procrastination, worry and avoidance are just some of the many benefits (refer to Chapters 1 and 2 for more on the benefits of compassion).

TIP

Having developed my own ways to integrate practices into my life, I actually think that I don't have time *not* to practice: with compassionate practice, I'm more efficient and my mind is calmer. I procrastinate and ruminate less, giving me more time to focus on the things it's helpful for me to do. Of course, like anyone, I can get swept away by the stress of a busy life or the difficulty of a situation, but a simple one-minute breathing exercise can make a lot of difference.

My personal list of everyday or weekly practices includes:

» Mindful dog walking.

» One minute of mindful breathing between therapy sessions.

» A compassionate imagery exercise, involving perspective-taking, whenever I realise I am heading for or in the midst of a confrontation.

» Compassionately asking myself, 'What can I do for myself today that will make tomorrow a better day?'

Most days I don't achieve everything I set out to, but my motivation to try, try and try again remains constant. I support myself in my efforts and day by day I get closer to the person I wish myself to be – while, importantly, appreciating and actually liking the person I am right now.

I'm not getting the results I hoped for

Compassion-focused exercises can bring with them difficult emotions such as sadness, anxiety and anger because compassion involves being in tune with our own difficulties, as well as those of other people. It also involves considering why we do the things we do and feel the way we feel. Instead of being on autopilot or in denial, we begin to face up to the challenges in our lives.

Delving into these difficulties may be quite different from the things we hoped to achieve through compassionate practices, such as peace of mind and happier mood states. However, by connecting with the difficulties we face, we create an opportunity to work through emotions that seem to overwhelm us or hold us back, and so we lay them to rest. Our mind becomes a more comfortable place to be as we warmly connect with ourselves (as well as others). We're then better able to look ahead with a calmer mind and body.

For some people, simply knowing that the route to connection, peace of mind and joy often involves touching fear, frustration and sadness can encourage them to be patient with themselves and to work through the many different feelings evoked by their practice. Others find that it can be helpful to enlist the support of a friend, relative or professional to assist them through the difficult times. There's no right or wrong. What's important is that you consider your options and act out of care for your wellbeing.

I don't have any support from the people in my life

Unfortunately, you can't control other people in your life (or anyone else for that matter), and sometimes people won't support or understand the changes that you're attempting to make for yourself. As such, all you can do is focus on the changes that it's helpful for you to make and hope that others will come to support your efforts and maybe make their own changes, with time.

If you think other people are spoiling your efforts, consider communicating how you feel (you can use some of the exercises outlined in Chapter 16 to guide you). You may need to persevere and repeat things a number of times and in different ways.

You may find that when you've successfully communicated your feelings to a close friend, relative or partner, they actually want to find out more – perhaps they just didn't understand what you were attempting to do. If you think that someone in your life may benefit from discovering more about compassion and how CFT is helping you, consider asking them to read Chapter 20, which introduces some of the basic concepts and, hopefully, will provide some useful background information.

TIP

Sometimes we need to move away from people who present obstacles to our wellbeing. This may involve ending a relationship, changing jobs or distancing ourselves from friends or relatives. Although difficult, this may be the most compassionate thing to do – for you and them. Of course, it's very difficult to accept that this may be what is needed, so the support of someone you trust or a professional may assist you in this process.

CULTIVATING A COMPASSIONATE GARDEN

What happens if a garden is left to its own devices? It may become over-run by certain plants, while others decline. If you want your garden to look a certain way, you need to cultivate it: you start with an idea of what you want to create and then you commit to developing it. You may occasionally spend a whole day on the garden, but you also need to do more frequent watering, tending and, of course, weeding!

In a similar way, if you leave your mind to its own devices, your threat-focused mind always dominates (refer to Chapter 4 for more on your threat system). But is this the way you want to live: listening to your self-critical thoughts, your worries and ruminations? The answer is probably no.

If you intend to develop a more compassionate version of yourself, focus your energies and make a commitment to this process. Nurturing your compassionate mind and compassionate self takes time and effort – but the payoffs are immeasurable.

5

The Part of Tens

Chapter 19

Ten Pointers for Seeking a Professional Therapist

Compassion Focused Therapy (CFT) is gaining popularity around the world for a number of reasons, one of which being that it takes a scientific approach to understanding ourselves. Instead of seeing ourselves as weird, dysfunctional or flawed, the approach stresses the struggles that we all face due to the complexity of our tricky brains and the challenges of our social environment (refer to Chapter 3 for more on our tricky brains). It stresses the importance of us all being 'in it together', and this central common theme of shared humanity is intuitively attractive to people.

Another great reason for the popularity of CFT is that research studies now demonstrate its effectiveness, and the growing evidence base means that more therapists are becoming trained in the approach, and more books, such as this one, are being written for people to learn about it and apply it to their lives.

This chapter helps you to consider if it may be helpful to gain the input of a professional CFT therapist, how to select the right one for you and, finally, how to get the most out of this therapy.

Knowing When a Professional May Be Able to Help You

A range of things can stand in the way of developing your compassionate mind and compassionate self. These include the beliefs you hold, strong or unexpected emotions, shame, self-criticism and the reactions of others. In addition, it's often difficult to maintain the motivation required to address your difficulties due to competing pressures and demands. Working with a professional therapist can help you to understand, address and negotiate these difficulties.

REMEMBER

Taking time to reflect on the things that shape you, considering the difficulties you face, and developing your compassionate mind and compassionate self is an emotional process. As such, gaining the support of another human being can help.

TIP

Instead of seeking a therapist, a CFT 'buddy' may help. Identifying a close friend or family member to go on the CFT self-help journey with you can provide both parties with a sounding board, a listening ear and a source of emotional support. Buddies can also help you to maintain your momentum when life gets in the way and your motivation is affected.

Understanding Different Professional Backgrounds

In the UK, anyone can call themselves a therapist or counsellor. Such terms aren't 'protected' for those who have undergone training. However, 'professionals' have qualified from a particular course and their training can let you know a little bit more about the way they work. None of these professional groups are better or worse than another: what's important is to find the right person for you.

Here are the most common groups from which you may find professionals trained in CFT:

>> *Clinical psychologists* study a broad range of psychological principles and theories in their initial psychology degree. They then study at doctorate level to help individuals understand, prevent and alleviate psychological distress. They can offer assessments, consultations and a range of different therapies.

>> *Psychiatrists* are medical doctors who go on to specialise in the detection and alleviation of psychological problems. They can prescribe medication and often specialise in specific forms of therapy.

>> *Counselling psychologists* have a degree in psychology and then train further in counselling and different types of psychotherapy.

>> *Nurse therapists* train in psychiatric nursing and then go on to specialise in a specific form of psychotherapy.

>> *Counsellors* usually train in listening and helping skills. They may then specialise in a specific way of working.

>> *Psychotherapists* usually train in a specific type of therapy, such as Systemic and Family Therapy, or Cognitive Behavioural Therapy (CBT).

TIP

Therapists in training offer therapy. Their job title is often prefixed by terms such as trainee, student or assistant. Most are very competent and work under the close supervision of a qualified member of staff. If the therapist you see is in training, it can be helpful to ask who they report to and who they're supervised by. That way, if you have any concerns, complaints or commendations you will know who to speak with.

Reassuring Yourself about Your Therapist's Experience

Professionals can access a number of courses in order to specialise in CFT. Currently, the most comprehensive training courses are the Certificate and Diploma in CFT. Both are run in the UK. The Compassionate Mind Foundation (www.compassionatemind.co.uk) also provides three-day intensive courses as well as bespoke or specialist courses.

A therapist's level of CFT expertise depends on a whole range of factors, such as the amount of training and additional study they've conducted, how long they've been using the approach, and the clinical supervision they receive. It's worth asking a potential CFT therapist about their training, supervision and self-practice.

REMEMBER

CFT advocates that developing and maintaining our compassionate mind and compassionate self is helpful for us all. CFT isn't an approach that's simply 'done' to those who are experiencing difficulties. CFT therapists therefore participate in personal self-practice that helps them to maintain their compassionate mind and compassionate self. By doing this, they're able to be of best assistance to you.

Considering Other Forms of Therapy

Many different forms of psychotherapy exist, and a number of therapists integrate CFT with other approaches. You can find a lot of information on the Internet regarding the broad range of therapy approaches, but here are a few:

>> *Person Centred Therapy* emphasises the warmth, empathy and non-judgement of the therapist. It's non-directive; in other words, the therapist doesn't direct the client one way or another but instead creates a space in which individuals can generate their own insights in the light of which changes may be made.

>> *Systemic Therapy* looks at the relationships between individuals and understands the difficulties that can arise as a result of this dynamic.

>> *Cognitive Behavioural Therapy* encourages individuals to look at their thoughts and behaviours and consider alternatives as a means to alleviate their difficulties. For more on CBT, check out *Cognitive Behavioural Therapy For Dummies* by Rhena Branch and Rob Willson (Wiley).

>> *EMDR* (*Eye-Movement Desensitisation and Reprocessing*) aims to work on distressing memories in order to reduce the difficulties associated with them.

>> *MBSR* (*Mindfulness-Based Stress Reduction*) and *MBCT* (*Mindfulness-Based Cognitive Therapy*) both teach mindfulness skills to help with physical and psychological health problems as well as the ongoing challenges that life creates for us. You can find out more about mindfulness in Chapter 9. You may also want to check out *Mindfulness For Dummies* by Shamash Alidina, or *Mindfulness-Based Cognitive Therapy For Dummies* by Patrizia Collard (both Wiley).

Considering Different CFT Formats

CFT is usually offered in one of two formats: *individual* (often called one-on-one) therapy or *group* therapy. Although considering attending a group can initially be anxiety-provoking, members almost unanimously report that hearing about the experiences and difficulties of others, knowing they're helping others on their journey, and learning about the approach together can be the most helpful way to overcome shame and self-criticism. It can also be a lot more fun!

Some therapists and services offer a mixture of these two approaches. In other words, people attend some individual sessions as well as meeting with a group.

TIP

Most groups are attended by a mixture of people. However, some groups are exclusively male or female, while others focus on a specific difficulty such as low mood, anxiety or physical health problems. You may find it helpful to speak to a CFT therapist to discuss the options available to you and to find out which approach best fits your needs.

Finding a Compassion Focused Therapist

Currently there is no specific directory for compassion focused therapists. As a starting point, consider speaking with your general practitioner (GP) to find out what services and therapists are available in your area. Your GP may then be able to refer you to an appropriate service. This may be with the NHS or your local authority.

CFT is offered in some schools and universities, through some occupational health or staff wellbeing services, and also through a number of charities. Therapists may also work exclusively or partly in private practice. Speak to friends and relatives or conduct an Internet search to locate some options.

TIP

Before meeting with your therapist for the first time, checking that they're registered with an appropriate regulatory body is important. In the UK, this body is the Health and Care Professions Council (HCPC). Most countries have an equivalent organisation to register and govern therapists.

Certain assumptions can underlie a wish to see a male or female, or an old or young, therapist. Similarly, certain assumptions can also lie behind requests for a therapist from a particular cultural or religious background. Although it's imperative for services to respect and offer choice, it can be beneficial for those considering therapy to be open and curious. You never know – you may even be surprised!

TIP

When asking for a therapy referral, take some information with you regarding the type of therapy you want to be referred for and any articles that outline its effectiveness. A source of up-to-date information can be found at www. compassionatemind.co.uk.

Most services have a waiting list for an initial assessment, and, if recommended, for any subsequent therapy offered. Waiting doesn't, however, mean that you have to be inactive. In fact, you may find that it's a good time to be more active in the development of your compassionate mind, safe in the knowledge that therapy is just around the corner.

Timing Your Therapy: How Many, How Long, How Frequent?

The number and length of individual and group sessions, as well as the gap between appointments, can vary greatly. Such factors depend upon the difficulties experienced and the blocks and barriers that need to be overcome. Whereas one person may benefit greatly from a one-off consultation, another may attend appointments for months or years or work through multiple cycles with a group. Certain sessions may comfortably fit into an hour, while others may benefit from being shorter or longer.

A therapist will be open to discussing your requirements with you, and, if you agree to an initial number of appointments, will build in specific review points to consider your progress and to allow you to plan ahead.

Towards the end of therapy, it can be helpful to leave increasingly longer periods of time between sessions. This allows you to develop confidence in your ability to maintain the changes made and to negotiate the setbacks that occur from time to time. Booster sessions at pre-planned intervals can also be helpful.

We're a social species and we develop meaningful relationships that are key to our wellbeing. It's helpful to know that, if the need arises, we can gain the support of others – so if life becomes difficult once more, you shouldn't feel any shame in seeking a re-referral or a further appointment. The key to a meaningful life is interdependence, not independence!

REMEMBER

We all need to be careful not to nurture long-term dependence on others. For example, it wouldn't be helpful if, at the end of therapy, you felt totally reliant on your therapist. But sometimes, in order to take the necessary risks and to develop our confidence, it's helpful to know that support is available if things prove to be tricky to overcome. After all, most trapeze artists don't learn without a safety net!

Asking Questions: Getting to Know Your Therapist

Before you make contact with your therapist for the first time, it can be helpful to jot down a few questions. Here are a few ideas:

>> Are you registered with a regulatory body such as the HCPC (in the UK)?

>> What is your professional background?

>> What training do you have in CFT?

>> Do you attend CFT supervision? (This involves regular meetings with another CFT-trained professional, with the aim of discussing their cases.)

>> Is there a maximum number of sessions that I'm entitled to (if the sessions are free at the point of delivery)?

>> Is there a minimum number of sessions (if private)?

>> What is the cost per session (if private)?

>> How long is each session?

>> Will session times and days vary?

>> How often will we review progress?

>> Have you seen other individuals who have similar reasons for coming to therapy?

>> If I need to cancel my appointment, how do I do this?

>> Are there any consequences associated with a missed appointment?

>> Are there any questionnaires that I can fill in that can help measure my progress?

>> Can I bring someone with me (if preferable to you)?

>> Do you engage in your own self-practice?

>> Do you have any initial or supplementary materials that I can watch or read?

Overcoming Your Fears about Therapy

We have an innate capacity to try to work out what other people think of us, and whether we can trust them. This tendency is triggered when we meet a therapist or other therapy group members to talk about important things.

Worries and concerns can jump into our minds as we contemplate attending therapy – like a *pre-mortem*, where you repeatedly think about what could go wrong – and therapy sessions may be followed by a *post-mortem*, where you go over and over what was said and how the session went. This can be extremely tiring, both emotionally and physically, and may lead to you deciding not to pick up the phone or ask for a referral (because you may also be worried about what your GP thinks of you!). Alternatively, you may consider dropping out of therapy.

You can find out more about why we often have such worries and concerns in Chapters 3 and 4. Chapter 5 may also help you to understand the origins of your worries and concerns in the context of your life, while Chapter 13 can help you cultivate more compassionate thoughts.

Some people become lost for words when trying to ask for a referral, call for an appointment or attend a session. The part of the brain that helps you with speech can go literally 'off-line'. So even if you feel motivated to speak, shame and anxiety may mean that, in the moment, you find it difficult to put things into words. Therapists understand this and will do whatever they can to put you at ease.

Other common fears include concerns that personal information will be shared with others, anxiety about 'opening a can of worms', and the experience of strong emotional responses. From a practical point of view, people worry about taking time off work to attend appointments, cost (if attending private sessions) and whether it's the right time for them to seek therapy.

Many people find that, once the session has started, their worries begin to fade. However, it can help to jot down your concerns so that you can remember to discuss them with your therapist.

CFT was initially conceived as a means of addressing shame and self-criticism. As such, CFT therapists are sensitive to such things.

At the start and end of every session, your therapist may ask for feedback, ask how you found the session, and may also ask you to raise any concerns you have and to identify things you would like to focus on differently. This is an opportunity to address your concerns and fears.

Some people find that it helps to bring someone along to their first appointment and, at times, subsequent ones. This is perfectly normal so it may be helpful to consider this.

Others find that it's really unhelpful for another person to be with them at their therapy appointment, but find it difficult to say no. Your therapist may ask to see you individually at some point in order to check out how helpful or unhelpful it is for you to have the other person attend. If they don't do this, it may help to give them a call to discuss your concerns.

CFT emphasises that we're more similar than different. Non-judgement, curiosity, empathy, sensitivity, tolerance of distress and a sense of common humanity are just some of the elements that CFT therapists both practise and advocate. For further information, head to Chapter 1 for an overview of CFT, and turn to Chapter 2 for more on what compassion involves from a CFT perspective.

Getting the Most Out of Therapy

Being open and honest in your therapy and approaching it with a sense of curiosity are just two ways to help you get the most from your time with your therapist. Here are a few additional ideas:

>> Sit quietly before and after each session for a period of time. This can help you orientate your mind and enhance your memory for, and emotional processing of, the session.

>> Ask for the guided exercises, practised in the sessions, to be digitally recorded so that you can repeat the exercises between sessions.

>> Make notes before, after and in-between sessions. This can both aid your memory and become the focus of subsequent exercises.

>> Provide your therapist with regular feedback. It's just as important to let them know about the things that are going well as it is about the things that are difficult for you – balance is the key!

REMEMBER

Many people find it difficult to give feedback. You may fear that you'll be judged, upset your therapist or look stupid. If you find it difficult, bring your attention to all the people that the therapist is yet to see in the future. With them (not yourself, and not the therapist) in mind, share what you think it may be helpful for future clients to know and consider.

>> Consider a time each day to orient your mind to the commitment you're making to enhance your wellbeing. Engage in exercises to build and maintain your compassionate mind and compassionate self.

>> Work with your therapist or your therapy group as you near the end of your therapy to develop a plan for the future. This can contain review points so that you can amend and adjust your plans as you go.

Chapter 20

Ten Tips You May Want to Share

Some people prefer to engage in self-help or therapy without letting anyone else know, while others feel it's important to share information or even to get certain people involved. If you've decided to let people know that you're attempting to make some changes in your life, consider sharing the key points in this chapter. (You may decide to do this verbally or simply ask them to read this chapter in their own time.)

Letting people know that you're trying to make some changes can help them to understand what's going on with you. It can also increase your opportunities for discussion and support. And, of course, it's possible that they'll discover ways to make helpful changes too!

That said, some people can be obstructive and may have a negative view of the changes you hope to make. (Head to Chapter 7 for more on the barriers you may face as you develop your compassionate mind and compassionate self.) In such cases, it may be helpful to engage in the exercises on your own at first, and to wait until you're part way through the process before you consider speaking with them about what you're doing. This may help you in a number of ways. First, your compassionate mind will provide you with the confidence and courage to broach difficult conversations (head to Chapters 15 and 16 for specific exercises to help with this). In addition, as you embody your compassionate self, others may see a positive change in you and be more open to discussion as a result. However, if others remain obstructive, your compassionate mind and compassionate self can help you consider another way forward and come to terms with the reactions of others.

But back to sharing your experience! The tips in this chapter provide some introductory ideas and Compassion Focused Therapy (CFT) concepts for you to share with others when you feel ready.

TIP

Because you may wish to share this chapter, I've written it *to* the person you've decided to share it with.

Self-Help Is a Good Thing

Most people are trying to make improvements to their lives in some way. Some do this via to-do lists, others through New Year's resolutions, job changes, house moves, gym enrolments, self-help or therapy. It's not something to feel awkward or ashamed about – self-help is just one way that you can try to improve things for yourself and for other people.

Self-Help Isn't About Being Selfish

Taking care of yourself and being aware of your needs shouldn't be confused with selfishness. *Selfishness* is behaving with a lack of consideration for others and profiting from it. CFT, on the other hand, focuses on your wellbeing so that you're better able to help both yourself and others.

REMEMBER

CFT emphasises the development, enhancement and maintenance of *self-compassion*, compassion *from* others and compassion *for* others.

People Need to Make Changes for Themselves

We have a tendency to think that other people need to make changes to their lives. You may even have ideas about what it would be helpful for them to do. Perhaps you want them to make these changes for the benefit of their own *and* your own wellbeing. But ultimately, people need to decide upon potential changes and make them for themselves.

It's therefore helpful to wait to be asked for your input and to, when the time is right, schedule in some time to regularly speak to your friend, relative or partner about these changes and how they're helping (or presenting challenges!). Good communication is the key to a healthy relationship!

You're Important!

If you're reading this, it's helpful to know that you're obviously important to the person who has asked you to read it. They consider you to be someone they can trust.

TIP

Be open about any support you feel able to offer. It may involve simply being aware that your friend, relative or partner is engaging in self-help, being responsive at the times when they wish to talk about it, or setting aside a regular time to talk things through.

REMEMBER

CFT is based on the principle of common humanity and aims to be of benefit to all. As such, it's likely that you'll experience a benefit too as you discover more about CFT and the benefits your friend, relative or partner is experiencing. The ripples created by CFT can travel far.

Plan Nice Things

Look for opportunities to do nice things with the person who's embarking on this journey. Plan some pleasurable or achievement-based activities: book a babysitter and have a 'date night', enrol on a course, engage in some exercise or, together, get involved with a local group.

Nice activities can provide the perfect opportunity for conversations about the process of therapy – and can also be a fun distraction if the therapy is proving difficult! Enjoyable activities can also be of benefit to you – life can all too often get busy and stressful, so it's helpful to remind yourself about what matters and get back to basics, spending meaningful time with those you care about.

REMEMBER

Busy lives can lead to lost momentum, so keep on planning ahead.

Change Takes Time and Effort

Learning anything new takes time and dedication. The process can be up and down, stop and start. At times we can all feel back at square one, and this can affect both motivation and confidence in the process. Be aware of the effort your friend, relative or partner is making and offer gentle encouragement – and if you decide to start making changes in your own life, keep this important point in mind for when your motivation is challenged.

TIP

Questions such as 'How can I help?' and 'What do you need?' can be far more beneficial than statements starting with 'You need to do . . .'. Refer to the earlier section 'People Need to Make Changes for Themselves' for more on this important point.

Change Can Feel Like an Emotional Rollercoaster!

Taking time out of our busy lives to reflect on our experiences and make changes can be an emotional endeavour. Working through emotions such as sadness, anger and frustration while allowing experiences of hope, joy and gratitude is part of the process. As your friend, relative or partner engages in CFT, they're asked to gently create space in their lives to experience such emotions. Wellbeing is not about feeling good all the time – it's about experiencing the wide range of human emotions and being okay with them.

TIP

If your friend, relative or partner experiences strong emotions or mood fluctuations, let them know that you've noticed and gently ask if you can be of help.

You're a Unique Human Being

From the moment of conception, we're each unique. Throughout our lives we're then influenced by both specific experiences and the culture we're born into. Everyone tries to get by in the best way that they can – you included!

You may have aspects of your life that you want to improve. At times you may not act in the way that you want to behave. We all say things we don't truly mean, and this can have an impact on ourselves as well as other people.

CFT doesn't require anyone to apportion blame, although it's important for us all to reflect and take the appropriate level of responsibility for the impact we have on ourselves and the people around us. CFT involves being sensitive to our own distress and that of others, and developing a motivation to do what we can to prevent and alleviate this distress.

Get Involved with the Journey

TIP

Consider how you want to be involved in the process as your friend, relative or partner begins to make compassionate changes. You may simply like to become more aware of what this person (who considers you to be important to their life) is engaging with, perhaps by reading this book chapter by chapter with them – a bit like a compassionate book club!

The central message of CFT is that we're more similar than different, we all struggle, and our lives can be enhanced through the development and maintenance of our compassionate mind and compassionate self. If you take part in this journey with your friend, relative or partner, it may be an eye-opening experience for you too.

Overcoming Your Misconceptions

You're likely to be reading this chapter because you're interested in how CFT can help you develop and maintain your compassionate mind and compassionate self. However, you, or other people with whom you may in turn want to share these tips, may be uncertain about its potential benefit. You (or they) may feel overwhelmed by the idea of reading a whole book, or hold negative views about the approach.

If this is the case, why not consider reading an additional example chapter to help you get a sense of how CFT can help you, and others? Chapter 6 reviews some of the views that can act as barriers for us, while Chapter 3 clearly outlines the challenges that we face and makes a case for why compassion can help. You can even start with Chapter 1, which provides an overview of the whole book.

REMEMBER

Be guided by what you want to find out about CFT. If you're aware of your doubts or misconceptions, talk to your friend, relative or partner, ask their advice on what to read first, or take a look through the Table of Contents at the front of this book to help find the right starting point for you.

Chapter 21

Ten Ways to Change the World with Compassion

Be the change you wish to see in the world.

—MAHATMA GANDHI

Practising compassion is a dynamic process. The 'flow' of compassion involves three elements: compassion for oneself, the experience of compassion *from* others and the extension of compassion *to* others. This chapter uses these three components to outline ten additional ways in which you can help to change the world with compassion. Changing the world may sound like a huge, impossible task, but everything you do creates a ripple, inside yourself or in others. The practice of compassion aims to change lives in helpful ways.

REMEMBER

We're all the product of our experiences and our biology. However, we also have a unique capacity to intentionally stop, consider, choose and then act in a particular way. Instead of constantly reacting to our internal world (thoughts, images, emotions, sensations) and external world (other people, our environment), we can proactively pay attention to particular aspects of life and choose a compassionate response.

Ask Yourself an Important Question

Having evoked your compassionate mind and embodied your compassionate self, ask yourself 'What can I do for myself today that will make tomorrow a better day?' Take time to develop ideas and actions that truly have your wellbeing at heart. You may be surprised by what you put on your list of 'things to do'. It may include the phone call you've been avoiding, the room you need to sort out or the conversation you know you need to have.

TIP

The things you decide upon may be the very same things that appear on your regular to-do list. However, instead of being motivated to do them by self-criticism or a sense of threat, you're motivating yourself through a sense of care for your own wellbeing – and therefore you're much less prone to avoidance!

Bring Compassion into Different Areas of Your Life

As you become more familiar with compassionate practices, it's helpful to consider applying the principles and practices to other areas of your life and different relationships. Ask yourself whether a compassionate focus may help enhance or maintain them.

Consider your neighbourhood, the place you work or your school, the groups you attend, the activities you're enrolled in, and your friendships and other relationships. Use your compassionate mind to develop ideas about changes your compassionate self can make to your thinking, emotions and behaviour in relation to these areas of your life.

REMEMBER

We can easily be motivated by a desire to compete (and win!), achieve and acquire, and to stay safe and deal with threat, so be compassionate to that too rather than getting frustrated with yourself!

Feel Like You're Part of Something Bigger

Being in contact with flora and fauna is incredibly important to our wellbeing. Taking this a step further, nurturing plants, feeding birds or sharing your life with an animal can have an incredibly positive impact all round.

REMEMBER

Instead of 'going through the motions', be mindful of the connection you have with other living things and choose to interact in a meaningful way.

Widening things still further, consider visiting a scenic vista, be it an expanse of land, sea or ocean. Stop, breathe and experience a sense of profound connection with the planet and everything it supports.

Savour Kindness from and for Others

So much of our lives can be spent quickly moving from one thing to another. Sometimes we don't allow enough time for significant experiences to 'sink in'.

Be mindful of times when someone has acted out of care for your wellbeing. Savour the experience. It may have a positive impact on your own wellbeing. In addition, when others see the positive effect that they've had on you, it can enhance their wellbeing too.

Random acts of kindness towards others can bring benefits to the receiver of a kind act as well as the giver. Just type random acts of kindness into any search engine and you'll find charities such as the Random Acts of Kindness Foundation (www.randomactsofkindness.org) that provide a good starting point for ideas and inspiration.

TIP

Many of us, on a weekly or even daily basis, see individuals offering their time to seek charitable donations for specific causes. They may include the local Scout group, life boat provision, animal rescue, or physical or mental health research. If affordable, consider carrying with you a small amount of change and using this to make donations. It can be so much nicer than avoiding eye contact or participating in an awkward exchange. Savour the experience of giving as well as the interaction you have with the individual.

Experience Gratitude

When we're having a bad time, well-meaning people can tell us to 'look on the bright side', 'count your blessings' or 'consider those worse off than you'. We may even say such things to ourselves. Unfortunately, this can lead to us feeling criticised, and we may go on to criticise ourselves further.

What people are often hoping is that we'll experience a sense of gratitude for the things we do have. Instead of coldly telling ourselves to look on the bright side, gratitude is associated with a warm sense of appreciation. Intentionally cultivating a personal feeling of gratitude and expressing it to others has been shown to increase wellbeing, energy, optimism and empathy.

Using your compassionate mind and evoking your compassionate self, warmly bring your attention to those things for which you can experience a sense of gratitude. They may be your health, your relationships, your skills or your environment. Maybe you're grateful for the expanse of the sky, the warmth of the sun, the sound of birds or the smell of blossom.

REMEMBER

We don't engage in any of these practices to eradicate difficult experiences and emotions from our lives; we do them *because* we experience such things. Our compassionate self can help us approach, be with and navigate our way through the difficulties we have.

TIP

Type 'gratitude practices' into a search engine and try some of the many different ideas out there.

Join a Community Group

Whether volunteering for a charity, singing in a choir or being part of an allotment community, such activities can all involve compassion in action! Choosing to be around like-minded people may be an act of self-compassion, while such activities can also give rise to experiences of compassion *from* others and, of course, compassion *towards* others. Savour all such actions and experiences.

Share Your Experiences and Insights

Some people shout good ideas from the roof tops if they personally find something helpful; others share their experiences more subtly. There's no right or wrong. However, good ideas and good practices are worth spreading, so if you find things in this book helpful, spread the word in keeping with the person that you are and the way that you choose to live your life.

Provide Feedback and Make Suggestions

The aim of this book is to improve your wellbeing, and hopefully other people's too. It compiles many of the things that Compassion Focused Therapy (CFT) therapists have discovered from research, and clinical and personal practice. But, if the approach is to be enhanced further, we need more feedback and more ideas.

TIP

Help us make things better: visit www.compassioninmind.co.uk/Dummies to share your thoughts, experiences and ideas. Feedback will come directly to me and it will help us consider what aspects of CFT people find useful and what people struggle with. You can request that your feedback is kept confidential or agree for it to be shared with others. Over time, feedback, combined with the growing body of research on what makes therapy effective, can help us develop compassion focused approaches further. It may make a difference to so many other people.

Offer a Smile

Maybe the simplest but most effective way to change things on a moment-by-moment basis, for yourself and others, is to connect with others, make eye contact and share a warm smile with those you meet.

Connecting with others can be difficult. This may be because you're preoccupied with what's going on in your own head or body, or you're concerned about what others may be thinking of you. Begin by gently remembering that other people are also a product of their biology and their experiences. Warmly feel a sense of connection between yourself and other people, as fellow human beings. When ready, bring your attention to them. It doesn't matter how fleeting is your eye contact or smile. The more you practise, the more comfortable you'll feel with these connections – and they'll grow.

TIP

Start slowly. This may involve making more eye contact and gently smiling at work, with your family or in your neighbourhood. Equally, it may be easier to start in places where you don't know anyone – the important thing is to slowly build your confidence and your connections, so start where it's relatively easy for you!

Grasp the Nettle!

Compassion involves sensitivity to distress, be it our own or other people's, plus a motivation to alleviate it. It's not all hearts, flowers and smiles. Acts of compassion can often be difficult. It may involve setting and maintaining boundaries (for yourself and others), allowing yourself to grieve, letting people know how their actions are impacting on you or standing up for your principles when everything inside you is telling you to comply!

REMEMBER

Daily compassionate practices can help to keep you on course. They give you the strength, courage and commitment to be motivated by compassion and to learn from the deviations you experience. So grasp the nettle and create some time in your life for compassion.

Appendix
Additional Resources

In this Appendix I list a variety of books, websites and organisations that provide you with further reading and information. I don't intend this list to be comprehensive, but I hope it will point you in the right direction.

Books about Compassion Focused Therapy

The following books provide you with some in-depth extra information about Compassion Focused Therapy (CFT):

>> *The Compassionate Mind* by Paul Gilbert, published by Constable & Robinson Ltd (2009)

>> *Compassion Focused Therapy (CBT Distinctive Features Series)* by Paul Gilbert, published by Routledge (2010)

>> *Mindful Compassion: Using the Power of Mindfulness and Compassion to Transform Our Lives* by Paul Gilbert and Choden, published by Constable & Robinson Ltd (2013)

>> *The Compassionate Mind Approach Guide to Beating Overeating* by Kenneth Goss, published by Constable & Robinson Ltd (2011)

>> *Improving Social Confidence and Reducing Shyness Using Compassion Focused Therapy* by Lynne Henderson, published by Constable & Robinson Ltd (2010)

>> *The Compassionate Mind Approach to Managing Your Anger* by Russell Kolts, published by Constable & Robinson Ltd (2012)

>> *The Compassionate Mind Approach to Recovering from Trauma* by Deborah Lee (with Sophie James), published by Constable & Robinson Ltd (2012)

>> *The Compassionate Mind Approach to Postnatal Depression: Using Compassion Focused Therapy to Enhance Mood, Confidence and Bonding* by Michelle Cree, published by Robinson (2015)

>> *The Compassionate Mind Approach to Building Self-Confidence Using Compassion Focused Therapy* by Mary Welford, published by Robinson (2012)

>> *The Compassionate-Mind Guide to Overcoming Anxiety: Using Compassion-Focused Therapy to Calm Worry, Panic, and Fear* by Dennis Tirch, published by New Harbinger Publications (2012)

Additional Reading

You may find that you also want to read more about compassion and mindfulness, or perhaps even discover more information about the way your amazing mind works! Consider checking out these books to find out more:

>> *Compassion: Conceptualisations, Research and Use in Psychotherapy* by Paul Gilbert, published by Routledge (2005)

>> *Shame: Interpersonal Behaviour, Psychopathology, and Culture* by Paul Gilbert and Bernice Andrews, published by Oxford University Press (1998)

>> *Human Nature and Suffering* by Paul Gilbert, published by Lawrence Erlbaum Associates (1989)

>> *Why Love Matters: How Affection Shapes a Baby's Brain* by Sue Gerhardt, published by Routledge (2004)

>> *The Neuroscience of Human Relationships: Attachment and the Developing Social Brain,* Second Edition, by Louis Cozolino, published by W.W. Norton & Company (2006)

>> *Mindfulness For Dummies,* Second Edition, by Shamash Alidina, published by Wiley (2014)

>> *Mindfulness: A Practical Guide to Finding Peace in a Frantic World* by Mark Williams and Danny Penman, published by Piatkus (2011)

>> *Mindsight: Transform Your Brain with the New Science of Kindness* by Daniel Siegel, published by Bantam Books (2011)

Helpful Websites

You can also find plenty of useful information online. Take a look at the following websites:

>> **Compassionate Mind Foundation (www.compassionatemind.co.uk):** The Compassionate Mind Foundation was set up in 2006 by Paul Gilbert and a number of colleagues (including myself). The charity aims to promote wellbeing through the scientific understanding and application of compassion. The website provides an array of resources (including videos, audio exercises, papers and questionnaires) and information on further training.

>> **Compassionate Wellbeing (www.compassionatewellbeing.co.uk):** Compassionate Wellbeing hosts events and supports research and activities that promote and explore compassionate approaches to health, wellbeing and society. Workshops are developed for the general public and healthcare professionals, and these workshops aim to introduce the theories and techniques developed by leading figures in the field of compassion research and practice.

>> **Mind & Life Institute (www.mindandlife.org):** The Dalai Lama and Western scientists came together to develop a more compassionate way of living. More information on this can be found on this website.

>> **Center for Compassion and Altruism Research and Education (http://ccare.stanford.edu):** Set up by Professor James Doty for international compassion work and the advancement of compassion-based therapies.

>> **Compassion in Mind (www.compassioninmind.co.uk):** Compassion in Mind was set up in 2014 by Mary Welford and Jason Friend to offer compassion-focused initiatives to individuals, groups and organisations. The website provides information on training, supervision, therapy and self-help. Head to the website to register to become part of a growing community.

Index

C

calm awareness, sense of, 74, 113, 122, 155, 171, 181, 245, 252

care, our need to, 51

care for wellbeing, as compassionate attribute, 29–30

CBT (Cognitive Behavioural Therapy), 8, 12, 289, 290

Center for Compassion and Altruism Research and Education, 311

CFT (compassion focused therapy). *See* compassion focused therapy (CFT)

chair work

  introduction, 266–267

  practising compassion for self-critic and criticised self, 268–271

  understanding mixed emotions, 272–275

changes

  as feeling like emotional rollercoaster, 300

  managing resistance to, 258–259

  people as needing to make changes for themselves, 298–299

  as taking time and effort, 300

Charlie (example), conflicting emotions, 225

Charlotte (example), efforts blocked by others, 114

Cheat Sheet, 3

Chloe (example)

  circle diagram of, 69

  deservedness for compassion, 99–100

Christianity, compassion as key aspect of, 28

circle diagram, 68–72

classical conditioning, 110

clinical psychologists, defined, 288

Cognitive Behavioural Therapy (CBT), 8, 12, 289, 290

Collard, Patrizia (author)

  Mindfulness-Based Cognitive Therapy For Dummies, 290

common humanity, as cornerstone of CFT, 9, 177

common terms, of CFT, 9–10

community group, joining of, 306

compassion

  as abdicating responsibility?, 101–104

  allowing compassion in, 165–178

  asserting yourself with, 251–258

  birthplace of, 52

  breaking down beliefs about, 95–106

  bringing of into different areas of your life, 304

  components of, 232

  connecting with, 24

  considering beliefs about, 91–106

  defined, 8, 12

  deservedness for, 98–100

  development and cultivation of as way of living, 13

  early writings on, 28

  enhancing experience of compassion from others, 178

  evaluating beliefs about, 93–95

  experiencing of for other people, 152–153

  facing barriers to, 107–118

  fear of, 92

  feeling positive as not always easy, 92–93

  having a need for, 101

  as having no more negative thoughts or difficult emotions?, 97

  as having people take advantage of me?, 106

  as involving doing, 97

  making case of, 12–13

  one set of rules for others, another set for ourselves, 94

  for people we overlook or dislike, 161–163

  for perceived flaws, 183–185

  placing of at centre of life, 278–279

  practising of for others, 151–163

  preparation for, 133–150

  reason for practise of, 97

  receiving of from author, 177

  responding to from others, 166–167

  for self-critic, 160–161, 183–184

  as set up for fall?, 105

  showing of for others, 157–163

  for someone similar to you, 159

  for someone you love, 158

  as taking strength and courage, 9, 154

  ten ways to change world with, 303–308

experience
  developing account of, 84–86
  learning from, 26–28
  recognition of, 74–76
expression
  examples of, 254
  finding words to express yourself, 252–254
  preparing to express yourself, 256–257
external shame, 16
external world, worries, fears and concerns relating to, 77
Eye-Movement Desensitisation and Reprocessing (EMDR), 290

F

facial expressions, exploration of, 136–138
faking it, 238
fears, exploration of, 76–78
feedback, 260–263, 307
focused, defined, 8

G

Gandhi, Mahatma (lawyer and leader), 303
genes, as our nature, 74
genotypes, 50–51
Gestalt therapy, 8
Gilbert, Paul (originator of CFT approach), 2, 11, 28, 46, 47, 102, 103, 195
goals
  discovering of, 235–238
  examples of, 236–237
Goss, Ken (clinical psychologist), 82
Graham (example)
  becoming aware of thoughts, 204–205
  capitalising on motivation, 211–212
  gaining perspective of compassionate mind, 206–208
  getting deeper into compassionate mind, 209–210
gratitude, experiencing of, 305
group therapy, as one format of CFT, 290

H

habits
  as factor affecting speed at which we can change thinking, 197
  old habits as dying hard, 199
Harborview Burn Center (University of Washington Seattle), 130
Health and Care Professions Council (HCPC), 291
health anxiety, 45, 127
Helen (example), illustrating compassion as paired with sadness, 108–109
hindsight, 89
Hinduism, compassion as key aspect of, 28
hormones
  adrenaline, 57
  cortisol, 57
  dopamine, 62
  norepinephrine, 57
house building analogy, 80
Hugh (example), triggering emotions, 111
human needs, acknowledgement of, 50–51
humiliation, use of term, 17

I

icons, explained, 3
Immersive Virtual Reality, 130
individual therapy, as one format of CFT, 290
influences
  recognition of, 74–76
  subtle influences, 76
inner support
  generating of, 214, 244, 245, 258
  sense of, 114, 218, 233, 238
inspiration, taking of from others, 234
intelligent design, 42
intended consequences, 80–81, 82
intentions, understanding of, 80–82
internal shame, 16, 77
internal threats, 57
internal world, worries, fears and concerns relating to, 77
interpersonal therapy, focus of, 12
Islam, compassion as key aspect of, 28

About the Author

Mary Welford qualified as a Clinical Psychologist at the University of Manchester in 1999. For over a decade she worked with many of the Cognitive Behavioural Therapy (CBT) greats, such as Professor Adrian Wells and Professor Anthony Morrison. However, it was her interest in the enhancement of therapy for those who didn't do so well using traditional forms of CBT that brought her to the work of Professor Paul Gilbert.

Compassion Focused Therapy (CFT) offers insights, hope and, most importantly, solutions for many individuals and communities. Working as part of a team, Mary helped to develop the approach, was a founding member of the Compassionate Mind Foundation, and in 2012 authored *The Compassionate Mind Approach to Building Self Confidence using Compassion Focused Therapy*.

Mary now lives and works in the South West of England. For a born and bred northerner, this was quite a change! However, the biggest changes in Mary's life have been brought about by CFT. Her self-critical mind is a lot quieter these days, while her compassionate one is getting stronger. It's a nicer mind to be in and one she would highly recommend.

Dedication

This book is dedicated to everyone who struggles.

Author's Acknowledgements

CFT wouldn't exist if it weren't for Paul Gilbert. I thank him for his support, guidance, inspiration and encouragement. I hope this book does his work justice and brings CFT to a wider audience. Paul has a brilliant mind and a deep-rooted desire to alleviate suffering – it's not just his work, it's his life.

I thank every individual who has courageously shared their experiences and difficulties with me, be it in the context of therapy, training, supervision or friendship (and yes, that includes family!). I've been inspired and humbled; I've learned, laughed and cried. And in those moments, when distress and despair seemed overwhelming, I've learned the most. I've experienced a profound sense of connection that can't be put into words. I feel truly privileged.

Thanks to the CFT community for their passion, generosity and fun. Key to that community is Deborah Lee. I thank her for her brilliance, humour (I break into a smile just bringing her to mind), compassion and friendship. Deborah is this book's technical reviewer and her input has been invaluable.

Finally, thanks to the Wiley team for the opportunity and support to write this book.

Publisher's Acknowledgments

Acquisitions Editor: Annie Knight

Project Editors: Rachael Chilvers, Iona Everson, Tracy Brown Hamilton

Development Editor: Kerry Laundon

Copy Editor: Kate O'Leary

Production Editor: Kumar Chellappan

Technical Editor: Deborah Lee

Art Coordinator: Alicia B. South

Cover Image: Konstantin Chagin/Shutterstock